# BEHAVIOR MODELING TRAINING

## Principles and Applications

Phillip J. Decker and
Barry R. Nathan

## PRAEGER SPECIAL STUDIES • PRAEGER SCIENTIFIC

New York • Philadelphia • Eastbourne, UK
Toronto • Hong Kong • Tokyo • Sydney

**Library of Congress Cataloging in Publication Data**

Decker, Phillip J.
    Behavior modeling training.

    Bibliography: p.
    Includes index.
    1. Behavior modification.   2. Role playing.
3. Bandura, Albert, 1925-        I. Nathan, Barry R.
II. Title.
BF637.B4D39    1985       153.1′52      84-18155
ISBN 0-03-069883-9 (alk. paper)

Published in 1985 by Praeger Publishers
CBS Educational and Professional Publishing
a Division of CBS Inc.
521 Fifth Avenue, New York, NY 10175 USA
© 1985 by Praeger Publishers

56789 052 987654321

Printed in the United States of America
on acid-free paper

This book is dedicated to

Kay Severson and Milt Hakel, Phil's most influential models,
and Maria Nathan.

# Foreword

It's all here! What more could a scientist/practitioner want but more of the same. Decker and Nathan have brought theory and application together.

This book presents a comprehensive treatment of Behavior Modeling, the most important perspective on adult training and development. It presents theory, especially as represented in Bandura's work. It presents research as drawn from the literature in Industrial/Organizational, Counseling and other branches of psychology. It presents application as illustrated in actual use of Behavior Modeling procedures in organizations.

A decade ago there were two books which served as the major resources for Behavior Modeling applications. The first to appear was Ivey's *Microcounseling: Innovations in Interviewing Training*. Ivey was concerned with shaping and maintaining effective counselor behaviors as minute (hence, "micro") as eye contact and verbal following. He identified specific behaviors underlying such concepts as attention, empathy, and interpretation and devised programs to teach those particular behaviors. His motto: "You don't know what you are doing unless you can teach it to someone else."

The second major resource to appear was Goldstein and Sorcher's *Changing Supervisor Behavior*. Goldstein and Sorcher emphasized training supervisors to manage *effectively*, with emphasis on both improved employee performance and improved employee satisfaction. They reviewed research on modeling, role playing, social reinforcement and transfer of training, and inter-related these components as Applied Learning. Their book concludes with examples of actual industrial programs.

Ivey's book placed great emphasis on illustrations of how to conduct microcounseling training. Goldstein and Sorcher's book placed great emphasis on the theory underlying successful use of Applied Learning. Between them, the two books covered the waterfront of theory and application. Their publication marked the beginning of a great surge of program development in both industry and education, as well as research on fundamental learning processes.

Both books stand as significant milestones in the development of our theoretical and operational knowledge of training. Given the advances of the past decade, both are now seriously dated.

Now here is *Behavior Modeling Training* by Decker and Nathan. The theory, research, and application of the past decade is all integrated in one comprehensive treatment. Best of all, the book models, in so far as it is possible to do so in a printed medium, the very principles and procedures it espouses. It begins with theory and understanding of the "big picture," if you will, the learning points or key behaviors in the modeling sequence. It continues with sections which model how to handle modeling, rehearsal, and feedback. And as in actual Behavior Modeling programs, transfer of training is dealt with by focusing on real problems. This assures participant attention and motivation, which in this book is handled by presenting real training content as well as dealing with evaluation and follow-up issues.

This book is not the final word on Behavior Modeling. Rather it will stimulate the next decade of theorizing, research, and application. It is certain that there is more to come. For now, however, if your need is to master the state of the art on any facet of Behavior Modeling, this is where to find it.

Milton D. Hakel
Columbus, Ohio

# Preface

Behavior Modeling, as a technique, has been used throughout history to train complex skills ranging from swordsmanship to salesmanship. The first formal presentation of the elements we now call behavior modeling was made by Charles Allen (1919) while directing instructor-training work for the Emergency Fleet Cooperation program conducted during World War I. Allen's approach was adapted by Glenn Gardiner into the Job Instruction Training (JIT) method of the Training Within Industry Program of World War II (Dietz, 1982). Eventually, 23,000 trainers were using JIT during World War II.

Behavior Modeling, first formally used in the counseling context to teach interviewing skills and later used in the industrial context to teach supervisory skills, has been described in books by Goldstein and Sorcher, *Changing Supervisor Behavior* (1974), and Ivey, *Microcounseling* (1971). In the industrial context, Behavior Modeling has been referred to as Applied Learning and Interaction Management Training. In counseling contexts, it has been called Micro-Counseling, Structured Learning, Social Learning Therapy, and Micro-Training. As a formal training procedure, this technique has been used for at least 15 years in the counseling context, 13 years in the industrial context, and informally it has been used since the earliest of times by all of humanity.

Behavior modeling, which is based on the social learning theory research of Bandura, is a sequence of five activities: 1) *modeling*, in which individuals or groups of trainees watch filmed models portray the behavior or set of behaviors which one wishes them to learn; 2) *retention processes*, in which trainees go through a series of formalized activities designed to help them retain what they saw in the modeling display; 3) *behavioral rehearsal*, in which trainees take part in extensive practice and rehearsal of the specific key behaviors demonstrated by the models and generalize the key behaviors across contexts; 4) *feedback*, in which praise or constructive feedback is provided by both the trainers and other trainees for accurate behavioral rehearsal and successful solution of problems presented in behavioral rehearsal; and 5) *transfer of training*, which is the inclusion of principles that enhance transfer of learning from the classroom to other training contexts (a job in the industrial context, counseling clients, or actually using the new behavior in real life situations for a counseling client).

In this book, we attempt to combine the literature from both the industrial and the counseling areas. Our bias, however, is industrial; we are industrial psychologists. We would also characterize ourselves as trainers. You will see that the literature in the counseling area is more extensive than that of the industrial context; yet, there are findings from both areas which contribute to our understanding of why behavior modeling works, how it can be used effectively in different contexts, and how it can be improved for future use. Consequently, this book is designed to describe the theoretical basis for behavior modeling as well as how to develop and use behavior modeling training in different contexts.

This book is about learning new behavioral strategies in the andragogical context; that is, teaching adults new behavior. Consequently, it can be used by a wide variety of audiences. It would be of primary interest to both industrial psychologists and business professors teaching training courses, as well as to industrial trainers who want to do behaviorally based training in all types of organizations. This book will also be of interest to those in schools of education for teaching education students about adult education (particularly in the organizational context). Finally, in counseling, this book can serve as a resource for those interested in teaching students or clients new behavior.

The book is divided into four basic sections. The first section reviews the basics for understanding behavior modeling. Section II covers the basic components of behavior modeling: modeling, retention, behavioral rehearsal, feedback, and transfer of training. Section III emphasizes the practical: how to develop key behaviors, how to choose models and develop modeling displays, how to do behavioral rehearsal, and how to put it all together to design workshops. This is the practical section that really is a cookbook for developing and using behavior modeling. The fourth section is future-oriented; it covers evaluation of behavior modeling training.

No book can be written without the efforts of many people other than the authors. This book is no exception. Many thanks go to Sue Dare, Teresa Higdon, and, especially, Marilisa Percich and Maryellen Amos for their patient typing. Also, thanks go to Jane Heitman and Sharon Presnell for their work on the word processor. Kay Severson and Audrey Easton edited the first drafts. We are very indebted to Susan Myers, Jim Breaugh, Milt Hakel, and Milt's Winter 1983 Training Seminar graduate students (Mary Brickner, Terri Coombs, Michael Coovert, Gary Dean, Jan Eriksen, Nancy Laitman-Ashley, Sallie Sherman, and Bill Woods) for their critique and advice on intermediate drafts. The School of Business and Department of Psychology, University of Missouri-St. Louis, deserve thanks for providing the support needed in writing this book. We also thank our editors, George Zimmar, Sheldon Cooper and Maruta Mitchell for a superb job.

# Contents

# I

# Introduction to
# Behavior Modeling

# —1—
# Introduction to
# Behavior Modeling

This book is about a relatively new training technique, behavior modeling. Yet the principles behind behavior modeling are ancient, and were possibly best expressed over 2,000 years ago by the Chinese philosopher Confucius, when he wrote:

I hear and I forget.
I see and I remember.
I do and I understand.

Confucius related the acquisition of knowledge and understanding directly toward living and experiencing. This is what behavior modeling is all about: "see and remembering," "doing and understanding."

Human beings are very limited information processors. We cannot attend to all that is going on around us. At a party, we can listen to only one person at a time, though we may hear many people talking. A magician's trick works because we attend only to what he wants us to see, and not to all that he is doing. In skills training, the trainer tries to do the same thing, he focuses our attention on what is important. In learning to use a computer, or any other piece of equipment, the first time we observe the instructor, we do not know what to watch. We become lost in a field of buttons, lights, switches, and instructions. However, when the instructor breaks the task down into a series of steps, the elements making up the total task become separate and distinctive, and can be ordered in a meaningful way. Rather than try to understand the complex whole, the learner needs only remember each distinct element, and practice performing each simple step in order, until the correct sequence required for operating the machine becomes a habit.

Behavior modeling training used for developing supervisory skills, or any other set of skills, is no different. Without training, a new supervisor trying to learn how to discipline an employee or conduct a performance appraisal interview will try to recall either a situation that he/she was involved in or one which was observed; in either case, without knowing what to look and listen for, the critical behaviors leading to a successful conclusion may have been overlooked, or else behaviors which were irrelevant or even detrimental may be recalled. It could take many observations, either of oneself or of others, before the most appropriate behaviors are figured out, and many more before they become habits. Behavior modeling speeds up the process. Learners are presented with a model, that is, someone who performs the appropriate behaviors so that each is distinctive and easy to follow. The modeled behavior is followed by an opportunity to practice these behaviors with others in a simulated setting to facilitate their being understood and remembered. This should lead to their being easily recalled, and hopefully used, when a similar situation arises on the job.

Modeling has been referred to by a variety of other names including imitative behavior, copying, observational learning, imitation, and vicarious learning. The critical factor in modeling that distinguishes it from other techniques, such as behavior modification, is that individuals are not dependent upon direct experience and reinforcement for behavior change to take place. Instead, people learn from observing others. Almost a half a century ago, Miller and Dollard (1941) made it clear that we can learn a variety of things by imitation (i.e., new skills, information, fears, or fear reduction). They were also among the first to draw attention to the fact that imitation is an economical form of learning because it enables individuals to learn large amounts of information without the need for trial and error.

## The Behavior Modeling Process

Behavior modeling training is based on the theoretical work of Bandura. He suggests that, to be effective, modeling must consist of four component processes: attention, retention, motor reproduction, and motivation (Bandura, 1977). Stated in more informal terms, in order for people to learn from behavior modeling training, they must *observe* what the model is doing, *remember* what the model did, *do* what the model has done, and later when the appropriate time comes, *want to use* what they have learned.

The four processes are included within the five components of behavior modeling training, as can be seen in Figure 1.1 (i.e., modeling, retention processes, behavioral rehearsal, feedback, and transfer of training). *Modeling* is an important element of the program because it involves the presentation of a set of behaviors by a model. These are called *key behaviors* and are the training content. The method of presentation of this performance can be live, videotaped, filmed, or audiotaped and is called the *modeling display*. The objective of modeling is to facilitate the trainer's attention towards the key behaviors.

The second component of behavior modeling is the *retention processes*. The retention processes include symbolic coding, cognitive organization, and symbolic rehearsal, all of which help the trainee remember and retain what was seen in the modeling display. *Symbolic coding* is the process of reducing the diverse elements of the modeled performance into verbal symbols or images that the trainee can mentally store and use later to guide behavior. *Cognitive organization* refers to presenting the written description of the key behaviors in an organized form that is congruent with the trainees' mental, or cognitive, information storage system. *Symbolic rehearsal* describes the process of mentally practicing the modeled performance before the trainee physically attempts to perform it.

*Behavioral rehearsal* is the third component of behavior modeling. In this component, the trainee actually practices the modeled performance. The person may reproduce and/or try to generalize the key behaviors to other situations. Although often confused with role playing, behavioral rehearsal does not require the participant to play a new role; rather, the trainee rehearses the modeled behaviors as they would be used in the person's own position on the job.

The fourth component is *feedback*. Feedback is provided by a trainer and by other participants in the workshop as the trainee attempts to use the modeled behaviors. Constructive feedback is necessary for the trainee to fine-tune the behaviors the trainee has observed and learned cognitively through modeling. At the same time, feedback, as social reinforcement, plays an important role in the initial acceptance of the new behaviors.

The last component is *transfer of training*. A variety of strategies are used throughout the behavior modeling components to facilitate transfer. The modeling display and behavioral rehearsal should resemble the job as much as possible, supplying identical elements. The behavioral rehearsal should include overlearning (practice beyond the first accurate reproduction of the key behaviors). Where possible, reinforcement for the modeled behaviors is given to the trainee on the job or in other real-life situations. All of these elements enhance the possibility that the training will transfer to the

**Figure 1.1**   The Behavior Modeling Training Process

job. It is also expected that the new behaviors will produce their own rewards when used correctly in real-life situations.

## Behavior Modeling in Industry

The first research studies examining the efficacy of behavior modeling in industry were reported by Goldstein and Sorcher (1974). Their research concerned a program developed at General Electric to reduce the turnover of "hard core unemployed" employees by helping these employees develop skills to adapt to and cope with industrial jobs. Behavior modeling was used to train both the new employees and their first-level supervisors. The six month turnover rate of the employees not trained was 72 percent. Those individuals who received training and who worked for supervisors who had also been trained had a turnover rate of 28 percent. Because of this early success, the initial training program at GE was expanded to include all first-level supervisors. This program (Burnaska, 1976) involved 62 middle-level managers from six different locations who were randomly selected to receive training, and 62 middle-level managers from the same six locations who were randomly selected to serve as a control group. Nine separate sets of key behaviors were included in the training. Behavioral observations were made of a role play situation similar to the training situations by 25 trained observers one month and four to five months after training. Trained managers were rated higher than untrained managers both one and four months after training, with four month scores even higher than one month scores. In addition, one week prior to training and then four months after training the employees and managers involved completed a questionnaire designed to determine if employees of the trained managers could perceive changes in their managers' overall behavior. Only employees of the trained managers in two locations perceived any improvement.

Moses and Ritchie (1976) evaluated a behavior modeling training program at AT&T for first-level supervisors. Two groups of managers were matched on sex, age, department, experience, and number of subordinates. One group of 90 managers received training on handling employee problems and one group of 93 managers did not. Two months after training, both groups' performance in handling three different employee problems were evaluated. Three different employee problems not used in training were role played by the supervisors and evaluated by trained assessors in a special assessment center. Trained supervisors received significantly higher ratings than did untrained supervisors. Of the trained supervisors, 84 percent received ratings of "exceptionally well" or "above average" in the handling of the problem discussions. Only 32 percent of the untrained supervisors received these ratings. In addition, the trained supervisors were able to use the skills learned in the training program and transfer this training to novel and difficult problems (e.g., a theft problem).

Byham, Adams, and Kiggins (1976) evaluated a behavior modeling training program designed to help first-level supervisors better handle interactions with subordinates. This program consisted of nine modules covering different employee interactions. Sixteen supervisors in two operations of the organization were chosen for the study. Eight supervisors in one department were trained and eight supervisors in a roughly matched department were not trained. Subordinates' perceptions of their supervisors' handling of interactions in the areas trained were assessed. Data were collected by interviewing a 20 percent random sample of the available subordinates (n = 62), using a highly structured interview guide. Interviews were conducted before training and seven months after training. Consequently, it was possible to make a pre–post comparison within the trained group and a post comparison across the trained and untrained groups. Supervisors' handling of interactions with subordinates significantly improved both in comparison to their own pretraining measures and in comparison to the untrained supervisors. Positive results were attained in seven of nine areas.

Smith (1976) conducted two studies evaluating behavior modeling training procedures at IBM. The first program was designed to train branch office managers to communicate the results of an employee survey effectively to individual employees and groups of employees. Eighteen managers were trained and thirteen managers matched on district size, geography, and employee satisfaction were not trained. Four months after training, a questionnaire measuring manager effectiveness was given to all employees. The results indicated higher perceptions of effectiveness for trained managers. In addition, an opinion survey administered to employees indicated that employee morale improved in the branch offices managed by trained managers.

A second study presented by Smith (1976) concerned the evaluation of a behavior modeling program designed to train managers in basic communication skills. This study compared three training treatments: traditional training, behavior modeling, and behavior modeling plus team-building training. Prior to training, three groups of managers were matched on level of customer satisfaction, sales performance, and geography; one group was trained in each condition. Subjects included managers from 12 branch offices of the organization. The criteria consisted of assessment of communication skills, customer satisfaction, and branch office sales performance. Communication skills were measured immediately before and after training by ratings of written answers to customers' comments. The author reported a significant increase in the quality of answers of the trained managers and no increase for the control group. Customer satisfaction was measured by surveying a random sample of branch customers. The level of communication effectiveness of managers after training was correlated with the level of customer satisfaction four months after training. There was a direct, positive relationship between communication skills after training and later levels of customer satisfaction for all trained managers. Sales performance measured ten months after training was not significantly different in the behavior modeling group and the control group, but had significantly improved in the modeling plus team-building group.

While the studies discussed above present an impressive amount of evidence in support of the effectiveness of behavior modeling, they have not always been received uncritically. For example, McGehee and Tullar (1978) suggested that the reported results could be attributed to faults in the design and analysis of the studies rather than to behavior modeling training.* McGehee and Tullar suggested that Burnaska's (1976) study was subject to at least three threats to internal validity (regression towards the mean, selection history interaction, and mortality). McGehee and Tullar criticized Moses and Ritchie's (1976) study for lack of randomization of subjects to condition and the use of role playing in both the training and evaluation. The Byham, Adams, and Kiggins (1976) study is criticized for the use of a nonequivalent control group design (which is subject to several threats to internal validity and is difficult to interpret). Neither Smith (1976) study is a true experimental design. Furthermore, in the second Smith study, the length of training was one day for the control group and two days for the behavior modeling training group. In summary, McGehee and Tullar made several conclusions relevant to these studies and suggested there is no clear-cut evidence for the effectiveness for behavior modeling as an industrial training technique.

Latham and Saari (1979), however, reported a study of behavior modeling which addressed all of these potential threats to internal validity. The study involved four levels of evaluation: trainees' attitudinal reactions to the training program, a written test to see how well they had learned the key behaviors presented in the program, exercises in which their skill in using the new behaviors was tested, and finally, performance appraisal ratings back on the job. Forty first-line supervisors were randomly assigned to a behavior modeling training program or to a control group. The program, which consisted of nine separate training modules, was designed to improve supervisors' interpersonal skills in dealing with their subordinates. Each training session followed the same format: introduction to the topic, presentation of a modeling film with learning points (learning points are written descriptions of the model's key behaviors), group discussion of the effectiveness of the model, behavioral rehearsal, social reinforcement, and transfer principles.

---

*See Chapter 12 for a discussion of internal validity and the threats to experimental designs in training evaluation.

Trainee reactions to the training program were highly favorable both immediately after training, and again eight months later. The learning measure consisted of a test containing 85 situational questions developed from critical incidents contained in a job analysis of supervisory behavior. This test did not contain questions restricted only to the nine areas covered in the training, but rather, examined all possible interpersonal situations that had been identified in the supervisory job analysis. The mean score on the test in the training group was significantly higher than that of the control group, showing that trainees could generalize the learning across situations.

The behavioral criteria measures consisted of role plays in which supervisors resolved supervisor/employee problems. The trained supervisors were given index cards containing the appropriate learning points to be used during role playing. Of the 24 in the control group, 10 were given the learning points which had been seen by the trained managers. This was done to determine whether knowledge alone of what one was supposed to do is sufficient to increase desired behavior. These role plays were recorded on videotape and evaluated by 15 superintendents (supervisors' superiors who were blind to the identity of each supervisor and condition). Analyses indicate ratings of the trained group were significantly higher than those of the control group with and without the learning points.

Finally, a comparison was made between superintendents' ratings of supervisors' job performance one month before and one year after the training. No significant differences were found in performance ratings before training between the trained and untrained groups. However, analyses of the job performance ratings after training indicated that the training group performed significantly better on the job than the control group. This was true for both specially developed job related behavior observation scale ratings (Latham and Wexley, 1977) as well as the company's traditional appraisal instrument. Furthermore, one year after the training had taken place, the 20 supervisors of the control group received the same training as the original training group. After their training, there were no significant differences between the two groups on any of the four criterion measures.

Meyer and Raich (1983) describe an evaluation study in which behavior modeling was used to increase sales performance. Salespersons from fourteen retail stores participated. The stores were matched on size, sales, and geographic area; the training program was then introduced into seven stores, one from each matched pair. Fifty-eight sales associates received the training which consisted of a program focusing on specific aspects of sales situations such as "approaching the customer"; "explaining features, advantages, benefits"; and "closing the sale." The typical behavior modeling paradigm was followed. The control group subjects received other kinds of sales training during the study period. Sales performance was compared for the six months before and six months after training. Sales representatives who received the behavior modeling training increased their sales by an average of 7 percent during the ensuing six month period while the control groups' performance declined 3 percent. Training also affected turnover; only 7 percent of the trained sales associates left the company during the study period compared to a turnover rate of 22 percent for the untrained sales associates.

The significance of the last two studies is that they support the earlier applications of behavior modeling training for first-line supervisors (Burnaska, 1976; Byham, Adams, and Kiggins, 1976; Moses and Ritchie, 1976; Smith, 1976), and are free of the objections raised by McGehee and Tullar (1978). Additionally, Porras and Anderson (1981) have shown the effectiveness of a ten module behavior modeling program for first-line supervisors of a forest products company. Their study is interesting because the program was offered in a condensed format to all levels of management above the participants, and upper-level managers participated in the training of their subordinate supervisors. Finally, Sorcher and Spence (1982) describe an eight module behavior modeling program given to white male supervisors in a South African company with a reciprocal program given to their unskilled black subordinates. This study is interesting in its geographic application. At least two firms offering commercial behavior modeling programs advertise that their products have been evaluated and are proven effective in changing behavior. Several of these studies are probably sound, valid studies done in field settings. None of them, however, have been published in their entirety. Consequently, they have not been discussed here. The studies offered by commercial firms simply extend the available evidence. Taken together, these studies indicate that leadership skills can be taught effectively and in a relatively short period of time using behavior modeling techniques. As can be seen, behavior modeling is a powerful training technique for developing interpersonal skills in industrial settings. Likewise, its effectiveness in clinical and counseling settings is well supported. This research is reviewed in Appendix A.

In summary, the behavior modeling technique has been shown to be an effective method of producing rapid behavior change in trainees. There have been numerous studies in the industrial (and counseling/clinical contexts) using both quasi-experimental and true experimental designs comparing the behavior modeling technique against no-treatment control groups and other training techniques. The consistent results of these studies indicate the efficacy of the technique for changing behavior, maintaining that change over time, generalizing new behaviors to different contexts, and transferring the training content to the job or other transfer contexts. Few training techniques have received as many detailed and successful attempts to evaluate its efficacy as has behavior modeling training. Across numerous studies and several contexts, the behavior modeling technique has shown a surprisingly strong ability to change behavior.

## What Can Be Accomplished by Using Behavior Modeling?

In training, we can teach individuals to achieve six basic learning states: 1) new attitude, 2) manual (psychomotor) skills, 3) social skills, 4) verbal skills, 5) cognitive skills, and 6) memory for factual material. All training programs attempt to affect one or more of these basic human states. An attitude is the belief or feeling one has towards a given object. Manual skills are simple psychomotor skills (typically not including any verbal response) such as riding a bicycle or operating machinery. Social skills are a combination of verbal and manual skills which are usually used in interactions with another person. Examples of social skills include interviewing, asking someone out for a date, or coaching an employee. Verbal skills include the use of the English language (or any other language) by applying grammatical rules. Cognitive skills are modes of thinking or analyzing information such as conceptual thinking, inductive and deductive logic, and decision making. Factual material refers to increasing memory for facts and figures presented to the learner such as in reading a book or listening to a lecture.

There are different training techniques that are more or less appropriate for helping trainees attain each of these given human learning states. For instance, behavior modeling is not the most appropriate technique for learning factual material because other methods are much more efficient and effective: lectures, books, films, and programmed learning. One uses many of the components of behavior modeling (retention processes and cognitive rehearsal) to learn factual material, but most of the components are not particularly needed. Transmittal of the factual material is all that is needed.

The research on the efficacy of behavior modeling has looked primarily at two skills: manual and social skills. Cognitive skills have not been studied as extensively as these, although behavior modeling can be an effective method to learn cognitive skills. Only one study has attempted to study the effects of behavior modeling on changing attitude (Stone and Kelly, 1980) so there is little evidence available. It is possible to learn abstract material through modeling. When someone observes a model performing responses embodying a certain rule, across different contexts, the observer will not mimic the specific responses observed, but will learn to apply the given rule by using different behaviors in different contexts. Behavior modeling is used to teach decision making in social contexts but the majority of research evidence concerns manual and social skills. Consequently, this book describes a training method used primarily to teach new manual or social skills (with some decision making/problem solving). Other applications have yet to be shown, but are very possible.

## Summary

The major purposes of the modeling process are to: 1) transmit information to observers about new responses and 2) transmit information about how responses can be combined into new patterns to improve performance. This information can be conveyed by physical demonstration, pictorial representation, and/or verbal description. In any given instance, the failure of an observer to match the behavior of a model may result from any of the following: not observing the relevant activities, inadequate coding of events for memory representation, failing to mentally rehearse and thereby failing to retain what was learned, physical inability to perform, lack of reproduction attempts, or lack of reproduction accuracy feedback. The failure to maintain the behavior over time or use the behavior in a transfer context may result from the lack of reinforcement for the behavior's use.

In Chapter 1 we have presented an overview of the behavior modeling process and a review of the empirical support for behavior modeling training in industry. In the chapters which follow, the component processes of behavior modeling (attention, retention, performance reproduction, and motivation) will be explored in depth.

# —2—

# Foundations for Behavior Modeling Training

We are living in an age of very rapid change; an age of new discoveries, new knowledge, new theories, new methods, new problems, and new solutions. Toffler (1970) has warned that this increase in the pace and complexity of new knowledge is likely to produce a state of cultural shock. The evidence indicates that this warning cannot be lightly dismissed. It seems that we must find ways to improve our acquisition of knowledge and our ability to choose quickly and accurately what we really want and need to know. We must learn how to make these kinds of decisions and carry them out with others who are affected by them. These concerns have raised questions about the goals and purposes of our basic educational system, human and organizational development, and training in all contexts.

Most early educational theories were based on the belief that the fundamental purpose of education is the transmission of the totality of human knowledge from one generation to the next. This is probably a workable assumption provided that the quantity of knowledge is small enough to be collectively managed by the educational system and that the rate of change occurring in society is small enough to enable the increase of knowledge to be packaged and delivered. In modern times, however, these conditions do not exist; we are living in a period of knowledge explosion in which cultural change is rapid. The increase in the quantity of knowledge in the world today leads us to question the viability of basic educational theory. We simply cannot transmit all of what is known; we can't even keep up year by year. There are two consequences: first, the responsibility for deciding what is to be taught and learned is going to shift increasingly away from the teacher and towards the learner; and second, education will no longer be primarily or exclusively an activity for children.

In this age of expanding knowledge, we need to become more concerned about the process of learning how to learn (especially learning from
experience). One of the primary ways adults learn is through observing
others (modeling). A major precept of modeling is that humans model faster
and more effectively when they have been reinforced for modeling others'
behavior in the past. One of the things we, in our society, need to do is increase the ability of the average adult to learn even in day-to-day situations.
Behavior modeling is a tool not only for the transmission of certain skills
that need to be learned, but it's also a tool for teaching us how to learn. If we
are exposed to a behavior modeling program, we learn something about how
people learn. When a person goes back to everyday life after training, the
person understands a little more about the concepts of modeling: who to
watch, when to watch, and how to learn from watching. Consequently, behavior modeling can be a primary tool in helping us learn how to learn.

## Adult Education

It had been assumed, in the training area, that anybody who knew anything about basic education and was reasonably good at managing the development and logistics of educational programs could be a good trainer of
adults. However, in the last twenty years, educational theory has been changing rapidly with varying techniques for helping adults learn being developed.
Knowles (1970) suggests four basic concepts which differentiate adult education (andragogy) and child education (pedagogy): trainee self-concept, experience, readiness to learn, and time perspective.

The first of these concepts is the self-concept of the individual. Children have the self-concept of being dependent persons. But, as children
move towards adulthood, they become increasingly more aware of themselves and their own decision-making ability. They become very capable in
their self-direction. This change of self-concept from dependency to one of
autonomy characterizes the maturity of adulthood. Adults tend to resent being in situations where they are treated with a lack of respect—being talked
down to, being judged, or otherwise being treated like children. The implications are that adult educators should be facilitators rather than dominant
teachers, adult education should be cooperative rather than competitive, and
also that the adult should have some input into what is taught.

The second concept is experience. Adults, in the course of living, have
accumulated vast quantities of experience where children have not. That experience can lead adults to make more meaningful choices about what is
taught and in what format it is taught. In adult education, the experience of
adults should be valued because the teacher can use theory to integrate and

formalize this experience. However, in the tradition of child education, the tendency has been to regard the experience of students as being of little worth to the educational process. That is why child education is oriented towards one-way communication, assigned readings, and audio-visual presentations, and is content-area centered. Adult education, on the other hand, should include experiential learning, two-way and multidirectional communication such as group discussions, role playing, teamwork exercises, and skill practice sessions and is problem-area centered. This way, the experience of all participants can be brought out and focused on the problem being discussed.

The third concept is readiness to learn. It is known that, in child education (we have all seen it in our high school and college education), educational development occurs best through a sequencing of learning activities that fits the developmental steps of the content. We simply can't learn certain topics or activities before we are ready to assimilate them. The main task of child education is in dealing with the sequencing and interrelating of subjects. Adults, however, should have already completed the basic requirements of their education by developing competency in reading, writing, speech, etc. Their developmental tasks increasingly relate to social roles that form their immediate concerns: working, living, family, recreational activities, etc. In child education, the teacher decides both the content of what will be learned and takes the responsibility for deciding how and in what sequence the learning will take place. In adult education, the group of learners can identify what they wish to learn and the sequence of learning. The adult trainer acts as a resource person to help learners form interest groups to diagnose their learning needs.

The last concept is the time perspective. We used to think of education in terms of preparation for the future rather than preparation for the present. Child education is the business of having students store up information for use on some far-off day following graduation. Teachers present information neatly packaged so students can use it later. But, as Confucius said, "All living is learning." That is particularly true in modern society with our explosion of knowledge. In adult education, learning is problem-centered rather that subject-centered. Thus, adult education is a process for defining problems and solving them for the present.

Two major forces have contributed to the increasing use of behavior modeling programs in industry. The first was the realization on the part of many key individuals in corporations that traditional management programs were not very effective because they did not incorporate adult education principles. The second was a very practical concern for more emphasis on improving the human element in corporations. The primary concern faced by many organizations in the 1970s was a significant change in employee population as a function of affirmative action and the attitudes of returning Vietnam War veterans. Many demands were made for training programs to deal with the social and attitudinal issues resulting from this new work force. Trainers and consultants were eager to supply training programs for this new environment and these, as noted by Goldstein (1974), met with little success. Consequently, modeling principles were examined and used. These principles are discussed below.

## The Theoretical Basis for Behavior Modeling

Behavior modeling training provides behavioral guidance, not a theoretical perspective, about the nature of the task to be learned. While perspective may be helpful, it is not sufficient for appropriate action to follow reliably. There is evidence that if behavior can be directly changed, there is a probability that new attitudes will be developed that are consistent with the new behavior. The new behavior, however, must be successful in its proper context. Early models of industrial training, shown in Figure 2.1, suggest that attempts to influence attitudes will lead to superior behavior. Goldstein and Sorcher (1974) have suggested that behavior modeling assumes a different model for accomplishing behavior change. In contrast, the behavior modeling approach (also shown in Figure 2.1) is based on the logic that training begins with the learning of new behavior. If that new behavior leads to superior results, attitude will become consistent with the new behavior.

Contrary to the opinion of many trainers, the evidence shows clearly that attempts at changing attitude by lecture, verbal persuasion, or logic do not always easily succeed (Campbell, 1971). The major roadblock to attitude change is the existence of defense mechanisms which come into action when customary beliefs or attitudes are threatened. While changing attitudes is feasible, it will usually only happen in long-term therapy, not in a one-day training workshop. However, if you change a trainee's behavior first, and that behavior is successful on the job, the trainee will move his or her attitude to be consistent with the new behavior that works on the job.

These conclusions about changing behavior are consistent with cognitive dissonance theory (Festinger, 1957), which suggests that people dislike having their attitudes and behaviors out of harmony. Individuals will actively seek to reduce this dissonance (nonmatching of attitude and behavior). Festinger and Carlsmith (1959) provide an example of this in a study where two groups of students were asked to do a very boring task. One group was paid $20 to tell the next group of subjects that the task was interesting and the other group was paid $1 to do this. When asked what they thought about the

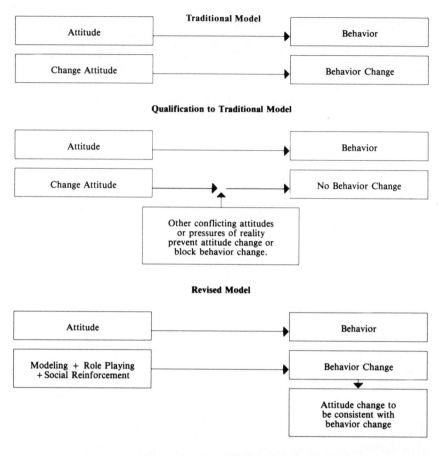

**Figure 2.1** Models of Industrial Training

*Source*: Adapted from Kraut, A. I. (1976) Developing managerial skills via modeling techniques: Some positive research findings. *Personnel Psychology, 29* 325–28.

task after it was completed, those who received $20 said it was boring and they did it for the money. The individuals in the group who received only a dollar reported that they did not mind doing the task and it wasn't so boring. Those individuals who did the task and received a dollar were not comfortable with the idea of doing such a boring task and receiving so little money. They had to reduce the distance between behavior and attitude by changing their attitude, in that they believed the task was not too boring. The group who did the task and received $20 did not have to restore this imbalance between attitude and behavior.

## Social Learning Theory

One theory incorporated in behavior modeling training, and probably the most significant, is social learning theory. Social learning theory has its roots in operant conditioning (reinforcement theory), which states that learning occurs when behavior, exhibited through trial and error, is reinforced. Through this process of differential reinforcement, behaviors leading to rewarding consequences are retained while those leading to no consequences or to punishing consequences are suppressed. Thus, in a new situation, a behavior which had led to a positive consequence (positive reinforcement) will be tried again, whereas a response that had led to a negative consequence (punishment) is not likely to be repeated. Reinforcement theory cannot, however, account for all aspects of human learning. In particular, it can explain neither the quickness of human learning, nor learning that occurs without evidence of behavior (no-trial learning). It is clear that individuals are not always dependent upon direct experience of their behavior for change to take place. People learn from observing others. Bandura (1977) has suggested that our ability to learn by observing others enables us to avoid needless and often fatal trials and errors. This means that we do not simply react to external stimulation. Instead, external influences affect behavior through our cognitive interpretations of the surrounding events. These cognitive processes determine which external events we observe, how we perceive them, whether they are retained, whether they have value, and how that information is organized and stored for future use.

In the Social Learning perspective, response consequences have three basic functions: 1) they impart information which can be stored to guide later behavior, 2) they serve as motivators through their incentive value (as explained by operant conditioning theory), and 3) they strengthen responses. In the course of learning, people not only respond, but they also notice the consequences that they produce. This information serves as a guide for future action and is used to selectively strengthen future responses. For example, observing the experiences of others creates expectations that certain behaviors will bring valued benefits, others will bring no benefits, and still others will bring punishing consequences. By observing these consequences, representing them symbolically, and storing them in memory, people initiate behavior which helps them avert future negative consequences or gain positive consequences. In this perspective, environmental consequences serve principally as informative and motivational feedback rather than to strengthen behavioral responses. We should be talking about regulation, rather than reinforcement, from environmental consequences.

In Bandura's social learning analysis of behavior, information about oneself and the nature of the environment, is developed and verified through four different processes (Bandura, 1977a). First, people derive much of their knowledge from direct experience of the effects produced by their actions (as explained by operant conditioning). Second, information about the nature of the environment is frequently extracted from vicarious experience when people observe the effects produced by someone else's actions. This then serves as a source of verification for the nature of the environment. Third, when direct vicarious experience is limited and we don't have access to it, people can develop and evaluate their conceptions about the environment in terms of the judgement voiced by others. Lastly, people can take the information gained in active, vicarious and social sources of verification (all of which rely on external influences or sources) and use this as a basis for making inferences about the nature of their environment. That is, through either inductive or deductive thought they derive new knowledge based on their past experiences or experience of others which they have observed. Bandura (1971, 1977) has taken the basic concepts of operant conditioning and built in cognitive components to produce what is now called social learning theory. Social Learning is shown in Figure 2.2.

Social learning theorists suggest that if a person anticipates reinforcement from watching and learning a model's actions, that anticipated reinforcement will cause the observer to directly attend to the model's actions. This suggests that observational learning will be more effective when one informs observers in advance about the benefits of adopting a model's behavior rather than by waiting until the observers produce imitative behavior and then rewarding them. However, attending to a model's behavior, while necessary, is insufficient for the behavior to be learned and retained. Other elements (i.e., rehearsal and feedback) must also be present. According to social learning theory, behavior is learned symbolically through cognitive processes before it is performed. By observing the model, an individual forms an idea of how response components must be combined in a sequence to produce a desired new behavior. People guide their actions by prior notions rather than by relying on outcomes to tell them what they must do. Bandura (1971) has shown that after watching models perform novel behaviors, people later described the behavior with considerable accuracy, and, given appropriate inducements, they often achieved errorless enactment on the first trial.

## Components of Social Learning

Social learning is governed by four component processes. They are: attentional processes, retentional processes, reproductional processes, and motivational processes. These are shown in Figure 2.3.

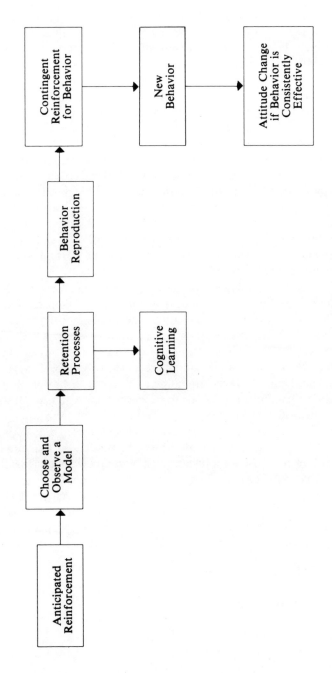

**Figure 2.2** Social Learning Theory

*Source*: Adapted from Bandura (1977) *Social Learning Theory*. By permission of Prentice-Hall, Inc., Englewood Cliffs, NJ.

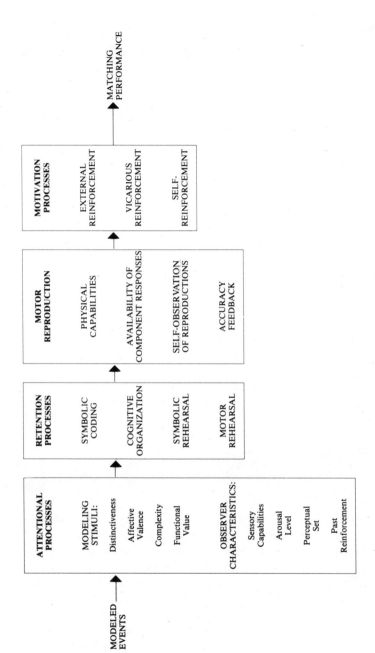

**Figure 2.3**   Processes of Social Learning Theory

*Source:* Adapted from Bandura (1977) *Social Learning Theory.* By permission of Prentice-Hall, Inc., Englewood Cliffs, NJ.

## Attentional Processes

People cannot learn much by observation unless they attend to, and perceive accurately, the significant features and key behaviors of a model's performance. Attentional processes determine what is selectively observed in the profusion of environmental events and what is extracted from such exposure. Factors involved in the attentional processes include the modeling stimuli and observer characteristics.

Among the various attentional determinants of the modeling stimuli are patterns of association. People we regularly associate with are readily observed. Also, those who are considered experts, or have elevated status, or are simply people who usually succeed in obtaining positive consequences for their actions, are all likely to receive greater attention. These people are *distinct*, they stand out from the crowd. In addition, their actions are perceived to result in some desired outcome, which also has value, or *valence*, to the observer. Children observe and copy not only the behaviors but the mannerisms of their parents. Advertising works directly on this premise; if we wear the right fashions, eat the right food, buy the right cologne, or drive the right car we will have fun and attract the right person, just like the people in the commercial.

There are also observer characteristics which are important in the attentional process. The observer must have the sensory capabilities (eyesight, hearing, consciousness) to observe and learn a model's behavior. Past reinforcement for observational learning will produce a perceptual set for attending to a model. If a person has been reinforced by learning successful behavior through vicarious means in the past, the observer is more likely to attend in the future. Finally, if a person is reinforced for attending by any external means, attention will increase.

## Retentional Processes

Having attended to a model's behavior, the observer must also code and retain the behaviors through cognitive processes. People cannot be influenced by observed behavior if they do not remember it. The first thing that an observer will do in the retention process is code the observed key behaviors, those behaviors assumed to have been responsible for the desired outcome, by symbolically reducing the various components of the behavior into a set of symbols (codes) which are easier to store, retrieve, and use later to guide performance. These codes can be either visual images or verbal statements. Sometimes the codes will be a description of the model's key behaviors, other times they will be in rule form. The observer mentally rehearses either the codes and/or the images from the observation process in order to store them in long-term memory. Motor rehearsal also helps in the retention process. Once the observer has attended to the model, stored what has been observed (either with images or verbal coding or both) and rehearsed it mentally so that it has been retained in long-term memory, cognitive learning has occurred.

## Reproductional Processes

The next stage involves actually trying out the behaviors to see if they lead to the same reinforcement that was obtained by the model. The amount of observational learning of complex behaviors that will be exhibited behaviorally depends upon the extent to which the observer has cognitively learned each element or step required to rehearse a sequence of behaviors. Learners who possess all of the elements can arrange them to produce the modeled patterns. But if some of these response components are lacking, behavioral reproduction will be faulty. The observer must also have the physical capabilities to perform the model's actions. A person can observationally learn how another person shoots baskets; but if the person is very short, that person will have difficulty practicing the technique in order to accurately reproduce it.

Furthermore, ideas are rarely transformed into correct responses on the first attempt. Accurate matches are usually achieved by corrective adjustments in practice. Discrepancies between a symbolic representation and execution of the modeled behavior provide cues for corrective action. So a person observes his or her own reproduction to gain accuracy feedback in order to fine-tune his/her motor reproduction of the modeled behaviors. For athletic performances, modeling will only provide a close approximation of the new behavior; the person must refine that performance through self-corrective adjustment on the basis of informative feedback derived from performance after performance.

## Motivational Processes

People do not enact everything they learn. They are more likely to adopt a modeled behavior if it results in valued outcomes. Once a person has learned and reproduced the observed performance, that performance will lead to two types of positive or negative consequences: 1) external reinforcement (reinforcement from events or persons in the environment), and 2) self-reinforcement (reinforcing oneself). If these consequences are positive, the behavior will be maintained and used in the future.

## Summary

In any given instance, the failure of an observer to match the behavior of a model may result from any of the following: not observing the relevant activities, inadequate coding of events for memory representation, failing to mentally rehearse and thereby failing to retain what was learned, physical inability to perform, lack of reproduction attempts, or lack of reproduction accuracy feedback. The failure to maintain the behavior over time or use the behavior in a transfer context may result from the lack of reinforcement for the behavior's use.

Social learning and the impact of a model have been found to occur in natural settings with virtually no prompting. For example, Lefkowitz, Blake, and Mouton (1955) showed the impact of a model on the frequency of pedestrians' jaywalking. These researchers had an individual cross the street either with the "walk" signal or during the "wait" signal. Half of the models were dressed in a freshly pressed suit, shined shoes, white shirt, etc. (high status model) and the other half of the models were dressed in scuffed shoes, patched trousers, and an unpressed blue denim shirt (low status model). The behavior of 2,103 pedestrians was observed and recorded. Their results indicated that significantly more pedestrians crossed against the wait signals when the model crossed than when the model waited or no model was present. They found that pedestrians crossed against the wait signal significantly more times with the high status model than when the low status model was used.

Bryon and Test (1967) showed that positive real-life behavior was also modeled. In their first study, an automobile with a flat left rear tire was parked on a Los Angeles street with a young woman standing next to it. During half of the time of this experiment, a second car was parked one-quarter of a mile behind the car described above. This car was raised by a jack under its left rear bumper with a woman watching a man (the model) changing the flat tire. Every driver that saw the car with the model saw the second car also. Of the 4,000 vehicles that went by, significantly more drivers stopped at the second car and offered to assist the stranded motorist when the model was present at the first car than when no model was present.

In another experiment, these researchers studied modeling effects at a Salvation Army donation kettle. Three hundred sixty-five times during the course of the experiment, the model walked up and placed a donation in the kettle and then walked away. Observers recorded the number of donations made by passersby 20 seconds immediately after each donation made by the model and 365 other 20 second periods with no model present. Significantly more passersby made donations when the model had done so than when no model was present.

## The Effectiveness of Modeling

The previous studies show that the presence of a model can have a significant impact on people's behavior in natural settings. The majority of modeling research has been conducted in clinical, counseling, and child development settings, investigating modeling as a means to teach social skills, manual skills, and rule-oriented behavior.

Several studies have shown that modeling facilitates the learning of manual skills. Gerst (1971) found that modeling was useful in teaching persons to use physical responses drawn from the manual language of the deaf. Bandura and Jeffery (1973) used modeling to increase the retention of manual responses consisting of lateral movements covering 1, 2, or 3 interval distances on a pattern board. Bandura, Jeffery, and Bachicha (1974) and Jeffery (1976) showed the effectiveness of modeling in teaching the construction of complex configurations using wooden rods and joints (tinker toys).

In the clinical area, modeling has been used to teach socially adapted behavior to adults and children. For example, researchers have shown that modeling has been successfully used to teach people to engage in more vocational self-exploration, i.e., make more self-referent vocationally relevant statements (Heitbrink, 1971), to modify adult aggressiveness behavior (Tureen, 1972), and to increase self-referent verbal behavior in students (Rosengren, 1972). It has been used with children to increase sharing behavior (Paulos and Liebert, 1972), to teach children the ability to delay gratification (Dean, 1975), and to increase cooperative behavior of second- and fifth-grade children (Sagotsky, 1977). Behavior modeling training has been found to be an effective method for teaching various counseling skills including the best way to communicate empathy (Dalton, 1973; Perry, 1975; Dalton and Sundblad, 1976; and Rosen, 1978).

Zimmerman and Rosenthal (1974) have reviewed the research examining the observational learning of rule-governed behavior by children and have found that modeling procedures have been effective in teaching a variety of generalized language rules, abstract concepts or principles, conservation responses, problem-solving strategies, and creative responses in children. Studies reviewed by these authors have shown that modeling procedures, both alone and in conjunction with other variables, were found to be effective in teaching children drawn from diverse populations to respond according to generalized linguistic rules. Observational modification of language usage has been successful when no reinforcement has been given to either the child or the model. Thus, these reviewed experiments demonstrate the utility of modeling for establishing conceptual behavior, that concepts learned can be generalized both immediately after training and after long delays, that observationally instated abstract concepts are relatively independent of the particular stimuli of experimenters involved in their original training, that coding procedures play an important part in observational learning, generalization and retention of abstract concepts, and that the generalization of concepts is dependent to some extent upon multiple models.

An important finding from the Zimmerman and Rosenthal (1974) review is evidence that modeling is effective in teaching conceptual strategies and cognitive styles. Both Loughlin, Moss, and Miller (1969) and Lamel (1971) found that modeling was effective in significantly altering the problem-solving strategy of children. This evidence of the effect of modeling on rule-oriented behavior is extremely important in behavior modeling. In these situations, the observer is free to complete the specific task with whatever specific response the person choses, as long as it is consistent with the rule pattern. What appears to be modeled or imitated is a rule-governed pattern or template which constrains the selection of the specific response components without specifying their exact character. For example, Rosenthal, Zimmerman, and Durning (1970) showed that children adopted the underlying criteria governing the model's diverse styles of inquiry with very little repetition of the model's exact word content. Liebert and Swenson (1971) found that after vicariously learning a conceptual rule, observers could accurately predict performance of the model on an unfamiliar task. In essence, these studies take modeling far beyond the simple concept of imitation, and have implications for how we encode and store information which is obtained observationally.

Models do more than teach novel styles of thought and conduct. Modeling strengthens or weakens inhibitions on behavior that observers have previously learned. Rachman (1972) and Bandura (1971, 1977) have reviewed the effects of modeling on observer phobias. Bandura suggested that behavior restraints are most strongly developed by observing the consequences experienced by models. Seeing models punished seems to inhibit behaviors in others; conversely, seeing others engaged in threatening or prohibited activities without adverse consequences can reduce inhibitions in observers. Such effects are revealed in therapeutic applications of modeling principles. Exposure to models performing feared activities, such as handling snakes, without any harmful effects weakens defensive behavior, reduces fears, and allows the observer to engage in the feared behavior. As an example, Kleinsasser (1968) has used modeling to reduce public speaking anxiety; Ritter (1969) has used modeling to reduce fear of heights; and Bandura (1969) has used modeling to reduce fear of snakes.

## The Trainee as Decision Maker

Traditional learning theorists have long argued that behavior will change automatically when paired with an appropriate consequence (reward or punishment) of the behavior. Thus, to increase the likelihood of a particular behavior, all that is required is that the individual be rewarded for exhibiting the behavior. Conversely, to reduce the likelihood of an undesirable behavior, one simply punishes the individual or withholds a reward from the individual for exhibiting the behavior. While the importance of reward and punishment are certainly important factors in the motivation to change, they are not the sole processes which regulate behavior. Theories emphasizing these reinforcement mechanisms for changing behavior have given way to theories emphasizing the role of cognitive processes in understanding motivation (Bandura, 1977, 1977a; Locke, 1968). Whether the trainee employs the skills presented and learned in a behavior modeling training program involves a number of decisions on the part of the trainee, not just whether or not the model was observed and the trainee's practice was rewarded or punished. Expectancy theory (Porter and Lawler, 1968; Vroom, 1964) serves as a useful heuristic for outlining the considerations made by a trainee that skills presented in the training program should be attempted back on the job. First, the outcomes proposed by the trainer and used as rewards for the model must also be seen as desirable to the trainee. In other words, they must have *valence*. Second, performing in a manner similar to that of the model must be seen as *instrumental* in leading to the trainee receiving those outcomes. Finally, the trainee must *expect* that he or she will be able to perform like the model. Thus one can believe that performing in a particular way will lead to a certain outcome, but if there is doubt that one can perform the necessary activities there will be little motivation to change. Bandura (1977a) has referred to this belief that one can successfully perform the activities necessary for obtaining the desired outcomes as self-efficacy.

## Self-Efficacy Theory

The importance of self-efficacy for the likelihood that skills presented in a training program will be applied in a new setting has been summarized by Bandura (1977a):

> The strength of people's convictions in their own effectiveness is likely to affect whether they will even try to cope with given situations. At this initial level, perceived self-efficacy influences choice of behavioral settings. People fear and tend to avoid threatening situations they believe exceed their coping skills, whereas they get involved in activities and behave assuredly when they judge themselves capable of handling situations that would otherwise be intimidating. (pp. 193–94)

Bandura identifies four sources of efficacy expectation (See Figure 2.4): performance accomplishments, vicarious experience, verbal persuasion, and emotional arousal. Performance accomplishment will typically be the most influential because it is based on personal mastery situations. Mastery expectations are increased by success, decreased by failures. This is, of course, the purpose of skills practice in behavior modeling; the trainee must actually perform the requisite behaviors which lead to successful perfor-

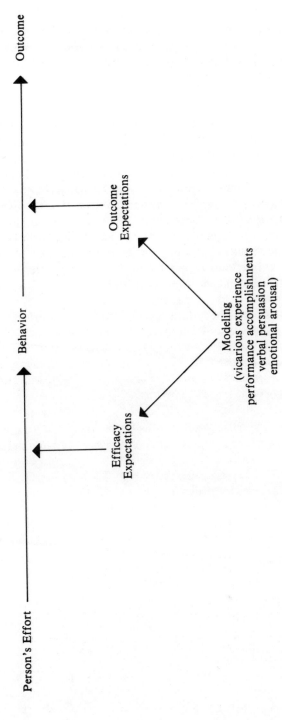

**Figure 2.4**   Effects of Efficacy and Outcome Expectancies

*Source*: Adapted from Bandura (1977) *Social Learning Theory*. By permission of Prentice-Hall, Inc., Englewood Cliffs, NJ.

mance. In an early test of the role of self-efficacy on behavioral change, Bandura, Adams, and Beyer (1977) obtained ratings of perceived self-efficacy about interactions with snakes of adult snake-phobics. As predicted, they found that those receiving participant modeling (where actual contact with snakes occurred) had higher efficacy expectations in a new situation and had higher performance in threatening tasks than did those in the modeling only condition, who were likewise better than those subjects in a nontreatment control condition. Furthermore, high correlations were found within each condition between successful snake approach responses and the strength of the efficacy expectations.

The next most influential source of efficacy expectations is, of course, observational learning. The observer draws an inference, from observing others, that job performance will improve if enacted like that of the model. Weaker in influencing self-efficacy is verbal persuasion. Since verbal persuasion relies solely on suggestion, it alone may have an effect on self-efficacy only as long as no disconfirming real or observed situation takes place. Finally, emotional arousal such as tension or anxiety may result in an attribution of limited mastery of the situation.

Behavior modeling training addresses all four efficacy expectations. Verbal persuasion is used to present the key behaviors and general rule codes, vicarious learning through the presence of a model, performance accomplishment during skills practice, and as a result, reduced emotional arousal when the trainee is faced with a previously emotionally arousing situation which he or she now believes can be mastered.

## A Model of Human Learning

The information provided in the remainder of this chapter serves as a useful summary of how humans learn new manual and social skills (and possibly, some simple cognitive skills) through the process of behavior modeling training. The core of the model shown in Figure 2.5 is six elements related to social learning: attention to modeling stimuli, observational learning, retention, behavioral rehearsal, reinforcement, and transfer. The ultimate aim is to teach trainees new behavior and have that behavior transfer to a context outside the training environment (i.e., as on the job).

The first major element is *attention to the modeling stimuli*. One is not going to learn observationally without attending to the modeling stimuli. There are four basic elements that enhance an observer's attention to modeling stimuli: the modeling display characteristics (e.g., type of media, organization), the key behavior characteristics (e.g., distinctiveness, number), characteristics of the model (e.g., expertness, age, sex) and the observer's characteristics (e.g., arousal level, anticipation of reinforcement). If an ob-

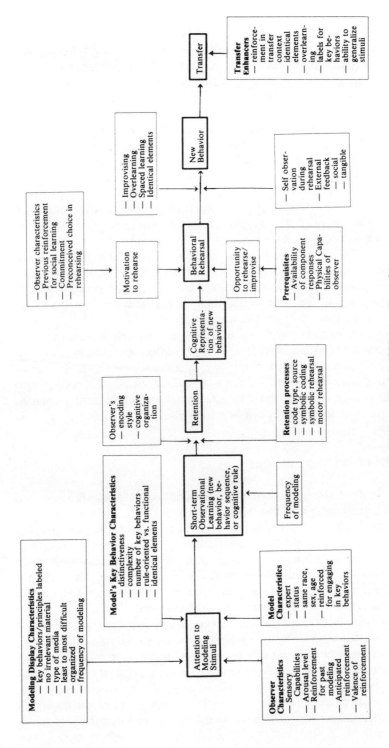

**Figure 2.5** A Model of Human Learning

server attends to a modeling stimuli, the resultant observational learning will, at least, go into *short-term memory*. The type of observational learning (learning abstract rules to apply across contexts or learning to reproduce a sequence of behaviors) is dependent upon modeled behavior characteristics such as the type of behavior (rule-oriented vs. simple behavior sequence) and how distinctive the behavior is in addition to other factors like the frequency of seeing different modeled performances.

Once the trainee has observed the training content, the person must use several *retention processes* in order for that learning to be transferred into long-term memory. Retention processes depend to a large extent on the observer's encoding style (whether the observer primarily codes visually or verbally or uses some kind of a dual coding system) and on the observer's cognitive organization (how information is stored). Given the observer's encoding style and how the person cognitively organizes material, there are several processes a person goes through in order to retain the material. The first is symbolic coding. Symbolic coding is the process of organizing the diverse elements of the modeled performance into symbols in order that the material can be stored, retrieved, and used efficiently to guide performance at a later date. Symbolic coding is a process that a person must go through to learn a large amount of information. It can be initiated and helped externally by providing some kind of description of the models' key behaviors. We will see later that code type and source have important functions in symbolic coding. Another retention process is symbolic rehearsal. Symbolic rehearsal is the process of mentally rehearsing the modeled performance. Finally, motor rehearsal (which is the actual performance of the behavior) is done.

These processes (symbolic coding, symbolic rehearsal and motor rehearsal) tend to develop cues for retrieval of information, put the information into a form that can be stored easily in memory, and move the information into long-term memory. After the trainee has: 1) attended to the modeling stimuli, 2) observationally learned either a sequence of behavior or rules underlying a series of model performances, and 3) gone through the retention processes to store and build retrieval cues for this information, the person has completed the cognitive components of long-term observational learning.

The next step is *behavioral rehearsal* (actually trying out and fine-tuning what has been learned observationally). There are two prerequisites in order for behavioral rehearsal to occur. The first is availability of the component responses. In both abstract modeling and in functional modeling there is some sequence of behavior. In order for a person to behaviorally rehearse rule-oriented behavior or a series of behaviors learned in functional modeling, the component responses of that sequence must have already been learned and symbolically practiced. If these have not been previously learned, then the trainee has to remedially learn the component responses. Secondly, the observer must have the physical capabilities to perform the behaviors.

Behavioral rehearsal will result in new accurate behavior if the new behavior is given reinforcement during behavioral rehearsal and certain needed characteristics of the behavioral rehearsal are present. Behavioral rehearsal must be done in a way that the person is committed to the behavior. One way to do this is to make behavioral rehearsal public. If a person publicly rehearses the behavior, he or she cannot later disown it. The more perceived choice a trainee has in behavioral rehearsal, the more likely the trainee is to be committed to the behavior. The practice should be spaced so that the trainee has a chance to rest between behavioral rehearsals, and should include all stimuli that would be applicable in the transfer context.

With adults, reinforcement of a response is a motivational tool more than a learning tool. Consequently, during behavioral rehearsal, reinforcement acts in two ways: 1) it provides accuracy feedback such that the trainee can fine-tune the behavior; and 2) reinforcement helps motivate the trainee to use the behavior in the future. Reinforcement can be applied in several different ways: 1) self-observation (the trainee observes his or her own behavior and compares it to the observational learning), 2) tangible external reinforcement (e.g., money), and 3) social reinforcement (praise from trainer and other trainees). Accuracy feedback will help the person fine-tune the behavior and it can also be a motivating tool.

Finally, the last component is *transfer*. In any training program, the ultimate aim is to have the learning transfer to the site where it will be used. This is especially true in formalized classroom training. There are several known transfer enhancers. One of the primary enhancers is reinforcement on the job, either through self-reinforcement or external reinforcement. When a trainee attempts a new behavior in the transfer context, it may not always lead to the reinforcement that was anticipated. Thus, external reinforcement for attempting the behavior is an extremely important transfer tool. Next is the concept of identical elements: to the extent that the training looks like the transfer context, it will be easy for the new behavior to be transferred from the learning context to the transfer context. Overlearning (practicing beyond the point of first accurate reproduction) is important. Furthermore, overlearning increases the chance that the behavior will be used in the transfer context under stress or high performance situations. Where labels for the key behaviors of the training context are provided, it helps the individual not only cue retrieval of the information but also helps in transferring both in normal and stressful situations.

## Implications for Training Programs

At minimum, the learning process involves three primary components: 1) presentation of the material to be learned, 2) opportunity for practicing the material presented, and 3) feedback about the practice. These components can be seen in Figure 2.5. Training techniques can therefore be characterized in terms of the presence/absence and type(s) of: 1) transmittal method(s) utilized (i.e., how learning material is actually presented), 2) type of simulation (i.e., practice) formally or informally utilized, and 3) feedback concerning the practice which is received by the learner (including amount and specificity). Furthermore, training techniques can be judged by the extent to which the practice component incorporates practice of the desired terminal behavior (i.e., learning/increased memory, new manual behavior, verbal behavior, social skill, or cognitive skill).

Many training techniques do not formally include all required components (transmittal, practice, feedback) and/or do not allow practice of the desired terminal behavior (end state). For example, lecture, films, and books do not include practice or feedback. Role play and some simulation games do not formally include transmittal of learning material or specific feedback. Programmed instruction, computer-assisted programmed instruction, and interactive video do not allow for behavioral practice (only mental practice), consequently not always supplying practice with the desired terminal behaviors. Behavior modeling includes all required components (transmittal of learning material, practice, and feedback) and formalizes practice of the desired terminal behavior. For teaching manual or social skills, behavior modeling is probably the most effective method.

# II

# The Components
# of Behavior Modeling

# ─3─

# The Components of Behavior Modeling

Before each component of behavior modeling is examined in detail, the literature examining the additive importance of the components to the overall method will be reviewed. There seems to be adequate evidence for the inclusion of each component, given various conditions.

## Comparison of the Components of Behavior Modeling Training

The relative importance of several components of the behavior modeling technique has been systematically studied by numerous researchers. Basic research evidence justifying the place of each of the components in behavior modeling has been reviewed by Goldstein and Sorcher (1974) and Twentyman and Zimering (1979). Spool (1978) has reviewed training programs designed to train observers of behavior and has discussed several studies which lack one or more components of the behavior modeling technique. In each instance, the programs studied were less effective than programs containing all of the components.

Several studies have focused on the modeling component. Fyffe and Oei (1979) compared no modeling and no feedback (social reinforcement) conditions with a condition including modeling and feedback from a supervisor. Behavioral rehearsal was constant across these conditions. Results indicated that the condition combining modeling and feedback from the supervisor was superior to the other conditions incorporating only behavioral rehearsal for increasing the use of counseling skills. Lira et al. (1975) investigated the relative efficacy of modeling, role play, and a no-treatment control group on the reduction of avoidance behavior. They found that role play showed a greater reduction of avoidance behavior than did modeling or control conditions. McFall and Twentyman (1973) examined the relative combinations of behavior modeling components in an assertiveness training program. These researchers found that role play and social reinforcement both made additive contributions to performance on self-report and behavioral measures. Stone and Vance (1976) compared training procedures containing modeling, role play plus social reinforcement, instructions alone, and all possible combinations of the above, in an attempt to increase written empathic communication of college students. All components together were superior to any components alone or partial combinations. Rehearsal plus social reinforcement were superior to modeling which was superior to instructions. Nelson (1982) showed that rehearsal contributed more than modeling in a study with alcoholics. Petroski, Craighead, and Horan (1983) found no difference between modeling and behavioral rehearsal in increasing grooming skills. Stroll (1982) compared modeling only, modeling–instruction, and modeling–instruction–rehearsal conditions as they are related to increasing cooperative game behavior in children. He found that the latter two conditions did not produce different levels of cooperation but were both more powerful than modeling only. All three strategies produced higher levels of cooperation than a no-training control group. Willis and Gueldenpfenning (1981) found that a handouts–practice–feedback condition increased specified tutoring skills more than a handout–modeling condition which in turn was better than a lecture handout condition.

This series of studies seems to show that modeling may be the weakest component of the behavior modeling technique. When the contribution of each component is determined relative to other components either separately or in combination, modeling seems to add the least to training effectiveness. Decker (1980) has given one explanation why modeling may have been the weakest component in these early studies. He showed that the early behavior modeling and microtraining techniques did not include formalized retention processes (symbolic coding, symbolic rehearsal, and cognitive organization). In a study where these retention processes were formalized into the behavior modeling training program, he found that modeling was significantly enhanced and the overall behavior modeling technique was much more effective than the behavior modeling program without the formalized retention processes.

Kazdin (1982) has shown that a condition combining behavioral rehearsal with mental rehearsal (covert rehearsal) enhanced assertive behavior (post-treatment and eight month follow-up) more than either behavioral rehearsal or mental rehearsal alone. Further evidence of this point was shown by Dorster (1972) in his work on facilitating self-exploration in counseling studies. In his studies, subjects underwent several instruction programs prior to behavior practice interviews: 1) minimal instruction on appropriate interview behavior; 2) detailed instructions; 3) observational model which consisted of observing a videotaped model demonstrate a vocal behavior with detailed instructions; 4) role rehearsal of appropriate interview behavior; and 5) detailed instructions, plus observing the model, plus role rehearsal. Results revealed the importance of the instructional component. Detailed instructions were the single most effective component for increasing the skill of self-exploration in counseling clients. Uhlemann, Lee, and Stone (1976) attempted to determine the relative importance of instructions, modeling and their combined effect on teaching reflection of feeling and empathy skills in counseling. The 50 subjects were randomly assigned to five training techniques: instruction only, modeling only, instruction plus modeling, modeling plus instruction (reversed order), and the control group. A subsequent interview with a coached client was scored for frequency of the skills. The results revealed that subjects in the instruction and the two instruction plus modeling groups reflected feelings significantly more often than the modeling only and control groups. With the more complex behavior of empathy, however, the instruction plus modeling and modeling plus instruction groups scored significantly higher than did the instruction only, modeling only, and control groups.

Perkins and Atkinson (1973) studied the relative merits of lecture plus discussion, lecture plus modeling, and lecture plus role playing, on teaching attending behavior, reflection of feelings, and summarization of feelings. All three groups maintained eye contact significantly longer than a control group and post-training interview reflection-of-feeling responses were recorded significantly more often for subjects in the lecture-discussion and lecture-modeling conditions. The most complex behavior of summarization, which occurred in less than 5 percent of the responses, occurred significantly more frequently only in the lecture-modeling group. Consequently, it can be shown that modeling is a powerful component of the behavior modeling process when there is some verbal description of the key behaviors shown with or in the modeling display. This is particularly true when one is trying to teach complex skills.

These results demonstrate that frequency of responses may be influenced by instructions alone on relatively simple behaviors but this does not necessarily hold true for more complex behaviors. The Stone and Vance study (1976) lends further support to the conclusion that efficient imparting of complex skills requires instructions, modeling, retention, rehearsal, and feedback.

O'Toole (1979) has examined the role of behavioral practice in a microtraining program used to teach counseling interviewing skills. Subjects were randomly assigned to five training conditions: 1) audio model followed by practice, 2) video model followed by practice, 3) written model followed by practice, 4) written model followed by no practice, and 5) a comparison training group. The results revealed that the frequencies of both the total use and total preferred use of interviewing skills taught were significantly higher for subjects in the practice training conditions than in the no-practice training conditions, regardless of the model. The importance of practice that is demonstrated in this study is consistent with other studies (e.g., Protas, 1981).

Overall, the studies examining the relative importance of the components of behavior modeling suggest that maximum treatment results in maximum behavior change. However, the complexity of the behavior to be learned may change the importance of some of the training components. Teaching less complex behavior may not require all components. In short, however, the complete behavior modeling technique appears to be the most effective method of imparting skills. The combination of modeling and behavioral rehearsal with feedback is extremely important. At minimum, practice and feedback are required. Adding modeling shows the trainee what the person is to learn and provides a standard for correct performance. The inclusion of some retention processes becomes extremely important with complex skills.

## Summary

We can see that the efficacy of behavior modeling has been examined in numerous contexts. It has also been examined with various training contents. The technique has invariably been found to be highly effective in changing trainee behavior. This is true across both the industrial and the counseling contexts. Virtually all of the studies of the effectiveness of behavior modeling discussed here have examined these techniques in teaching social skills. There is ample evidence, however, that these procedures are also effective in teaching manual skills (Jeffery, 1976; Bandura and Jeffery, 1973; and Bandura, 1977) and cognitive skills (Zimmerman and Rosenthal, 1974).

Given the research evidence examined, it seems that the behavior modeling technique is extremely effective in changing trainees' manual, verbal, and social behavior. The studies examined include both quasi-experimental designs (not controlling all threats to internal and external validity) and a sufficient number of true experimental designs to conclude that, across all of the studies, behavior modeling is an effective training technique.

Furthermore, in looking at studies examining the various components of behavior modeling, we must conclude that the basic components of modeling, retention, behavioral rehearsal, and feedback must be included in order to change behavior. There must also be some examination of transfer principles if one wants the behavior transferred from the learning context to the transfer context. Only in very simple skills have we seen a truncated version of behavior modeling be effective. We have evidence that behavior modeling training does work, and that all of the components of behavior modeling should be present whenever possible.

# ——4——

# Modeling

The critical claim in modeling is that individuals are not dependent upon direct experience of their behavior for behavior change to take place. People can learn from observing others. Bandura (1977) has suggested that the ability of individuals to learn by observing others enables humans to avoid needless and often fatal trials and errors. He also suggests that observers can learn faster than actual performers because performers need to devote considerable attention to performing required responses and, therefore, cannot attend as well to consequences. Basically, people guide their actions by cognition rather than by relying on outcomes to tell them what to do. Humans formalize rules from past experience and observation which suggest when and how to use behavior to obtain desired results.

In a classic review of imitation and modeling, Miller and Dollard (1941) compiled a number of findings about imitation learning: one more readily imitates a more prestigious model; we generalize between models; imitative learning is assisted by verbalizing responses; and directing the subject's attention to the vital elements is helpful. They suggested that failure to imitate would occur when any of these major conditions was not met. Though Miller and Dollard drew attention to the importance of the modeling phenomenon, Bandura (1971,1977) has extended the value of the concept as an explanatory tool. Bandura pointed out that imitative behavior can occur even in the absence of the occurrence of real behavior or its direct reinforcement. He also drew attention to the importance of symbolic processes in modeling. The early work of Bandura and his associates is reviewed by Rachman (1972) and summarized by Bandura (1977).

## Modeling Enhancers

There are characteristics of the model, the model's behavior, the modeling display, and the observer which have been demonstrated to significantly affect the degree of learning by modeling. These are described in detail below.

### Model's Characteristics

Modeling is facilitated when the model, or the person to be imitated, in relation to the observer, 1) is: of the same age, sex, and race, etc., 2) is of apparent high competence or expertise, 3) is of high status, 4) controls resources desired by the observer, 5) is apparently friendly and helpful, and 6) of particular importance, when the model is rewarded for engaging in the behaviors. Each of these is discussed in detail below.

While much of the early modeling research that compared sex of model in relation to the observer found that male models were superior (Bandura, Ross, and Ross, 1963; Hicks, 1965; Rossenblith, 1959; Krumboltz, Varenhorst, and Thoresen, 1975), these differences can probably be discounted. For example, Rickard and Joubert (1968) found a significant sex of model by sex of observer interaction. Modeling was enhanced when the sex of the model and observer were the same. Robinson, Froehle, and Kupius (1979) found no difference in model behavior related to the sex of model. Noel (1976) used behavior modeling techniques with high school students to teach direct mutual communication and found improved communication effectiveness but no sex or race differences. Sodetz (1972) also found no sex differences in behavior modeling training. It must be pointed out that many of the early studies looked at gender type behaviors, such as aggression, when they found that male models were superior. It is also possible that the influence of women as models has changed significantly as women have moved into more prestigious positions such that the sex difference is not as important as are the perceptions of status or expertise. This has not been examined.

Kloba (1975) manipulated model status in teaching counseling skills and found that increased model status as perceived by the observer increases the modeling effect. Cook and Kunce (1977, 1978) used behavior modeling to teach counseling skills by showing subjects either a model perceived as being an expert or a model perceived as just coping with the problem shown. Both studies examined the reduction of anxiety towards participation in a counseling interview by a counseling student. In both studies, a model who was perceived as an expert reduced the anxiety towards participation more than the coping model.

At least two studies have shown a "coping and then mastery" sequence to be helpful in modeling (Meichenbaum, 1971; Kazdin, 1975). The model initially shows uncertainty and apprehensiveness about applying the skill (is like the trainees), and then demonstrates increasing confidence and competence with the skill. This sequence has been shown to be more powerful than the mastery mode alone in reducing snake avoidance behavior. Consequently, this technique has not been used in skill acquisition training, but may be useful in such programs when trainee anxiety is high.

Dowling and Frantz (1975) have shown that facilitative models who appear friendly and helpful generate significantly more imitative learning than control-oriented models or unfacilitative models. Facilitativeness, the independent variable, was defined along the two dimensions of empathy and respect. Baron (1970) manipulated attraction towards the model by varying the apparent degree of attitude similarity between subjects and the model. In this study, he showed that both attraction towards the model by the observer and model competence influenced the rate at which subjects learned to match the behavior of the model. However, the results indicated that attraction produced no effect by itself upon learning, while the model's competence did influence matching behavior. The two independent variables interacted so that the high level of attraction facilitated imitation when the model was relatively successful in performing the experimental task (i.e., high competence) but interfered with imitation when the model was relatively unsuccessful on this task (i.e., low competence). Goldstein et al. (1973) have shown that when a model was characterized as "cold," that treatment had an insignificant impact in comparison with controls.

Hamilton, Thompson, and White (1970) have shown the importance of rewarding the model in a modeling display. Modeling is effective when the observers see the model either rewarded or punished for the behavior but is not effective when the reward or punishment is inconsistent and when there are no vicarious consequences. Furthermore, Kazdin (1974, 1975) has shown that modeling with imagined favorable consequences had a significantly greater impact upon behavior than modeling without them.

## Model's Behavior Characteristics

Greater modeling will occur when the model's behavior is: 1) distinctive, 2) meaningful to the observer, 3) not too complex, and 4) is observable. Mann and Decker (1984) have suggested that the attention to and retention of modeling stimuli appear to be affected by the distinctiveness of the stimuli. Distinctiveness may occur naturally (e.g., a red shape against a black background) or it may be induced. A key behavior that is repeated several times or because of other reasons stands out in contrast to the background of a modeling display would be naturally distinctive. Mann and Decker (1984) suggest one can induce distinctiveness by 1) displaying key behaviors out of context, 2) exaggerating the behaviors, 3) repeating the behaviors, and/or 4) including written labels or descriptions of the behavior in the modeling display. These researchers showed that the latter strategy enhanced recall and generalizability of modeled behaviors. Mann and Decker (1984) also summarize research showing that meaningful behavior is more readily modeled. Bandura, Jeffery, and Bachicha (1974) have shown that letters assigned to modeled behaviors significantly enhance the reproduction of those behaviors when the letters form a meaningful word.

Finally, we have seen that behavior modeling has been used primarily to teach manual and social skills. A few studies have shown the use of this technique to teach cognitive skills such as grammar rules and decision making. Fine-tuned muscle activity such as an athletic performance may be very difficult to teach via behavior modeling. They key behavior(s) must be readily observable for imitation or generalization to occur.

## Modeling Display Characteristics

Modeling is facilitated when the modeling display depicts the behaviors to be modeled: 1) in a vivid and detailed manner, 2) in order from least to most difficult behaviors, 3) with sufficient frequency and repetitiveness to make learning probable, 4) with a minimum of irrelevant details, 5) when several different models rather than a single model are utilized, 6) when a live or video-tape acted model is used, and 7) when a positive modeling display is shown (with or without a negative modeling display) rather than a model only depicting what not to do.

Bandura and Mischel (1965) have shown that matching performance can be achieved without a live model if the essential features of the model's behavior are accurately depicted pictorially. To the extent that a filmed modeling display and a live model present the same amount of information and are equally effective in commanding attention, comparable results may be expected. Performances that entail strong inhibitions may be more easily established through live modeling (Bandura and Menlove, 1968). There are other aspects of live modeling which facilitate the behavioral rehearsal component of behavior modeling and will be discussed in later chapters.

Walter (1976) has explored the relative effect of acted vs. natural models upon the behavior of observers. In this experiment, 72 undergraduate students saw either an acted model (i.e., a live model enactment developed to show only the behaviors to be taught) or a natural model (a model tape of an interacting group). He found that acted models were more effective in promoting behavior change than were natural models. He concluded that the relative effectiveness of acted models to induce behavior change leads one to reason that the clear presentation of behavioral cues is central to social learning of complex behaviors. Consequently, Walter's research relates to the retention processes that are described in the next chapter. He concluded that the value of modeling depended greatly on a demonstration of concrete cues. Such cues improve subjects' ability to perceive target behaviors. The complexity of the social learning process, plus the probable need for cuing, led Walter to suggest that acted models can be utilized effectively to increase the salience of the desired behaviors in the modeling display. What is clear from this research is that only the key behaviors (and cues or labels) should be presented. All irrelevant material should be deleted from the display.

Alssid and Hutchinson (1977) examined two modeling techniques in training counseling students to ask open-ended questions. These authors hypothesized that a pure video model (i.e., exhibiting only desired behavior) would result in greater learning than a corrective video model (i.e., exhibiting both desired and undesired behavior) given that both models contained cues to indicate the behaviors were desired or undesired. Eighteen counseling students were randomly assigned to these two conditions and a no-treatment control. The results indicated that modeling had a significant impact on the percentages of open-ended questions and that the pure model was significantly different from the corrective model. The findings support the hypothesis that the pure video model would result in greater learning and they indicate that pure video modeling is the most efficient (less training time) means for training. The authors conclude that the corrective model (including both the desired and undesired behaviors) interferes with learning.

Kanfer and Goldstein (1980) have reviewed the characteristics of the modeling display which enhance modeling. Using different or multiple models which vary along such dimensions as sex, age, race, etc. enhances the presentation by showing both the generalizability of the key behaviors as well as their appropriateness for each particular observer. Graduated modeling displays, in which the model begins with performance at the level of the observers and gradually progresses to more complex behavior, should be used where the modeled behavior is complex or observers are anxious about use of the key behaviors. Bandura and Menlove (1968) found that observance of multiple models with different dogs was significantly more effective than observance of one model with a single dog in reducing avoidance behavior with dogs. Other studies have shown the superiority of multiple models in teaching assertiveness (Kazdin, 1975) and error reduction in reading a micrometer (Lumsdaine, Sulzer, and Kopstein, 1961).

## Observers' Characteristics

Greater modeling will occur when the observer: 1) is instructed to or expected to model or perform the behavior, 2) is similar to the model in relevant attitudes or background, 3) is favorably disposed towards or attracted to the model, and most importantly 4) is rewarded for engaging in the model's behaviors. Other personality variables which tend to enhance modeling have also been investigated.

Research studies have shown that modeling is enhanced when the observers are instructed to model and/or are told that they will be expected to perform the behaviors. Kanfer et al. (1971) and Tibbitts (1974) have shown that when observers expect to perform the behavior seen in the modeling display imitation is increased.

Satterwhite (1971) has investigated the interaction between the model's and observer's cognitive style. The degree to which the observer imitated the model depended upon whether the two were similar or dissimilar in cognitive style (reflective vs. impulsive). Cognitive style was measured by the Matching Familiar Figures Test. Furthermore, Dolly, Meredith, and Saunders (1977) had potential observers do a task on which they were all provided negative feedback concerning their ability to identify the personality characteristics of others. The observers were then given the opportunity to imitate models competent on the task or models poor on the task. The poor models' performances were more similar to the subjects' performance. Most subjects imitated the poor models, indicating that observers tend to model or imitate models that are similar to themselves. Finally, Meisel (1972) performed a study in which 60 college males were led to believe that they had attitudes which were either similar to or opposite from the political and social attitudes of the model. The control group received no information about the model's attitudes. Again, observers tended to imitate the models which they perceived to be similar to themselves. Consequently, observers tend to imitate models to which they are attracted and models who are rewarded for the model behavior.

Finally, there are several individual differences which have been found to enhance modeling. Observers rated as highly authoritarian have a significantly greater tendency to imitate models (Candler and Goodman, 1977). Internal locus of control subjects demonstrate significantly greater attention to, awareness of, and utilization of vicariously presented, task relevant information (Stone and Jackson, 1975; Primo, 1974). Observers rated as independent rather than dependent tend to imitate models more readily, especially high status models (Kloba, 1975). Kloba and Zimpfer (1976) also found that independent trainees imitate models better than dependents. Rennie and Toukmanian (1974) compared the acquisition of counseling skills by introverted and extroverted counselor trainees. They found that there is basically no difference in observational learning between introverts and extroverts. Chasnoff (1976) studied the relationship between ambiguity tolerance and the learning of video modeling interview behavior and found that high ambiguity tolerance trainees performed somewhat better.

Kanfer and Goldstein (1980) have reviewed this literature and have suggested other characteristics of the observer which influence modeling. An observer who is unsure about the appropriateness of his or her behavior is more likely to attend to a model. Too much anxiety on the part of the observer may interfere with observation or retention of the model's behavior.

Weiss (1977) has examined the effect modeling plays in the socialization of persons as they move into organizations. He hypothesized that modeling is more pronounced for low self-esteem observers, and therefore, self-esteem moderates the relationship between model characteristics and the model/observer behavior similarity. He found strong support for the moderating influence of self-esteem, in that he found perceived supervisor success was significantly and positively correlated with similarity between the supervisor and the subordinate behavior after socialization for low self-esteem subjects. Supervisor success was not correlated with similarity for the high self-esteem subgroup. Furthermore, Weiss suggests that because external incentives motivate behavior for people with specific value or personality profiles, while other people are motivated by intrinsic satisfaction associated with the correct behaviors, that the former group will be more likely to imitate models on the basis of characteristics which convey extrinsic reward-probability information. The latter group will be more influenced by model attributes. Weiss and Nowicki (1981) looked at the interactive effects of model task performance and observer field dependence on the observers' adoption of models' expressed attitudes. The results of this study show that the influence of information on task attitudes is an interactive function of model and observer characteristics. Research on the relationship between field dependence and independence and social behavior has generally characterized field dependent persons as more interpersonally oriented and more likely to take the attitudes of others into account when forming their own opinions. He found that the task attitudes of field dependent subjects were significantly influenced by the expressed attitudes of a model and that the model's competence didn't matter. Field dependent subjects were just as likely to adopt the attitudes of a low performing model as the attitudes of a high performing model. The results showed that field independent observers responded to the model's attitudes but were selectively influenced. They were willing to accept the attitudinal information of the competent model but were quite unwilling to accept the information of the incompetent model.

What we can conclude from this research is that some observer personality characteristics do affect modeling and to some extent the effectiveness of the behavior modeling training technique. This research is in its infancy and more work needs to be done. We know very little about the connection between observer personality characteristics and attention to models or modeling behavior. This needs to be explored.

## Coaching

Coaching is the process of subjects receiving information verbally about appropriate responses. It could be considered a verbal description of the modeling display. Whereas modeling presents one (or more) responses and allows the client to select from among these, coaching presents guidelines for the client to make his or her own response (and thereby enhances generalization).

Coaching of subjects in social skills training has taken a variety of forms. McFall and Twentyman (1973) presented concise audio instruction. Van Sickle (1975) used coaching which included specific information about what constitutes effective responses, information directing subjects' attention to their needs, as well as information about negative self-statements.

Coaching has been presented by the therapist (Parr, 1974), by audio tape (Goldsmith and McFall, 1975), and video tape (McFall and Twentyman, 1973). In a large majority of the studies, subjects were coached toward performance of the appropriate target behavior, while in some studies subjects were coached on both appropriate and inappropriate ways to handle situations (Berenson, 1975).

Several investigators have examined the effectiveness of coaching. Jaffee (1974) compared the effects of modeling and rehearsal with coaching and rehearsal to an attention control group. His results showed that both were equally effective and superior to the control in improving patient interactive behaviors. Cobb (1974) used three treatment groups and two control groups in training cooperative behaviors in first-grade boys. Each of the treatment groups contained coaching, either alone, in combination with modeling, or with modeling, rehearsal, and reinforcement. The results showed significant differences on the behavioral measure at posttest, with the full-treatment group showing the most change.

Consequently, coaching may be a substitute for modeling when teaching simple skills. More importantly, coaching can be used to augment modeling. This can be done during behavioral rehearsal if the trainee seemed to miss elements of the modeling tape. This would save rerunning the modeling film when in a workshop format. Also, coaching may be useful to increase generalization of the skills to be taught.

## Summary

The results showing the efficacy of modeling for teaching new behaviors and motivating the use of those behaviors is overwhelming. It is possible to look at modeling alone as an effective technique. However, modeling alone is insufficient over and above the fact that it yields positive training gains, because these gains are not enduring. Hayes, Rincover, and Volosin (1980) have examined variables influencing the acquisition and maintenance of aggressive behavior using modeling and sensory reinforcement. Sensory reinforcement is visual, tactile, or auditory feedback. Forty-eight preschool children participated in the study and were shown either no modeling film, a film of a limited-movement doll being struck, or a film of a flexible doll being struck. Subsequently, the children participated in a period in which they were given access to a similar doll. Frequency of aggressive behavior was monitored. Effects showed that modeling increased imitative aggressive behavior but that sensory consequences served different functions in the support of aggression: modeling primarily influenced the initial acquisition of aggressiveness where sensory reinforcement determined maintenance of the behavior. Consequently, modeling may not be sufficient. It must be followed by other reinforcing consequences in order to enhance maintenance of the new learned behavior.

Observational learning gained from modeling will not endure without including behavioral rehearsal, retention aids, further motivation, and transfer principles. Several studies (Lira et al., 1975; McFall and Twentyman, 1973; Spool, 1978) have shown that when comparing the components of behavior modeling, modeling is one of the weaker components. Consequently, modeling alone is not sufficient. Several researchers have found that modeling alone has only a short effect (Sutton, 1970; Friedenberg, 1971; Walsh, 1971). Basically, viewing the modeling display teaches the trainee what to do. What the trainee needs, in addition, are retention aids, sufficient practice to learn how to do it, accuracy feedback, and aids for the transfer process.

# —5—

# Retention Processes

Once an observer has attended to and observed a model, the next process in behavior modeling is to enhance the extent to which the observer remembers what was seen in the modeling display and to organize it in a fashion easily used to guide performance. As noted in Chapter 2, Bandura (1977) delineated the processes that affect the learning and reproduction of behavior presented through modeling as: attentional processes, retentional processes, motor reproduction processes, and motivational processes. Goldstein and Sorcher (1974) formalized all of these processes with the exception of the retention processes, in their original description of behavior modeling. Decker (1980) has shown, however, that retention processes enhance behavior modeling and should be specifically included.

Bandura included four retention processes in his social learning theory: 1) symbolic coding, 2) symbolic rehearsal, 3) cognitive organization, and 4) motor rehearsal. *Symbolic coding* is the process in which individuals organize and reduce the diverse elements of the model's performance into a pattern of verbal symbols that can be easily stored, retained intact over time, quickly retrieved, and used to guide performance. *Symbolic rehearsal* is the process in which individuals visualize or imagine themselves performing behaviors that were previously seen performed by another individual. *Cognitive organization* is the process of developing codes that easily fit into the observer's cognitive network. *Motor rehearsal* is behavioral rehearsal. Incorporating all of the retention processes strengthens the effectiveness of the modeling component and consequently the total behavior modeling technique (Decker, 1980, 1982). Therefore, formalized retention processes should be included as a component in behavior modeling training.

People cannot be influenced by the observation of modeled behavior if they do not remember it. Consequently, the retention processes are an extremely important activity that enhances the behavior modeling technique. These processes have been left out of much of the behavior modeling training that has been done in previous years because they were not formally included in the original description of behavior modeling.

In order for observers to profit from the behavior of models when those models are no longer present, the response patterns must be represented in the observer's memory in some symbolic form. It is this advanced capacity to form symbolization and store symbols in memory which enables humans to learn much of their behavior by observation. Bandura suggested that observational learning relies upon two representational systems, imaginal and verbal. He suggested that repeated exposure to modeling stimuli produces enduring and retrievable images of modeled performances. Visual imagery plays an especially important role in observational learning during the early childhood period when verbal skills are lacking. However, when the verbal system comes into play at the later adult stages, the capacity to model becomes very fine-tuned.

## Imagery and Coding

For many individuals, pictures are retained better than verbal labels or any verbal description of the picture. Much recent work has attempted to find out why. The dominant theory in this area has been Paivio's (1971) Dual Coding Theory which attributes the superior retention of pictures to the greater likelihood of inducing both imaginal and verbal codes when pictures are retained. Paivio suggests these two systems are created with connections between the two. Pylyshyn (1973) suggests, however, that memory for an image behaves as if it were interpreted. He suggests that since we can immediately retrieve visual information when given a meaningful description such as "my living room," it doesn't seem likely that we must mentally scan a series of pictures. In essence, Bandura's original Social Learning Theory is consistent with the dual code model of Paivio in that there are two types of representation: visual and verbal.

Anderson (1978) has reviewed arguments concerning representation and mental imagery. He suggests that an alternate theory to describe the efficacy of pictures in memory retention is the "level of processing" view. This approach suggests that pictures induce a deeper "encoding" (richer, more detailed representation in memory) and this in turn makes them more distinctive at the time of retrieval. Whether the richer encoding induced by pictures is specifically visual in nature, and whether both verbal symbols and pictures are coded in a common abstract form, is still a controversial point. Anderson argues for a dual coding system where pictures and words are connected in the same image much like that in Figure 5.1. Sterosahl and As-

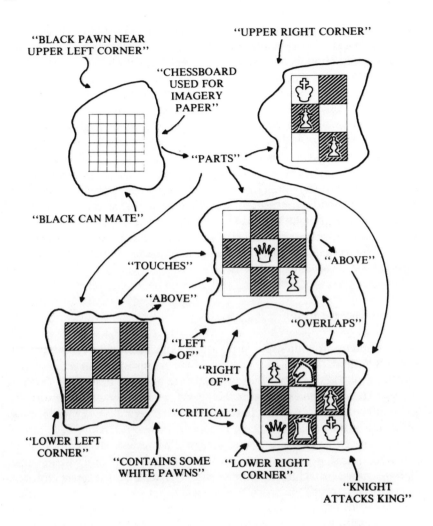

**Figure 5.1**    A Dual-Code Representation of a Chessboard

*Source*: Adopted from Anderson (1978) Arguments concerning representatives for mental imagery. *Psychological Review, 85*, 249–77. Used by permission.

cough (1981) argue, however, for a system where image and verbal coding are to some extent separated. Regardless, the information processing research implies that imagery may be much more complex than presupposed in the notion of an image being a mental photograph. Images not only convey information that would not be visible in a photograph, but it is likely that the visual and verbal process systems are active contributors to the sequence. It seems unlikely that the visual and verbal systems do not co-represent and share processing-of-response ability for incoming information.

Many studies published in the last decade have examined memory from the point of view of the depth, elaborateness, or extensiveness of the encoding induced at input. Some of these studies have adopted the "levels of processing" viewpoint. Some have adopted the "dual processes" viewpoint; and others have suggested alternate frameworks for describing their results. The "levels of processing" research has shown us that the more an item to be remembered is made distinctive and the more it is practiced, the more likely it is to be encoded, retained, and retrieved. Since this controversy between the depth of processing and dual coding theories in explaining the efficacy of remembering observed information is far from resolved, it seems that the best strategy for one who wants to practice behavior modeling is to incorporate both the processes into the procedure. Consequently, one would enhance the depth of processing by making sure that the model behaviors are distinctive and are processed extensively. At the same time, one should make sure that the information seen in the model is coded both with images and verbal symbols.

The discussions in this chapter take on the philosophy that one who is involved in behavior modeling should "cover all of the bases." In other words, one should make sure the modeled behavior is distinctive, that the model is seen repeatedly, and that the observer mentally codes both imaginally and verbally the information seen in the modeling display. Furthermore, to further increase the depth of processing, one should include symbolic rehearsal as a retention process to enhance the imagery and coding process.

## Memory Span

Once modeling stimuli have been attended to, seen and encoded, they must be stored in memory. There are two types of memory: short-term and long-term. Short-term memory is a system that stores information for current attention and where actual information processing is carried out. The amount of energy or capacity available to short-term memory is limited; thus, only a few storage or processing activities can be carried out simultaneously. Long-term memory represents the products of individuals' experience which have been processed through short-term memory and are stored for long-term use. Products in the long-term memory range from individual letter or word codes to more general things such as strategies for processing and maintaining information.

Many strategies have been found to increase memory span. Rehearsal is perhaps the simplest strategy that can be used as a processing and storage strategy to move things into long-term memory (Dempster, 1981). Rehearsal is generally viewed as an iterative process. It maintains information in short-term memory by insuring a sufficiently high level of activation, and thus facilitating the transfer of information to long-term memory. Adults have the capacity to rehearse several different items together; children under nine years old usually do not. The more rehearsal activity a person goes through, the better will be the performance in recall tasks.

There are at least several possible variables which affect the ability of a person in a behavior modeling training program to process information into memory, to store it and retrieve it at a later time. We should verbally identify the key behaviors in the modeling display. The information presented in the modeling display and in the verbal description of the key behaviors should be organized and should be shown or written in such a way that the observer can identify each element easily. It should be grouped. Where there is any ordering involved, the ordering should be specified in the modeling display and the verbal description that goes with the modeling display. We should make sure that the modeling display never shows more than approximately ten key behaviors at any one time. The modeling display and the viewing of the model should not be susceptible to any interference or irrelevant material presented. Finally, when we are presenting a model performance that shows rule-oriented behavior, we must present more than one modeled sequence guided by the rule(s). This will increase generalization.

## Instructions

There is evidence that adding instructions to behavior modeling programs enhances learning (Dorster, 1972; Uhlemann, Lee, and Stone, 1976; Stone and Vance, 1976). For example, Spiegler et al. (1969) developed a modeling film for use in reducing fear of unpoisonous snakes. They showed the film to matched groups with and without a taped narrative describing what the film depicted. A third group just heard the narrative, and a fourth, control, group received no treatment. Only the subjects who saw the film with the narrative did significantly better than controls.

While most studies have found instructions with modeling to be the most powerful condition, two studies (Friedman, 1971; Goldstein et al. 1973, Experiment 3) found that instructions alone were more powerful. As Fox (1983) has pointed out, the instructions used in these studies were less focused than a typical set of learning points. He suggests instructions are helpful, presumably, because they provide the trainee with ready made verbal labels (symbolic coding) for modeled behavior.

In integrating the results of several modeling studies, Zimmerman and Rosenthal (1974) suggest that what is learned from instruction and other formalized attempts to supply codes are rule structures which can be applied to a broad sample of stimulus instances, not the literal motor or verbal responses of the model. They conclude that verbal instructions, and other encoding parameters, play important roles in acquisition, generalization, and retention of observational learning.

## Symbolic Coding and Rehearsal

Bandura and his associates have investigated the effects of symbolic coding and rehearsal on reproduction of simple motor response. Gerst (1971) performed an experiment to test the hypothesis that symbolic coding of modeling stimuli enhanced observational learning and that different types of codes have differential effects over time. Subjects observed a filmed model perform simple motor responses drawn from the manual language of the deaf, each of which they either described in concrete terms, "reactivated imaginally" (mental rehearsal), or coded in the form of summary labels which encompassed the essential elements of the performance. All three coding operations facilitated immediate reproduction of modeled responses. However, subjects employing imaginal and summary label codes achieved higher reproduction scores than those in the concrete verbal description group. Also, summary labeling proved superior for retention of model responses. Consequently, Gerst found that symbolic coding did enhance the observational learning of simple motor responses and that summary labeling may have been the most proficient because it increased retention. This support must be qualified, however, because summary labeling did not differ significantly from imaginal labeling for immediate reproduction.

Bandura and Jeffery (1973) investigated the effects of symbolic coding and different types of symbolic rehearsal on the retention of observationally learned responses. The modeling stimuli used in this study were simple manual responses. Subjects coded the model's actions verbally or numerically and immediately rehearsed the memory codes. These combined operations helped subjects attain the highest level of reproduction. Physical practice, on the other hand, did not independently aid retention of model responses. Neither mental rehearsal without coding nor coding without mental rehearsal of the codes improved retention of modeled behavior in this study. In further tests conducted a week later, symbolic coding remained a significant determinant of matching performances. Consequently, this study shows that both symbolic coding and symbolic rehearsal processes are important in observational learning of simple responses.

Bandura, Jeffery, and Bachicha (1974) examined the influence of symbolic codes varying in meaningfulness, retrievability, and rehearsal on retention of observationally learned responses. Modeling stimuli used in this study were simple hand movements. The authors found that symbolic codes combining retrievability rules (letters assigned to responses) and meaningfulness (the letters formed words) facilitated reproduction of the observational learning. Responses were poorly retained in situations containing only one of these properties. Half of the subjects in each of the conditions engaged in symbolic rehearsal. Symbolic rehearsal enhanced the memory performance of movements that were input early and, consequently, had a primacy enhancement effect.

Jeffery (1976) reported that subjects who rehearsed mentally, either singly or in conjunction with motor rehearsal, reproduced tinker-toy configurations more accurately than those subjects who rehearsed only motorically or not at all. Bandura and Jeffery (1973) performed post hoc analyses on spontaneous subject generation of symbolic codes. In their noncoding conditions, they found that subjects who spontaneously generated codes achieved significantly better reproduction than did noncoders. The results of the research done by Bandura and his associates indicates strongly that symbolic coding and symbolic rehearsal enhance observational learning, at least of simple nonverbal responses. There are also indications that observer generation of the codes is better than having the codes supplied by the experimenter (Decker, 1980). Furthermore, the Gerst study suggests that simpler codes are more effective; that is, summary labeling seems to be the most effective coding type. Since behavior modeling in industrial settings is typically designed to teach complex social skills and generalization of responses to novel contexts, generalization is viewed as more important than simple reproduction. Consequently, simple labeling may not be sufficient.

Decker (1980) has investigated the effects of symbolic coding and rehearsal in behavior modeling training programs designed to teach complex social skills. Two experiments designed to assess the effects of symbolic coding and rehearsal, source of codes, and types of codes on reproduction of modeled behavior and generalization of observational learning in new situations were conducted. These studies were done to assess the efficacy, in industrial behavior modeling programs, of the results of Bandura and his associates. The two experiments, reported by Decker (1980), were done in a behavior modeling training program designed to teach college students assertiveness skills. The first study compared descriptive codes (codes in which the model's key behaviors are verbally described) and rule codes (codes that describe rules governing the model responses and/or present the relevant response-consequence connection). This study showed that descriptive coding produced more accurate reproduction than rule coding. Code type had no differential effect on generalization. A second study investigated the effect of symbolic rehearsal and the source of the codes (i.e., trainee generated vs. experimenter provided). This study also included a modeling-only control.

The latter experiment revealed that modeling alone and symbolic rehearsal facilitated reproduction and generalization. It also showed that trainee-generated rule codes enhanced generalization and that reproduction decay was least in the trainee-generated code conditions. The results of these experiments indicated that rule codes may tend to facilitate generalization and that descriptive codes facilitate at least verbal reproduction of a model. These are tentative results which show that trainee-generated codes, rather than experimenter-provided codes, are superior. The results reported in Decker's studies have clear implications for the practice of behavior modeling training: symbolic rehearsal instructions and the use of symbolic rule codes do facilitate generalization of observational learning to novel contexts. These instructions would add only a few minutes to any behavior modeling workshop.

These experiments were replicated by Decker (1982) in an industrial setting. Decker found that both formalized symbolic coding and symbolic rehearsal facilitated generalization of the observational learning to novel contexts more so than spontaneous trainee coding/rehearsal. Decker (1984) compared three types of coding (rule-oriented, behavioral, and summary labels) in terms of their effects on generalization of observational learning in a behavior modeling experiment. Subjects in this experiment were randomly assigned to four conditions: 1) presentation of rule-oriented learning points, 2) presentation of behavioral learning points (which described the model's behavior), 3) presentation of summary label learning points (which were simple one- and two-word labels of the model's key behaviors), or 4) a no-code control situation. Individuals who were assigned to the rule-oriented condition were able to generalize the model behaviors to different settings. Those who had received the behavioral codes were only able to imitate the model performance while those who received the summary label points were not able to reproduce or generalize the model's behaviors to different settings.

The implications of Decker's series of studies is that symbolic coding and symbolic rehearsal do have a facilitative effect on observational learning. These retention aids help an observer reproduce or accurately imitate a model's behavior and generalize that behavior to different situations where the same general kind of behavior is needed to solve a problem. Rule-oriented codes seem to be in order when one is interested in trainees generalizing skills from the modeling display to a new context; and behavioral descriptive codes seem to be in order when the desire is to have the trainees accurately imitate the model's behavior. It seems that summary label codes cannot capture the complexity of modeled social skills. Symbolic rehearsal appears to be a very powerful effect that should be included in any behavior modeling training program. Furthermore, it seems worthwhile to let the trainees or the observers participate, in some way, in the generation of the codes (learning points) (Decker, 1980; Hogan, Hakel, and Decker, 1984). It is suggested that trainees observe the model display and at least rewrite trainer-provided codes if they so desire.

Goldstein and Sorcher (1974) stated that learning by modeling would not occur unless the observer attended to the modeling display and, in particular, to specific key behaviors which are the focal training content. They do not specify how key behaviors are developed (one would infer through job analysis), what form they should take, or how they are used. Decker (1980) has shown that presentation of rule codes to trainees in combination with symbolic rehearsal does facilitate the modeling effect; yet Latham and Saari (1979) have shown that the presentation of codes alone is not effective in eliciting behavior change. The term "learning points" and the term "codes" are essentially the same. These terms refer to some attempt to verbally (in writing) reorganize the visual material seen in the modeling display and in particular the behaviors performed by the model which are the focal learning content. Decker (1982) has attempted to specify what these codes or learning points should be like. The term "learning points" will be used. Learning points can be used to: 1) develop the modeling film, 2) help trainees attend to the specific key behaviors in the modeling film, and/or 3) stimulate coding by the trainee. Consequently, learning points may affect both the attentional and retentional processes in observational learning. It must be pointed out, however, that the trainer has no control over whether the observer or trainee actually uses written learning points (either provided by the trainer or written by the trainee) in symbolic coding operations. Since Decker's results clearly show that the presentation or development of some kind of written description of the model's behavior does increase the learning that goes on in a behavior modeling training program, formalized symbolic coding operations of some kind should be included along with symbolic rehearsal operations.

Decker (1980) and Hogan et al. (1984) have provided support for the practice of inviting trainees to examine learning points for ambiguities and other language deficiencies so that they could rewrite the learning points to make them more understandable. This seems to enhance observational learning. Fox (1983) has pursued an interesting rationale in suggesting that we may reasonably infer support for instructions/coding from research on goal setting. Learning points provide the trainee with specific and easy to understand learning goals. Abundant research findings show that goal specificity, understandability, and acceptability are related to superior performance (Latham and Yukl, 1975; Locke et al., 1981).

Mann and Decker (1984) have built upon the earlier results of Decker (1980, 1982) and examined how learning points should be used in the behavior modeling training program. They created modeling displays using video tapes in which the observers saw the written learning points on the video-tape screen with the model performance. They carried out training programs where trainees: 1) saw only a model performance (no learning points), or 2) saw rule-oriented learning points presented in a group on film before they saw the model performance or 3) saw each rule-oriented learning point individually just before they saw the particular key behavior performed by the model. Thus, in the two learning point conditions, observers saw the list of learning points that covered the entire performance just before they saw the model or they saw the learning points interspersed so that the learning points came on screen just before the model performed the behavior. They found that the closer the attachment between learning points and the modeled key behavior, the more effective was the behavior modeling program. This result is stronger for key behaviors that are not very distinctive. The less distinctive the key behavior, the more important it is to induce distinctiveness by pairing learning points with the modeled key behavior. Mann and Decker suggested that interspersing the learning points within the modeling display may not be as efficient as superimposing the learning points. The results, however, are clear that learning points can be used to make the modeled key behaviors distinctive.

Furthermore, Nugent, Tipton, and Brooks (1980) have examined the effectiveness of using introductory organizers in presenting effective television materials to college level audiences. These researchers tested training films with program titles and advanced written organizers (much like the table of contents in a book) versus none of these aids, at the beginning of the film. Results showed that advanced organizers such as these significantly increased the student comprehension of the film content.

While symbolic mental rehearsal does appear to enhance interpersonal skill learning, it does not appear to be as useful for athletic performances. For example, Ryan and Simons (1981) found no difference in novel perceptual tasks between mental and no practice groups on a predominately motor task, while the physical practice group performed significantly superior to both. However, on a predominately cognitive task, the mental practice group performed as well as the physical practice group, and both were significantly superior to the no practice groups. Other studies involving only athletic or motor performances (i.e., dart throwing, pursuit tracking, swimming) in which one would expect physical drilling-type practice to be the most beneficial, have also failed to find any superiority of symbolic rehearsal over physical rehearsal (e.g., Epstein, 1980; Hrapsky, 1981; Yamamoto and Inomata, 1982). On the other hand, Ryan and Simons (1982) investigated mental imagery ability as a moderator of mental rehearsal in a single balancing task. They found that physical practice was best when followed by mental rehearsal, although ability to image did not affect performance scores regardless of rehearsal mode. Consequently, the research is mixed as to whether symbolic rehearsal enhances performance on physical or athletic tasks.

MacKay (1981) proposes a theoretical framework for the relationship between mental and physical practice which is physiological in nature. This paper may spur more research which may help to reconcile the differences reported above.

## Covert modeling

Preceding discussion has dealt with the influence of overt modeling, the observance of another person performing the key behaviors, or mental rehearsal, the imagining of oneself performing the key behaviors. Three studies by Kazdin (1973, 1974, 1975) have evaluated the effectiveness of covert modeling with adults. Covert modeling is the process of trainees imagining *another person* engaging in the key behaviors. In all three studies, covert modeling produced significant effects in comparison with controls. Furthermore, Kazdin (1973, 1975) reports that individual differences among subjects as to clarity or vividness of their covert modeling imagery is not related to resultant behavior change. However, it is important to point out that Kazdin's studies deal only with disinhibition or with simple refusal behaviors. It obviously remains to be seen whether covert modeling can substitute for overt modeling when the training task is complex social skills.

## Summary

Overall, one should include formalized symbolic coding and rehearsal operations in behavior modeling. It seems useful for the observers to participate in the development of the learning points and, where one wants the learning content to be generalized across situations (as would be applicable in most all industrial or counseling behavior modeling applications), one should use rule-oriented learning points. Instructions may be helpful in the training of very complex skills. Symbolic rehearsal must be used in teaching complex cognitive skills.

# —6—

# Behavioral Rehearsal

Behavioral rehearsal is defined as the process by which individuals practice new behavior in a setting not normal for the enactment of the role, but which simulates a possible job situation. This is similar to the definition of role playing, which is a situation in which an individual is asked to take a role not normally the person's own, and in a setting not normal for the enactment of the role (Mann, 1956). The term "role playing" represents at least four distinct concepts: 1) *theatrical,* where an actor/actress plays a role as defined by a playwright and the director, 2) *sociological,* which refers to the usual behavior of people in particular societies and how they act under certain circumstances and formal ways, 3) *dissimulative,* where people play roles with the intention of deceiving or of creating impressions contrary to their real feelings, and 4) *educational,* which has three general purposes— diagnosing, informing, and training (Shaw et al., 1980). The diagnosing function is to provide better understanding of the role players by seeing and hearing them in action. The informing purpose is to give the observer information about how certain roles should be filled. The training purpose is to provide role players with knowledge and skills by permitting them to experience a nearly real situation and to provide feedback about their behavior in the situation. Behavioral rehearsal is a subset of educational role playing; the difference being that the player plays his or her own role. Behavior rehearsal is reality practice and action planning. It involves realistic behavior under unrealistic conditions allowing a person to take on the person's own role and practice new behavior in an artificial situation.

Written reports on role playing and behavior rehearsal are numerous. Research has been conducted in counseling, clinical, and industrial settings. In the counseling area, role playing has been used to increase assertive behavior in unassertive patients, to alter attitudes of patients towards treatment, to reduce smoking, and to reduce inhibitions. Role playing has also received attention from social psychologists interested in attitude change. Finally, during the 1950s and early 1960s, role playing was used extensively in industrial settings in supervisory, sales, and labor/management conflict training. Studies in the counseling, social, and industrial context provide an impressive array of reports indicating the value of role playing for behavior and attitude change. Unfortunately, many of the reports are in the form of descriptive testimonials rather than empirical research. Furthermore, behavior change or attitude change resulting from role playing is likely to be transitory unless attention is given to other factors such as the other components of behavior modeling (especially that of feedback or reinforcement about the behavior rehearsal attempts).

## The Origins of Role Playing

It is likely that role playing was first used as a teaching method long ago—perhaps the first time someone told an apprentice/employee to "pretend I am a customer and show how you would treat me." If the two stopped after the behavioral rehearsal and the trainer evaluated and gave feedback to the trainee about alternate ways of interacting in that situation, then that was behavioral rehearsal. Moreno (1923) was the originator of the modern concept of role playing. He maintained that emotional problems could be corrected if people acted out troubling situations, analyzed the enactment, and practiced new solutions. To do this, he employed a version of role playing known as "psychodrama."

In 1933, the German army used role playing procedures in selecting and training army officers. The British army later used the same procedures in its officer selection program. The United States Office of Strategic Services used the same procedures in the selection and training of spies and people involved in other secret wartime work. Today, role playing and behavior rehearsal are used in both selection and training in many different areas. Role playing began to be used for teaching purposes in the United States during WWII, with early reports of its use in industrial training by Lippitt (1943) and French (1945). Shaw et al. (1980) provide a complete review of the role playing literature.

Lazarus (1966) was the first to use the term behavioral rehearsal. He used this term to describe a combination of modeling and role playing and initially used these procedures to increase patients' assertive behavior. The term behavioral rehearsal is much more appropriate than role playing for what goes on in behavior modeling because the trainee is not taking on another role, but in fact is using his own role and simply practicing new behavior which has been seen in the modeling display.

## The Rationale for Behavioral Rehearsal

In behavior modeling, trainees are not only shown a particular process of handling a problem, but have the opportunity to actually practice it. They get the feel of the problem and how to progress through to a solution. They can also experiment with alternate ways to use the key behaviors provided by a modeling display. This is particularly true when those key behaviors are defined by underlying rules. Behavioral rehearsal expands the awareness of the trainee about the skills the person is learning. This characteristic of behavioral rehearsal stems from the feedback aspect. Not only can trainees in behavioral rehearsal get feedback from a trainer and/or their fellow trainee(s) about how well they have reproduced or generalized the model's behavior, but they may also receive information about the feelings of the other individual involved in the behavioral rehearsal. If the behavior modeling program is not teaching a social skill but rather a manual skill, there may be no other person involved in a behavioral rehearsal. (The behavioral rehearsal will be an interaction between the trainee and some object such as a piece of machinery). In this case, the participant will not be provided information about the feelings of another person but will be provided with information about the feel of the machinery or object involved in the manual skill. It is also possible to "stop the action" here and there for evaluation or feedback, or to practice alternative modes of reacting, etc.

Behavioral rehearsal is the time-tested method for helping people learn athletic activities. A successful athletic coach may teach out of a book, but the coach also places a student or player in the actual situation to provide the individual with the opportunity to test himself or herself with feedback. The coach works with a person and helps identify mistakes. The coach also provides practice opportunity so that the rehearsal of alternative ways of reacting is possible.

In behavior modeling training, the aim is to teach skills—usually rule governed interpersonal skills. These skills are typically difficult to exhibit correctly without practice and feedback. When using role playing and behavioral rehearsal, other people, often members of the training group or persons interacting with the trainee, can tell an individual how the trainee's behavior appears to them. Consequently, individuals can discover how others would be affected by their behavior. In doing this, alternative ways of behaving can be explored under feedback conditions to identify behaviors which may or may not be conducive to solving problems or dealing with other people. Observers in a role play situation help the trainee to identify assumptions underlining the person's conduct, to assess the impact of the trainee's behavior on others, and to spot behavioral factors that are sources of difficulty in solving problems. Many of these aspects of behavioral rehearsal go above and beyond the opportunity to simply practice what is seen in the modeling display with feedback; however, they all add to the effectiveness of the method in teaching social skills in industrial and counseling contexts. Behavioral rehearsal focuses on skills that can be applied to problems that concern each trainee. It permits active participation supported by feedback and practice with freedom for experimentation of the kind made possible only by a laboratory setting.

## Research on Role Playing and Behavioral Rehearsal

Experimental support for applications of role playing in both the clinical and industrial realms is rather sparse. This is evidenced in the books on role playing (Corsini, 1966; Shaw et al., 1980). The literature in this domain is almost exclusively descriptive and impressionistic. The few existing studies reporting successful use of role playing to alter behavior often lack adequate experimental controls and must be considered suggestive.

One of the classic experimental studies was done by Janis and Mann (1965). This study was aimed at decreasing smoking. The subjects, all female smokers, were asked to assume that they were medical patients who had just undergone a series of diagnostic tests and were awaiting the results. The experimenter acted the part of the physician. Half of the subjects were asked to play the role of patients and the other half listened to recordings of these role enactments. All of the subjects were premeasured on attitudes toward smoking, cancer, and future plans regarding smoking. Immediately following the experimental conditions, the subjects' attitudes on the dimensions noted above were reassessed. In each instance, the role play subjects were significantly more negative toward smoking and smoked significantly fewer cigarettes than did the subjects who just listened to the role plays. This decrease in smoking behavior was still in effect 18 months later.

In a study reported by McFall and Marston (1970), role playing was used to increase assertive and independent behavior of counseling clients. The researchers developed a series of 24 role playing situations to which the subjects were asked to listen and respond assertively. After completing these sessions, role players were compared in several measures of assertiveness with other subjects who had been through a discussion section about assertiveness but had not role played. The role players were not only more assertive on these measures but were significantly less anxious about being assertive. Two weeks after the role play participation, each subject was telephoned by another experimenter posing as a magazine salesman. Working with a prepared script, the salesman delivered a hard sales pitch to sell a magazine subscription. Analysis of these telephone conversations revealed that subjects who had undergone the role playing showed resistance at a significantly earlier point in the telephone call than did the other groups of subjects.

McClure, Chinsky, and Larcen (1978) used modeling plus role play to enhance the social problem-solving performance of elementary school children. Role playing significantly increased the skills examined in this study and significantly added to the modeling component. Other studies have shown that role playing is effective in increasing empathic communication and attending behavior (Hundleby and Zingle, 1975; Huyck, 1975).

While the studies cited above used role playing to change behavior, most role playing research has focused on attitude change. Role playing has been successfully used to change attitudes toward integration and housing (Culbertson, 1957); strong religious opposition to the sale and drinking of alcohol (Harvey and Beverly, 1961); attitudes about the admission of the Peoples Republic of China to the United Nations (Zimbardo, 1965); attitudes toward other people (Davis and Jones, 1960); the value of compulsory religious education (Cohen and Latane, 1962); the need to increase college tuition (Brock and Blackwood, 1962); attitudes toward the police (Berham and Cohen, 1962); attitudes toward experiments and procedures (Carlsmith, Collins, and Helmreich, 1966); attitudes of male business students toward hiring women for management trainee positions (Schuh and Young, 1978); self-esteem attitudes (Altmann and Firnesz, 1973); and attitudes toward the physically disabled (Clore and Jeffery, 1971).

Role playing has been used in industry in various ways, but there are very few experimental studies examining the effectiveness of role playing. [The study by Schuh and Young (1978) cited above is one example.] However, role playing has been reported to be successful in nonempirical, descriptive studies of training uses such as in supervisory training, training business students, enhancing the flow and accuracy of communication within industrial organizations, enhancing communication in labor–management relations, and maximizing the personal awareness of the dangers of relying on word-of-mouth communication on important matters. Furthermore, role playing has been used in industry to train salesmen, train union leaders to resolve grievances, and increase interviewing skills (Goldstein and Sorcher, 1974).

Overall, the literature on role playing (in particular behavioral rehearsal) is wide and varied; however, very few controlled empirical studies are reported. Of those studies that are reported, we find that role playing does change behavior and, in at least one or two studies, has had a long-term effect. There are more studies evaluating the use of role play to change attitudes. In some of these studies, attitude change does occur. There is little research examining behavioral rehearsal alone, but where these studies have been done (and where studies have been done looking at behavioral rehearsal as a component of behavior modeling) it seems to be effective in changing behavior. Behavioral rehearsal without feedback, however, does not seem to be effective. Studies examining all components of behavior modeling have shown that all of the components must be present to have the most effect on learning new skills. Obviously, it makes sense that if you show trainees what you want them to learn, let them practice it, and give them feedback, skill development will be enhanced.

## Behavioral Rehearsal Enhancers

There is evidence that role playing is a valuable technique for changing a behavior or attitude. However, these changes seem likely to be transitory in nature. Obviously, role playing is an important component of learning, but is not sufficient alone. This is the major premise behind the behavior modeling technique and why it includes several components. Furthermore, role playing and behavioral rehearsal will not be effective unless sufficient attention is given to implementing behavioral rehearsal procedures which include enhancers that have been experimentally demonstrated to significantly increase the likelihood of behavior change. Behavior change has been shown to be greater and more enduring when the role player: 1) is given the choice to participate or not (Cohen and Latane, 1962); 2) plays the role or practices the new behavior publicly or otherwise commits himself or herself so that the behavior cannot be disowned (Davis and Jones, 1960); 3) is required to improvise in his own role enactment (Janis and King, 1954); and 4) is rewarded for role playing or for behaviorally rehearsing (Scott, 1957). These procedures have been shown to enhance role playing and behavioral rehearsal in the same way that the modeling enhancers have been shown to enhance modeling.

## Amount of Rehearsal

When training new behaviors, less rehearsal is needed than when attempting to displace well-established "old" behaviors with alternative behaviors. The absence of a competing behavioral system lowers the amount of rehearsal needed.

Maximizing rehearsal is sometimes called overlearning. Overlearning refers to providing trainees with continued practice beyond the point when the behavior(s) have been performed correctly. Overlearning is important in a training program where the task to be learned is not likely to be quickly practiced in the transfer context. Fitts (1965) suggests that overlearning is necessary to maintain performance during periods of emergency and stress. Wexley and Latham (1981) point out that overlearning is important for several reasons. 1) It increases the length of time training content will be retained. By continually pairing stimulus and response, the response is less likely to be forgotten. 2) It makes the learning less reflexive and more automatic. The trainee does not have to concentrate as much on the task. 3) It maintains performance during periods of emergency or stress. And 4) over-learning helps trainees transfer what they have learned to the setting in which the behaviors will be used.

## Other Conditions of Practice

Learning theory research has shown that when a task to be learned is very complex, it should be broken into its parts and one should learn each part separately (Sheffield and Maccoby, 1961). If possible, the parts should be learned from the simplest to the most difficult. When part learning is used, however, a combination with whole learning is in order. Trainees should be shown the whole performance so that they know what their goal is and where they are going. The training content should then be divided into integrated parts and each part should be learned in practice until it is retained intact and can be recalled accurately. Then, the trainees should be allowed to put all of the parts together and practice the whole performance.

## Summary

Behavioral rehearsal, as with the modeling and retention components, appears to be a necessary but insufficient procedure for affecting durable behavior change. Modeling provides an example of what we want the trainee to learn, retention aids place that learning into long-term memory and provide recall cues, and behavioral rehearsal provides the practice. Combining these three with feedback or reinforcement in the behavioral rehearsal component will affect durable behavior change. We have seen, in research, that behavioral rehearsal will cause behavior change; however, this research has failed to demonstrate any lasting behavioral changes without other elements.

# —7—

# Feedback and Social Reinforcement

The saying, "practice makes perfect," is only a half-truth. It is practice in combination with reinforcement or feedback that makes perfect, or at least enables people to learn. Feedback is essential for acquiring and developing any kind of skill.

The nature and consequences of feedback and reinforcement have received more examination than any other aspect of the learning process. Feedback is information, obtained by a performer from either internal or external sources, about the results of a performance (its effect or consequence) and the manner of the performance (the process or manner in which the performance was executed). Reinforcement is any event or state that serves to change the likelihood that a given behavior will occur. Reinforcement is a consequence which follows behavior and is contingent upon that behavior, which either increases or decreases the frequency of the behavior. In this chapter, we will discuss the available research and knowledge about corrective feedback and reinforcement.

Reinforcement and feedback can occur either in the training workshop or on the job. Obviously, reinforcement and feedback used in training will serve not only to improve the behavior ("improve" meaning to make the behavior like that of the model), but also to insure that the behavior will be used in the future. Reinforcement on the job relates directly to transfer of learning. When a behavior is learned in a training program and later there is reinforcement on the job for that behavior, the behavior is more likely to be repeated on the job. This is also a critical element of transfer of learning that will be discussed in the next chapter.

The generic term, "feedback," will be used to describe anything given or implied to the performer about the person's performance which is designed to improve the quality of that performance or change the quantity of that performance. This includes praise, approval, encouragement, attention, criticism, any other informative feedback, tangible reinforcers, self-criticism, praise, or vicarious reinforcement.

## Knowledge of Results: Feedback

Knowledge of results is critical for both learning and motivation (Ammons, 1954; Annett, 1961). Trainees should be informed when and how they have done something correctly. Wexley and Latham (1981) review the issues relating to feedback. They suggest that feedback, in any form (written or verbal) serves three functions: 1) it conveys information to the trainees as to whether their responses are correct; 2) it makes the learning process more interesting, thereby increasing their motivation to learn; and 3) it leads to the setting of unambiguous, specific goals used by the trainee to maintain or improve performance.

Luthans and Kreitner (1975) reduced the scrap rate of a manufacturing team with the use of feedback and reinforcement procedures. In this study, a supervisor had attempted to reduce the group scrap rate by posting equipment and maintenance rules and reminding workers about procedures. This had little effect. He then took a base line measure of the group scrap rate for a two week period. Based on this analysis, the supervisor decided to provide a new consequence for the workers' performance in the form of a chart showing the scrap rate. The chart was posted in a department work area. The consequences of providing feedback improved productivity 40 percent.

Michael and Maccoby (1961) presented a 14 minute film on civil defense to 1,029 subjects (in 12 groups) who were then required to take a test on the film's content. Before taking the test, a third of the subjects answered orally administered practice questions in writing during three breaks in the showing, others thought out answers, others received no such practice. Half of the practicing subjects were given knowledge of the correct response, half were not. Those who practiced without knowledge of results did do significantly better than those who had no practice. Those who receive feedback from their practice questions did significantly better than those who practiced without feedback. No significant differences were found between "think the answer" subjects and "written answer" subjects.

Feedback should be provided as soon as possible after the trainee's behavior. The feedback does not have to be instantaneous but the relationship between behavior and feedback must be made evident. Wexley and Thornton (1972) have shown that college students learned better when their instructor gave them verbal feedback, even with a delay of 30 minutes, as to the correctness of test answers.

Too much feedback at one time, or too early in the learning process, can be confusing to the trainee and lead to a decline in performance (Wexley and Latham, 1981). Likewise, too little feedback at critical learning stages will hamper learning. Too much information, whether in the form of a large amount of feedback or in another form, will overload trainees. If the trainees' capacity to cognitively learn new information is small, the capacity to perform new skills based on that learning may be even smaller. Giving someone feedback on half a dozen areas at the same time is unlikely to prove very helpful. Some people can only concentrate on one area at a time and it makes it very hard to change performance if several areas are discussed simultaneously. Each item should be concentrated on alone until that behavior is improved. In the behavioral rehearsal component, it is very useful to have trainees practice one key behavior over again if there is a problem rather than giving feedback on many key behaviors at the completion of a behavioral rehearsal.

Wexley and Latham (1981) also point out that positive feedback is perceived and recalled more accurately and accepted more readily than is negative feedback. Negative feedback may be denied, especially by low self-esteem trainees. Ilgen, Fisher, and Taylor (1979) concluded after reviewing the feedback literature that trainees are more likely to accept and respond to negative feedback from trainers whom they view as trustworthy, knowledgeable, and who have control over trainees' resources.

Overall, feedback should be constructive, specific, come fairly immediately *after* (not during) the trainee's behavior, be both positive and negative (depending upon the trainer–trainee reltionship), and be constructive, not critical.

## The Nature of Social Reinforcement

Having viewed a modeling display (the presentation of the key behaviors), the learner commences to rehearse the key behaviors under the guidance of a trainer. As the learner's behavior increasingly approximates that of the model, or his/her proficiency in generalizing the desired modeling rules presented in the display across contexts increases, the learner should be provided with social reinforcement in some form. This reinforcement can come from the trainer, other participants, or from the learner. There are also several forms that this reinforcement can take. Some of these forms have been researched, some of them have not. The different forms of reinforcement can be placed on a hierarchy of complexity. The lowest level of reinforcement is tangible reinforcement. Tangible reinforcement is simply a physical consequence contingent upon the performance, such as money or food. If a person is very hungry and is offered food for the performance of a certain task, the food will motivate the person to perform that task.

The next level of reinforcement is that coming from the social context, i.e., other people. Most social reinforcement is in the form of praise which includes simple comments like "that's good," "that was excellent," etc.

Self-reinforcement is information coming from the trainee him or herself about the performance. There is reinforcement inherent in the knowledge that one is correct or accurate (i.e., the same as the model) in one's behavior. In a behavior modeling program, the trainee always has the opportunity to compare his or her performance against the symbolic representation retained from viewing the modeling display. If this comparison reveals an adequate match, then the learner will praise him or herself mentally.

The term "vicarious reinforcement" is applied to changes in the behavior of learners that result from witnessing a model's actions being rewarded or punished. Vicarious reinforcement can affect the course of observational learning if repeated opportunities are given to observe modeled performances; the observer values the observed consequences, and assumes that performing matching behavior will produce similar outcomes. Imitative behavior is generally increased by observing reward and decreased by observing punishment. In the behavior rehearsal component of behavior modeling, the learners often have a chance to observe other learners' behavioral rehearsals; those behaviors performed by others and rewarded by the trainer are more likely to be attempted by the learner when it is his or her turn to rehearse.

Reinforcement can come from the trainer, other trainees, the individual trainee, or by observing other trainees' actions. This reinforcement can take several forms, such as praise, criticism, informative feedback, and tangible consequences. There are several variables which enhance the effect of reinforcement. These have been reported widely in the training/education literature and are, therefore, discussed in Appendix B for the interested reader.

Laboratory research has demonstrated that the relative effectiveness of given reinforcers for behavior change varies with the age and circumstances of the individual (Goldstein and Sorcher, 1974). At the earliest ages, or in times of physical need, tangible positive rewards may function effectively to alter behavior. In the adult years, reinforcement that is social in nature may serve as the most effective method to change behavior. While the effectiveness of both tangible and social reinforcement continues into later years, there is evidence that their relative effectiveness diminishes in relation to self-reinforcement. When one reaches the adult stage, knowledge about one's behavior and being told that one's performance is good or bad by a valued person (self-reinforcement and social reinforcement) tend to supersede the potency of tangible reinforcers such as food or money. In behavior modeling, it is particularly easy to build in vicarious reinforcement. A learner can receive vicarious reinforcement by watching other trainees perform the behavior in addition to the vicarious reinforcement that is obtained by observing the modeling displays.

## Reinforcement's Place in Behavior Modeling

It has been argued that neither modeling alone, nor retention processes, nor behavior rehearsal alone yields results nearly as effective as these components combined. We will take the same position with reinforcement—it is most effective when used in conjunction with other components of behavior modeling. It is also true that behaviors to be reinforced must occur with sufficient accuracy and frequency for reinforcement to have its intended effect of leading to an enduring behavior change.

In many instances rewards are bestowed, but they are not made conditional upon the behavior that the trainer wishes to promote. In many cases, these positive reinforcements are inadvertent or are made contingent upon the wrong type of behavior. For example, the act of spanking a child the next day for inappropriate behavior such as stealing may occur immediately after the child cleaned up his or her room without being told. The cleaning behavior may not be soon repeated. It is clear that any reinforcement given with the aim of increasing or improving behavioral rehearsal performance must be made contingent upon correct performance. Consequently, reinforcement alone is not enough for effective training. We must include modeling, retention aids, and behavioral rehearsal. Modeling provides the standards for the performance, retention aids will make sure that the trainee has the information symbolically represented (so that they can be reproduced accurately in behavioral rehearsal), and behavioral rehearsal provides the opportunity for feedback.

Reinforcement has indeed been shown to be a powerful tool for altering human behavior. The following are a number of studies in which reinforcement procedures have been successfully applied in a variety of business and industrial settings to change various kinds of work behavior. Marholin and Gray (1976) reduced cash shortages in a family restaurant with the use of a response-cost procedure. On any given day, a minimum of three and a maximum of six cashiers used either of two cash registers to ring up sales. Shortages averaged over 4 percent of the day's sales receipts. After collecting baseline data for five days, the cashiers were told that if any single day's cash shortages equaled or exceeded 1 percent of that day's sales receipts, the total shortage, divided by the number of cashiers working that day, would be subtracted from each cashier's salary for that particular day. This response-cost procedure lowered daily shortages to .43 percent of daily receipts.

Kohlenberg, Phillips, and Proctor (1976) reduced peaking in residential electrical energy consumption with a feedback and reinforcement procedure. "Peaking" results in inefficient use of electrical generation facilities and may force the use of older, less safe, and more environmentally damaging generating facilities. The morning peak begins at 8:00 am and runs to 1:00 pm. The afternoon peak is between 6:00 and 8:00 pm. In an attempt to change the electrical energy consuming behavior of families, current-sensitive relays installed in each home turned on a signal light when current levels exceeded the criterion level which would indicate peaking. The feedback condition using the signal light alone resulted in approximately a 20 percent reduction of peaking, while a combination of feedback plus incentives reduced peaking by about 50 percent.

There are literally hundreds of studies done in a laboratory showing the effects of reinforcement. Those of the most concern to behavior modeling trainers would be studies examining verbal reinforcement. Hildum and Brown (1956) showed that the word "good" used by an attitude survey interviewer would serve as a reinforcer and alter the interviewee's statements. They had interviewers respond with "good" to interviewee responses which agreed with a focal attitude during half of the calls made, while for the other calls the interviewer responded the same way to disagreeing statements. Those reinforced for agreeing responded with more agreeable attitudes; those reinforced for disagreeing attitudes increased in disagreement. Other examples of behaviors/attitudes shown to be changed by reinforcement include remembering personal experiences (Quay, 1959), expressions of feeling (Salzinger and Pisoni, 1957), evaluation of other people (Gelfand and Singer, 1968), attitudes towards capital punishment (Ekman, 1958), test taking behavior (Fahmy, 1953), social interaction (Milby, 1970), and many more.

## Feedback and Reinforcement in Behavior Modeling

Now let us take a look at the use of feedback and reinforcement in behavior modeling programs. Watts (1973) tested whether modeling reinforced by critics would reduce undervaluing in self-evaluation. The subjects were military personnel designated for duty as Air Force instructors. Each of the 98 subjects prepared a ten minute instructional lesson in which all elements of desired teaching behavior were to be displayed. Subjects presented their lesson in front of students and in the presence of a critic. The lesson was video-taped. The presence or absence of an instructor critique prior to playback and self-grading constituted the difference in experimental treatment. Students in the experimental group received a critique of their lessons individually before watching a play-back and filling out a self-grading form. In both groups, the advisers' forms for rating each trainee and each trainee's self-evaluation rating were made on identical forms. The subjects in the group that received no critique tended to undervalue their performance to a greater degree than those who were reviewed by a critic. Therefore, trainer critiques appear to be important for both helping to preserve the individual's self-concept, as well as simultaneously producing an appropriate modification of behavior.

Noble, Egan, and McDowell (1977) showed that video feedback helped deprived urban seven-year-olds adequately describe themselves projected into the future both verbally and nonverbally. Ten children were assigned to both an experimental and control group differing only on video-tape feedback. Drawings and verbal statements describing "I am" and "in ten years I will be" were collected before and after the experimental manipulations. Video feedback increased the children's ability to draw themselves in action accurately and increased consciousness of individual differences in verbal statements about themselves.

Ronnestad (1977) compared the effects of three techniques (modeling, feedback, and experiential intervention) in teaching counseling students to communicate empathic understanding. The students participated in three simulated counseling interviews during which their responses to standard clients were rated on the degree of empathic understanding conveyed. After each of the first two interviews, students in the experimental group were given one of the treatments; students in the control group received no treatment. Ratings of the last interview indicated that modeling was more effective than feedback and feedback was more effective than the experiential method in helping the counselors communicate empathy. Both the modeling and the feedback conditions were significantly better than the experiential and control conditions.

Thompson and Blocher (1979) randomly assigned 18 male undergraduates to either: a behavior modeling program that included a modeling audio tape, a skills practice interview with a coached client, a supervised audio replay of the interview, a second practice/replay cycle, and a posttest interview; a behavior modeling program with supervisors cocounseling during the first interview; or a control program consisting of a description of target skills with instructions to practice during three subsequent interviews. Trained independent raters rated a posttest using instruments measuring reflection of feelings and use of open-ended questions. Results indicated that behavior modeling including modeling and practice components, and receiving visual feedback of what they had done was significantly better than instructions alone. Cocounseling did not significantly add to the procedures.

Overall, there is substantial evidence to indicate that reinforcement/feedback enhances learning. This effect is even more powerful when modeling, practice, and reinforcement are combined.

## Traps in Giving Feedback

Now that the basics of reinforcement have been discussed, some hints about giving verbal feedback will be discussed. The most common feedback trap is the irresistible temptation which causes some people to put themselves in the other person's shoes and say what they would have done in that person's place: "If I were you . . . ." Such feedback is not feedback at all. It is a fantasy about how much better the trainer would have handled the problem. It is neither realistic nor motivating. Feedback of this kind creates the image of superiority and should be avoided. The most serious objection of all is that this kind of feedback seems to have a minimal effect on changing performance.

Feedback that concentrates on the goal rather than the process of reaching that goal is not really feedback. This type of feedback makes the assumption that *telling* the person how to perform will help the person improve. Although there are circumstances where this assumption is justified, presenting a goal without aiding the trainee in knowing *how* to achieve that goal is self-defeating. A training program which describes the destination while making no reference to the starting point or the process of getting there is an inefficient training program. Feedback of this sort is the same. Trainers must not use "should statements" to indicate goals.

Feedback is often given in the form of criticism, which tells trainees what they did wrong or did badly. There is undoubtedly a school of thought which believes the best method to get people to improve their performance is to point out their mistakes or weaknesses and to administer some punishment along with it. No one talks about the average events when there is an opportunity to talk about the extremely bad. When one is a trainer in behavior modeling, poor trainee performance floods the mind with possible comments and observations. It is remarkably easy to find things to say about bad performance; moreover, we can boost our egos at the same time and thus arrive at double satisfaction. The trap of criticizing is very wide for trainers. But it is a trap because an increasing amount of research shows that criticism is not nearly as effective as positive reinforcement or informative feedback. Many times, criticism is associated with blame and recrimination, which are forms of punishment. The way to avoid criticism is to give descriptive feedback on the performance without letting value judgments of "bad" or "wrong" creep in. One should never say what is wrong without being very specific about how to make it right.

The purpose of feedback is to improve performance. However it is done, be it quantified, balanced, and/or objective, there is no likelihood that it will improve performance unless it is relevant to the performance in question. Trainers in a behavior modeling program should give feedback which is related to the learning points and/or key behaviors. This is the essence of the training content. Any feedback, over and above that about the key behaviors, should be very relevant to the performance at hand, so that the feedback can be justified and thus meaningful.

Three other kinds of feedback should be avoided. First, is nongeneralizable feedback. This is feedback which might well be an accurate picture of what happened in a training situation, but which entirely fails to contain any link that helps the trainee generalize the experience to future performance. It is very common for trainers to give careful feedback about the training situation without giving much thought to whether it will be a useful carry-over to the job or transfer context. Second, one should also avoid irrelevant feedback. An easy way to avoid irrelevant feedback is to video- or audio-tape a behavior rehearsal. This way feedback can be tied to the replay of the video tape. Last, one also should be careful when giving prescriptive feedback. Prescriptive feedback inevitably involves evaluation. It is a trap which is difficult to avoid. The reason for this is that the trainer must invariably appear as something of an expert. This expectation of expertness from trainees is a hard one to resist, even in behavior modeling. Prescription may be proper, of course, but it must be based on impeccable evidence or great experience.

## Using Video-Tape Feedback

There have been a number of studies done examining audio- and video-tape feedback. Video-tape feedback has been found to be a viable means of improving behavior in a small group problem-solving context (Walter, 1973). It appears that the primary role of feedback in the behavior change process is similar to that of all social reinforcement; that is, one develops an awareness of the discrepancies between the intended behavior and one's actual behavior as revealed during playback of the video tape. This is particularly true in behavior modeling where both the intended behavior and the enacted behavior can be presented by video tape. It is particularly useful for examining many nonverbal behaviors about which one would not have been able to obtain feedback without the video tape. Wilson (1976) examined practice with video-tape feedback and practice without video feedback. Fifteen counseling students were randomly divided into experimental and control groups. Half of the subjects conducted video-taped individual interviews with coached clients; half did not. Subjects exposed to video tapes of themselves portraying appropriate role model behavior appeared to learn the three counseling behaviors that were measured better than subjects in the no video-tape feedback condition. Silverman and Quinn (1974) have shown that providing verbal feedback during a video-taped presentation is more powerful in changing behavior than providing verbal feedback after subjects viewed the video-taped replay. Finally, Melnick (1973) found that video-tape playback added significantly in improving dating behaviors, as did Prout (1974) with assertiveness.

Several studies, however, have found no difference between practice with video-taped feedback vs. practice without video-tape feedback in increasing assertive behavior (Gormally, Hill, Otis, and Rainey, 1975; Melnick and Stocker, 1977; White, 1977). Both treatments were similarly effective in increasing assertive behavior. Another possibility is that since the subjects in these playback studies had incapacitating (or severe) interpersonal problems, they may have been affected by anxiety arising from seeing (hearing) themselves during playback. Sarason and Ganzer (1973), who found that Test Anxiety Scale scores were significantly associated with the effects of playback, support this hypothesis. Furthermore, McFall and Galbraith (1977), who found that audio-tape playback was disruptive, showed this to be true only for low assertive subjects *and* only after the first rehearsal.

Decker (1983) has examined video playback in an industrial training program designed to teach "on-the-job training" behaviors. He found that video feedback significantly increased the ability of subjects to reproduce the eight key behaviors taught. He also found that this was enhanced when trainees behaviorally rehearsed in small groups. This study was done with evening business school subjects who volunteered for the study. Self-esteem and anxiety were not measured, but it is presumed that these subjects more completely mirrored the typical organizational training audience than the subjects of the assertiveness training studies reviewed above. Clinicians, however, may need to prepare highly anxious persons for working with feedback.

## Summary

In summary, we have seen that giving reinforcement to improve or change behavior and motivate the use of the new behavior is fairly complex in behavior modeling training. We have examined several different sources of feedback: the trainer, other trainees, self, and vicarious reinforcement. This amount of information looks overwhelming, but it must be remembered that people learn by observing the training content, by retaining it, practicing it in behavioral rehearsal, and obtaining feedback on their rehearsal attempts. A behavior modeling trainer should remember to attempt to give feedback to the trainee from every source: the trainer him or herself, other trainees (particularly trainees role playing subordinates), and the person enacting the behavior. Trainers should point out that one can be reinforced by watching others' behavior. When others behaviorally rehearse and are reinforced for it, the observer obtains vicarious reinforcement. Social reinforcement (especially from those perceived as competent and with high status) is very effective. Feedback should be positive when possible and should not include criticism unless very specific informative feedback is also given. And one should be aware of the traps of feedback.

It seems that video-tape feedback can be useful in behavior modeling. These authors always use it. The research about the effectiveness of video-tape feedback is not consistent. However, video-tape feedback would provide the most specific informative feedback possible about nonverbal behaviors. Trainers in behavior modeling typically attend to verbal behavior, particularly when one is teaching social skills. Video-tape feedback also enhances self-reinforcement in that the trainee compares the video tape of his or her performance to that of the models. All in all, reinforcement has been shown to be an extremely effective method for changing behavior, however, it is insufficient alone. We are making the case that modeling, retention, behavioral rehearsal, and social reinforcement are elements that must all be included for the most effective learning.

# —8—

# Transfer of Training

Transfer of training refers to the process of using what was learned during a formalized training program in the intended situation (the transfer context). The ultimate interest of any training program, and especially formalized training programs, is not the trainees' performance at the end of the training program, but whether what has been learned in the training program transfers to the context for which it is to be used. In industrial training, the obvious ultimate aim is for the training to have some effect on the organization's functioning and/or productivity. In the counseling situation, it refers to the extent that behavior learned in counseling sessions is used by the client in society in general. Wexley and Latham (1981) outlined three transfer possibilities: 1) positive transfer—learning in the training situation results in better performance on the job, 2) negative transfer—learning in the training situation results in poorer performance on the job, and 3) zero transfer—learning in the training situation has no effect on job performance. Training that results in zero or negative transfer is obviously of no value. Behavior modeling training, as any other training technique, must include the principles of transfer of training in order for that training to have the intended impact. In fact, lack of transfer of training may be where most training programs fail (Goldstein, 1974).

Atkinson (1972) conducted an experiment that illustrated the complex relationship between training performance and performance in the transfer context. His experiment clearly indicated that one cannot make the assumption that transfer of performance will be high if initial learning is high. In this experiment, the learning task consisted of sets of German/English words. In each step of the training, the German word was presented and the student responded with the English translation. Then the correct answer was presented. Three different methods were utilized in the presentation of the material. In the random-order strategy, items were randomly selected and presented by a computer. In the learner-controlled strategy, the student was permitted to decide which items were to be studied. In the response-sensitive strategy, a mathematical model was used to compute, on a trial-by-trial basis, the individual's state of learning. In this last strategy, students were presented repeatedly with poorly learned items. In the instruction session, each student was given 336 trials, and a second test was taken one week later. The random-order strategy resulted in the highest initial learning, i.e., immediately after training. The learner-controlled strategy was second, and the response-sensitive strategy produced the lowest initial learning. In the delayed test session, however, the response-sensitive strategy had the highest score with the learner-controlled strategy second and the random-order strategy last. In fact, the random-order strategy transfer scores were significantly lower than the initial scores. The random-order strategy resulted in good performance during the training because it presented many items that had been previously learned. The learner-controlled strategy allowed the student to concentrate on those items that he or she thought needed the most work. The response-sensitive strategy selected those items that had not been well learned by the student and consequently caused the most errors during learning. However, high transfer scores were attained. This experiment would suggest that high initial learning does not lead automatically to transfer of training.

### Transfer versus Generalization

Technically there are two types of transfer of training. In what could be referred to as pure transfer, the exact form of behaviors learned in training are exhibited in the transfer context. In the second type of transfer of training, referred to as generalized ability, trainees exhibit behaviors of a similar type to those learned in training or use learned behavior in response to similar, but not identical, stimuli to that presented in training. Those interested in behavior modeling must attend to both of these phenomena. Generalized ability becomes a very important issue when social skills are taught in behavior modeling training. When we teach social skills, we are usually teaching rule-oriented behavior. For example, the first thing trainees are taught to do in a selection interview is establish rapport. Establishing rapport at the beginning of an interview helps interviewees feel at ease and encourages them to reveal more about themselves. There may, however, be several different ways to establish rapport. Methods include having the interviewer talk about him or herself, or about finding the interview site, or the trip into town. Another way would be to talk about hobbies or interests that the interviewer and candidate have in common. The stimulus in this case is sitting down with the candidate at the start of the interview. One knows, given the stimulus, that the rule is to establish rapport. Given different candidates, however, there may be more or less appropriate ways to establish rapport, and different rapport-establishing techniques are used with different candidates. This would be generalization. On the other hand, a training program could be developed that taught new interviewers only one way to establish rapport— let us say in this instance, talking about him or herself. When the trainee went back to the job and actually interviewed candidates, we would expect the trainee-interviewer to talk about him or herself at the start of every interview. Of course, this might not be the most appropriate way to establish rapport with some candidates, nor would it be comfortable for all trainees. This would be an example of pure transfer, i.e., exactly what was learned in the training program was used on the job. In this case, the training is possibly less effective, because the trainee has not been taught to generalize. Unless otherwise specified, transfer of training as used here will refer to generalized ability not pure transfer.

## Transfer of Training Enhancers

Researchers have identified several different principles that enhance transfer of training (Wexley and Latham, 1981). All of these principles should be implemented in any training program because their combined impact greatly increases the likelihood of positive transfer. Transfer of training has been demonstrated to be facilitated: 1) by providing general principles governing satisfactory performance in both the training and the transfer site tasks; 2) by procedures that maximize response availability, or adequate opportunities to practice; 3) when the maximum number of characteristics in the training program and the transfer context are identical (identical elements); 4) when performance feedback is given in the transfer context; 5) when the stimulus and response elements are specified; 6) when a variety of stimulus situations are provided so that the student can generalize his or her knowledge; 7) when important features of the task or behavior are labeled or identified; and 8) when the training content is designed so that the trainees can see its applicability in the transfer context. Let's review these eight principles:

### *General Principles*

To the extent that general principles are taught in training, a student can focus on those general principles necessary to a task and then apply them to problems in the transfer situation. Hendrickson and Schroeder (1941) demonstrated the use of general principles in transfer of training. In their experiment, two groups were given practice shooting at an underwater target until each was able to hit the target consistently. At this point, the depth of the target in the water was changed. One group was taught the principles of refraction of light through water while the other group was not. In the second session, the group that was taught the principles of refraction of light performed significantly better than the group not taught these principles. In this case, by learning general principles, the first group was able to adapt what had been taught to a nonidentical transfer context. In fact, in some training applications, it may be more important to teach general principles than to have identical elements. Using general principles also refers to giving the trainee the organizing concepts and rationale that explain or account for the stimulus-response relationships in both the training and the transfer tasks.

In behavior modeling training, the concept of general principles is incorporated at several points. Learning points are presented before and during display of the modeling films and also during the retention processes. To the extent these are rule-oriented, general principles are presented. Recall of the general principles (key behaviors) is also an integral part of the behavioral rehearsal component (Decker, 1982). Cominsky (1982) has shown that the use of general principles enhances transfer in a behavior modeling program used to teach reflection of feelings to counselors.

## Maximum Response Availability

The principle of response availability is derived from research on overlearning; when the learner practices new behavior beyond the point of first accurate reproduction, long-term retention is greater. Consequently, enough practice or chances to respond must be available to make overlearning possible. Overlearning in training increases the probability of subsequent transfer. However, we cannot clearly say that more is better. It must be kept in mind that when more than one skill is being taught, negative transfer is likely to occur if training on the second skill is begun while the first is still only partially learned.

It has been amply demonstrated, other things being equal, that responses that have been performed frequently in the past will be enacted on subsequent occasions. Mandler (1954) trained subjects on a motor task until they were able to perform it without error either 0, 10, 30, 50, or 100 consecutive times. Transfer was then assessed. Positive transfer increased as the degree of original training was increased. Several authors (Mandler and Heinemann, 1956; Atwater, 1953; Gagne and Foster, 1949) have shown that the greater the amount of training, the greater the subsequent transfer. These principles can be used in behavior modeling by increasing the time allowed for behavioral rehearsal.

## Identical Elements

The principle of identical elements was first proposed by Thorndike and Woodworth (1901) who showed that transfer would occur as long as there were identical elements in both training and the transfer situations.

Identical elements refers to both the physical characteristics of the training environment and interpersonnel stimuli to which the trainee must respond. Identical elements have been shown to increase the transfer of both motor (Duncan, 1953; Gagne, Baker, and Foster, 1950) and verbal behavior (Underwood, 1951; Young and Underwood, 1954). In all cases, including behavior modeling training, the physical environment of the training should look, as much as possible, like that of the transfer context, including any apparatus or material that the trainee interacts with or manipulates. However, in situations where a broad range of stimuli is possible, such as in social interactions where individuals are required to respond to different persons in similar, but not identical, social situations, the task of providing all the possible stimuli and response elements in the training situation (in both the modeling display and behavior rehearsal) becomes formidable, if not impossible. It is for this reason that behavior modeling training has emphasized the teaching of rule-oriented principles which, while more general, are more likely to transfer from training.

Identical elements are incorporated in behavior modeling in several places. Obviously, the modeling display must be a very realistic portrayal of the training content. This point cannot be emphasized too strongly. If the modeling display appears too contrived, especially if the model succeeds too easily in obtaining the desired outcome in the social situation, the trainee is likely to discount the behavior of the model and instead focus attention on the artificiality of the situation. The success of the model will likely be attributed not to the key behaviors or general rules, but to the author of the script. Such a modeling display will do little to change the trainee's expectancy that the desired behavior will lead to a desired outcome. Use of actors as models is also often seen as artificial by trainees. Behavioral rehearsal must also reflect the realities of the transfer setting to every extent possible. Often role players will try to be "supportive" of the trainee as the person practices the new skills. To the extent that it is too easy to succeed with the new skills in practice, success will again be attributed to the artificiality of the training situation and not to the key behaviors. Succeeding at easy tasks provides the trainees with no new information by which to alter their sense of self-efficacy, and therefore, believe they have enhanced their self-competence. Trainees must experience mastery of the key behaviors in challenging situations if they are to reasonably expect the skills to succeed in the transfer context (Bandura, 1977a).

The degree to which the transfer setting can be realistically simulated is exemplified in an experiment by Porras et al. (1982). This study was conducted using 17 first-line supervisors and their 700 union employees. Training sessions of a behavior modeling training program designed to teach the supervisors 10 targeted supervisory skills were led by line managers senior to the participants. For each general principle underlying each supervisory skill, a short video tape was presented using actual company personnel filmed in their own plant. In this case not only were the modeling displays realistic, but the trainees' behavioral rehearsals were supervised by the same line managers who supervised their actual job performance. Results were impressive. The unionized employees reported not only increased use of the key behaviors both 1 week after training and 6 months after training as compared to before training, but they also reported less feelings of being manipulated by supervisors and an improved organizational climate at both posttraining measurement periods, as compared to untrained control groups. Furthermore, rates of employee absenteeism and turnover decreased while measures of performance increased.

## Feedback

One of the most important transfer enhancers is feedback in the transfer context. We have emphasized the importance of continued reinforcement to elicit and maintain behavior change. For example, Lovaas et al. (1973) report that, in long-term followup, autistic children sustain or increase training gains if parents continue the regimen at home, but revert to pretraining behaviors if placed in settings which do not support skill maintenance. Reinforcement must take place not only in the training program, but also on the job or in the transfer context. It cannot be stressed too strongly that the trainee must be reinforced for use of new behavior on the job for that behavior to be maintained. It is quite likely that when a trainee goes back to the transfer context, the first enactments of the new behavior will not produce the desired results. A common thing for that trainee to do in this situation is to revert back to the old behavior. To avert this, the supervisor of the trainee should be exposed to the training program content and taught how to reinforce the subordinates for the use of the new behavior on the job. Again the example presented by Porras et al. (1982) has shown the value of this type of top-down reinforcement. Another way to reinforce new behavior is to develop a buddy system where trainees are asked to meet with each other after the formal training is completed, in order to practice the new behavior and provide feedback to each other (Schinke and Rose, 1976). Almost every trainer would tell you, however, that it is best to provide training from the top on down. This kind of a training procedure enhances performance feedback to the trainee. The feedback should be of a positive nature.

## Specific Stimulus and Response Elements

To the greatest extent possible, stimulus and response elements involved in the training content should be spelled out to the trainees. It is very difficult to determine whether complex stimulus and response elements are similar across the training and transfer context. If the trainer does an adequate job of needs analysis, understands the training tasks and how behaviors are used on the job, and uses that knowledge in developing a training program, the trainer will be able to specify what key behaviors should be used in response to any given stimuli. If one does not do a good job of outlining the stimuli and response connections before designing the training program, negative transfer could result. As Goldstein (1974) has pointed out, when shifting from a mechanical to an electrical typewriter, there are some positive effects due to knowledge of the keyboard and some negative effects due to the different sensitivity of the keys. Thus, to teach individuals how to use an electric typewriter, one should specify the different stimuli and the different responses which will be required so that trainees know where both positive transfer and negative transfer can be expected. By doing this, trainees can know what to expect on the job, so that self-feedback will be possible and positive transfer can occur.

### Variety of Stimuli

The more stimulus situations used in the behavioral rehearsal component of the training program, the more likely is the trainee to see how the key behaviors can generalize, and therefore transfer. When a behavior modeling trainer supplies learning points (written descriptions of the key behaviors seen in the modeling display) and these learning points are rule-oriented, the stimulus and response elements may be specified. Stimulus-response elements can also be specified when behavioral rehearsal includes practice with all possible stimuli. This is enhanced when one uses unstructured behavioral rehearsal and the trainees are allowed to develop the problems where the key behaviors can be used as the solution. When supervisors are to learn coaching or discipline skills, they should be allowed to define the kind of employee with which they will use these behaviors, and with what kind of discipline and coaching problems they would apply these new behaviors. Here the trainees are, to a certain extent, helping to define the stimulus-response connection.

### Labeling

Labeling or identifying the important features of the task helps the trainee to distinguish the important features of the training content. In training someone to operate a piece of machinery, one might give a step-by-step description of the operation of that piece of machinery. In addition, one might label the various parts of the machine or give a picture of the machine to the trainee (Wexley and Latham, 1981). In behavior modeling, the important features of the task are repeatedly labeled through the use of learning points.

Transfer is also facilitated when the trainee understands the general principles that are needed in solving the problems that the training is designed to remedy. This can be facilitated in discussions about the modeling display and/or a complete explanation of the learning points and key behaviors by the trainer before the modeling display is shown.

## *Applicability*

Wexley and Latham (1981) also suggest that the training program should be designed so that the trainee can see its applicability. Positive transfer will be facilitated when trainees feel that the trainers understand their unique job problems. Conversely, training programs felt to be too difficult or poorly organized will generate less positive transfer. These authors suggest that individuals who feel that the training course helped them learn new skills and ideas directly related to their job situation are more likely to transfer their learning to the job. The trainee is a decision-maker who will decide whether the training can increase the instrumentality for obtaining desired outcomes (Vroom, 1964) or an enhanced sense of mastery of future situations (Bandura, 1977), or whether it will be simply an interesting activity with no applicability back on the job. To the extent that trainees see applicability directly on their jobs, they will be motivated to attend to and learn the training content.

Wittrock and Lumsdaine (1977) found that questions inserted in instructional materials can influence trainee motivation. Questions in a text that precede the training material containing the answers to those questions facilitate the trainee's learning and retention of the information. Wexley and Latham (1981) suggest that goal setting should be included in any training program. The questions presented before the training content can be used to facilitate such goal setting.

Finally, two other studies are of interest. Porras and Anderson (1981) report an elaborate transfer effort in a supervisory training program which was very effective. Workshop leaders were selected from line management, and training was conducted on company premises. The video modeling tapes were made in-house, utilizing organizational members as role players, and each new model was introduced by a well-known company executive. Trainees used problems they were currently facing for their rehearsal sessions, and then were asked to commit to using the new skills on the job. Upon reporting back to the group, remedial training was provided where needed. Similar "reporting back—remedial training meetings" were scheduled two months and four months after the training ended. Further organizational support for sustaining the new behaviors was achieved by introducing a version of the program to all managers, from the top on down. It stressed how they could encourage and reinforce others to use the skills being developed. Six months after training, there were important improvements in supervisory behaviors: average production had increased, and grievance and absentee rates had dropped markedly.

The second study entails use of a "buddy system." To encourage transfer of interpersonal skills from the training program, Schinke and Rose (1976) utilized a buddy system in which pairs of trainees committed themselves to trying new behaviors and then periodically phoned each other to report on success/failure relative to their goals. The contracting "buddies" showed significant improvement on a role play test three months after training.

## Maintenance of Behavior

Most of what we have previously discussed concerns transfer of training and generalization. Generalization has been used to refer to behavior changes that carry over to situations or settings other than those in which the training program was implemented. However, changes must also extend over time. This is referred to as maintenance of behavior, continuing to use the new behaviors once they have been transferred to and used in the transfer context. Consequently, transfer is not the only issue of importance. Behaviors can transfer and even be generalized, but they also must be maintained.

There are two primary reasons why new behavior may be transferred but not maintained in the transfer context. One of these is lack of reinforcement in the transfer context. Reinforcement in the training situation helps the trainees learn the new behavior; reinforcement in the transfer context immediately after training will help the behavior transfer to the transfer context. To the extent that the reinforcement is long-lived, the behavior will be maintained. The second reason why behavior is not maintained in the transfer context is that competing stimuli or competing behaviors may be present which are more powerful than those presented in the training program. In these situations, the desired behavior will not continue.

As noted previously, one method of enhancing maintenance of new behavior in the transfer context is to train from the top on down. If the supervisors of the trainees are trained, they will reinforce the new training behavior on a long-term basis. Latham and Saari (1979) did this and found supervisory skills were maintained as long as one year after training. As noted previously, Porras et al. (1982) used supervisors' superiors as trainers, thereby ensuring greater commitment to reinforcing skills learning in training. Six months after training, subordinates of the trainees still reported higher levels of skills and improved organizational climate. Objective labor relations and performance indices were found to have been maintained at the improved levels reported one week after training.

The trainer should do everything possible to change the contingencies in the transfer context that would inhibit maintenance of the new behavior. One strategy which will enhance behavior maintenance is the selection of target behaviors likely to be reinforced by events which occur naturally and reliably in the transfer context. To any extent possible, the target behaviors selected in a training program should be those that are relevant to the setting in which the trainee will move after training. Another method to enhance maintenance is punishment of the undesirable behavior in the transfer context. One method the first author has used in behavior modeling programs is to pair up the trainees into peer groups (i.e., the buddy system). These pairs or groups meet once a week or so for two to three months after the training program to discuss how they have used new behaviors learned in the training program and what success or failures they have had with them. These groups are designed to facilitate not only self-reinforcement but to provide reinforcement from the training peers.

Kazdin and Mascitelli (1982), in an assertiveness training program, compared "self-instruction training" (trainees engage in self-statements designed to promote assertive behavior) and "homework skill practice" (trainees engage in the key behaviors in extratreatment physical practice). These researchers found that both conditions enhanced use of assertive behaviors in immediate posttreatment measures but that, in a six month followup, only the effects of homework practice continued as a significant determinant of treatment outcome. Consequently, asking trainees to practice the key behaviors with each other where meaningful feedback can be given may not only motivate trainees to maintain use of the training content but may also increase their effectiveness in its use.

## Self-Control

One reason that changes in behavior do not transfer and are not maintained is that behavior comes under the stimulus control of external agencies (trainers, supervisors) in restricted situations (e.g., the training program). To the extent that a trainee uses the new behavior only when the external reinforcement is present or potentially present and that external control is not reliable, the behavior will not be maintained. Self-control procedures are used extensively in counseling situations and are reviewed by Kazdin (1980). Kazdin suggests that self-control is a set of behaviors, learned in much the same way as other behaviors, that individuals use to control their own behaviors.

Procedures for self-control can be developed through many methods. The first is stimulus control. A trainee who is aware of how certain stimuli control his/her behavior can structure the environment to maximize the likelihood that desired behavior occurs. If a supervisor yells at his or her subordinates in a given situation or an overweight person eats in a given situation, then those situations can be avoided with proper forethought. Control over one's behaviors can also be enhanced by self-observation. To the extent that individuals develop a standard for behavior, then when their behavior departs from that standard, the person observes the deviation, and can subsequently correct his/her actions to be more like the standard. Modeling helps develop standards for behavior and the modeling display should be pointed out to trainees as such a standard. It is hoped, then, that trainees will compare their own behavior in the transfer context to those which were shown in the modeling display. Self-reinforcement and self-punishment are also methods useful in self-control. Trainees can be taught to reward themselves for using the new behaviors taught in the training program and to punish themselves for not using the new behaviors.

Another method of self-control is alternative response training, that is, training a person to engage in responses that interfere with or replace the response which is to be eliminated and replaced with the new training content. For example, people can think of pleasant thoughts to control worrying or whistle whenever they feel afraid. In counseling situations, the most common focus of alternate response training is to control anxiety. Relaxation procedures have been widely used as a response which is incompatible with anxiety. Mental rehearsal has also been used as a self-control device. If a person pictures him or herself doing the correct behaviors before actually going out and attempting that new behavior, the training will be used correctly and maintained over time. It is useful to instruct trainees to picture themselves doing something before they actually attempt it, particularly the first few times they try using the new behavior taught in the training program. Trainees can imagine themselves engaging in undesirable behavior and desirable behavior. When an undesirable behavior is imagined and the image is vivid, the trainee will also see the adverse consequences associated with that undesirable behavior. Then, they can imagine themselves doing the training behavior and see positive results coming from it. This should lead to self-reinforcement for attempting the new behavior.

Marlatt and Gordon (1980) developed a relapse prevention model which is designed to increase long-term maintenance of newly trained behaviors. The model emphasizes helping trainees learn a set of self-control and coping strategies. This model has been adapted to the industrial training context by Marx (1982) and is shown in Figure 8.1.

The first step in this model is to make trainees aware of the relapse process itself. Most training programs are presented as being quite successful. Awareness of what may make the program vulnerable is neglected and trainees may not consequently be able to avoid situations in which the training content will be unsuccessful. Trainees are asked to pinpoint situations

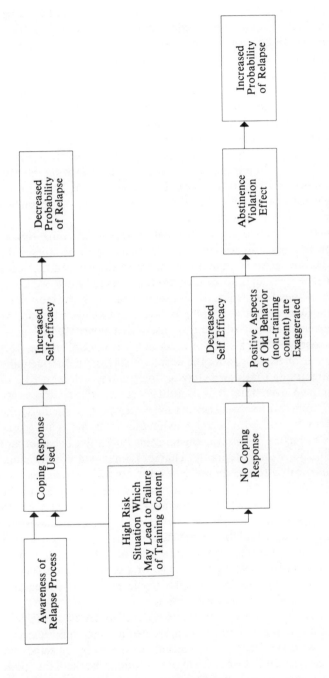

**Figure 8.1**  A Model of the Training Relapse Process

*Source:* Adapted from Marx (1982) Relapse prevention for managerial training: A model for maintenance of behavior change. *Academy of Management Review, 7(3)*, 433–41.

which are likely to sabotage their efforts. Trainees can then be taught: 1) to anticipate high-risk situations, 2) coping strategies for avoiding high-risk situations, and 3) that slight slips or relapses are predictable outcomes of any training paradigm and need not become full-blown relapses. These techniques should increase trainees' self-efficacy (feelings of control over the situation requiring use of the training content).

Most of the possible coping strategies which can be used have been described in previous sections. The importance of this model is in showing that trainees' exposure to possible failure situations will enable them to expect and prepare for such situations in advance. This advance mental preparation for trying situations will decrease the probability of small relapses turning into absolute failure due to the "abstinence violation effect". The effect occurs when guilt over a small violation of the training content leads a trainee through cognitive dissonance to deny the possible effectiveness of the training content or key behaviors. Such denial almost guarantees that a small slip will end up as a total relapse or non-use of the training content. Again, the keys are: 1) awareness of the relapse process; 2) identification of high-risk situations; and 3) the development of coping responses. The trainee should not be afraid, in behavior modeling, to discuss possible failure situations and ways to cope with them. Better yet, trainees should practice such situations using the key behaviors in the neutral environment of the training room. In this way the trainees prepare themselves for the difficult situations. But, the trainees will not be motivated to prepare for the difficult situations unless they know about the relapse process.

## Summary

Overall, the training content must be transferred to the job or other transfer context, must be generalized where needed and must be maintained for the training program to be truly effective. One of the most powerful methods to maintain new behavior in the transfer context is to include training modules explaining self-control techniques to the trainees. To the extent that the new behavior taught in the training program comes under the control of the individual, that behavior will be maintained over time.

The ultimate aim of any training program is to have the new behavior transfer to the job (or another transfer context) and have it be maintained over time such that there is some effect on the organization. There are three elements involved in this process. The first is transfer of training (the new behaviors learned in the training program are actually used in the transfer context). The second is generalization (stimulus and response). The training will be more effective and the behavior will be transferred when the trainees are taught to generalize their behavior across situations that they will find in the transfer context. Finally, maintenance is important. There are techniques that are aimed at maintaining the behavior over a long period of time in the transfer context. All of these elements should be considered by the behavior modeling trainer and included or discussed in the training program.

We have also seen that transfer is only one component of training. Effective training occurs when trainees have been shown the proper behavior to use and when to use it through viewing a modeling display, are aided in retaining this information cognitively, are allowed to behaviorally rehearse the new behavior, and are given feedback about and reinforcement for the behavioral rehearsal. Transfer/maintenance elements should also be included in the training program. This is behavior modeling.

# III

## How to Develop and Implement Behavior Modeling Programs

# —9—

# Developing Key Behaviors and Learning Points

The previous sections in this book have exposed the reader to the background and basic theory of behavior modeling training. This section is concerned with the pragmatic factors involved in developing and conducting a behavior modeling training program. This chapter discusses training needs analysis, the process of identifying key behaviors to be taught to trainees in a behavior modeling program, and the development of the learning points to be used in the training. Development of key behaviors and learning points is probably the most important part of the behavior modeling training process and must be done with the utmost care, because whatever is in the modeling display is what the trainees are going to learn. Also, the manner in which the modeling display is developed and presented to the trainees will, to a very large extent, determine how they learn what is in the modeling display, whether it is simply reproduced on the job, or is generalized, and to what extent it is transferred.

## How To Determine Training Needs

The first step in training is to determine that a need for a training program exists. Only then should training resources be expended. A company or corporation should commit its resources to a training activity only if, in the best judgment of its managers, the training activity can be expected to achieve some organizational result. Training must support some organizational goal such as more efficient production, distribution of goods and services, reduced operating costs, improved quality, or more efficient or satisfied personnel. Only educational institutions can legitimately view training as an end in itself. Such training can be looked at as a developmental tool to increase the general knowledge or ability of an individual for later use.

There are four levels of measurement in training evaluation: training reaction, learning, behavior change, and organizational result (Kirkpatrick, 1967). An educational institution in the business of "selling" training can legitimately use trainee reaction as its only evaluation measure. If trainees like the training, they will purchase more of it, and that meets the goal of that institution. Of course, educational institutions are also responsible for developing individuals to go into the work place. In this regard, educational administrators should be concerned with the learning and behavior change of the individual. In most private organizations, however, the ultimate aim is to increase the profitability or productivity of that organization. Training should therefore be designed to directly impact on those organizational result criteria.

This naturally leads to the question, "On what should I spend my training resources?" This is a decision that people interested in training must make aided by the best available data. In corporations, this data can come from training specialists, other knowledgeable people in the organization, and by continual systematic and accurate analysis of the training needs of that organization. In educational institutions, it comes from a monitoring of the kinds of behaviors that are useful in the sites to which students move after graduation. With behavior modeling in mind, the typical educational institution should be concerned with the criteria of behavior change. Yet, a corporation will look at behavior change as a means toward the goal of some organizational result. For the educational trainer, the process is fairly simple: determine what behaviors are needed by the trainees and teach those new behaviors. If learning is required, measure learning also. To the extent that the trainees change their behavior to that which is desired, the training is successful. For the corporation, it is a more complex problem. The first part of the problem of determining training needs is singling out those activities which can be made more effective by training efforts which change behavior. Also there is always a great deal of day-to-day "maintenance-type" or orientation training taking place in any organization. This type of training is used to instruct people who, as new employees, are brought into the organization or current employees who are promoted. A certain amount of training resources must be assigned to the training of these new or promoted employees. Those resources left over should be aimed at specific activities which will increase the effectiveness of the organization.

Too often, training programs are used in an organization simply because the program has been well advertised and marketed or because other organizations have found them to be useful. This has made training a very faddish business (Campbell, 1971). It does not make sense, however, for an organization to adopt an expensive training effort simply because other organizations are doing it. This faddish use of new training programs in organizations can be reduced by systematically determining training needs, and using those training needs to develop very specific training content. In this way, training programs are used efficiently and organizations use training programs only for those people and those situations where training is actually needed.

Sometimes the need for training is misunderstood. The sales manager may feel that salespersons need product knowledge training while a good analysis of the situation may reveal that the sales personnel need the skills to present the product rather than additional knowledge of the product. This kind of situation is eliminated by applying systematic procedures for determining training needs in organizations.

Any use of behavior modeling, at minimum, should be designed to change people's behavior and, in an organization, to produce some positive organizational result. Behavior modeling training is expensive and trainer-intensive. Consequently, one should not go into the business of behavior modeling training without a systematic and thorough needs analysis. Furthermore, in behavior modeling, the needs analysis does not end at specifying tasks that will enhance an organization or a person's ability. Training needs must be refined into very specific key behaviors which can be presented through behavior modeling training.

## Systematic Training Needs Analysis

McGehee and Thayer (1961) proposed an integrated, three-faceted program designed to provide a systematic, objective determination of training needs. The facets are organizational analysis, task analysis, and person analysis. Although there is some conceptual overlap, organization analysis focuses on the entire business enterprise examining organizational goals, management support, and available resources for training. Task analysis focuses on what tasks are required and what skills, knowledge, and abilities an employee must possess in order to perform the tasks at the desired level. Person analysis focuses on determining the degree to which each employee is able to perform the tasks and/or is actually performing the tasks. The development of needs analysis procedures has progressed little beyond description of various techniques used to collect data for the three analyses since McGehee and Thayer (1961) wrote their text. Moore and Dutton (1978) detail the various techniques used commonly for needs analysis. A full listing of these techniques is shown in Table 9.1.

Moore and Dutton (1978) suggested that the typical needs analysis still lacks a systematic and empirical approach, yet these researchers saw continued progress toward this goal. Some notable conclusions can be made from

**Table 9.1 Techniques Used in Training Needs Assessment**

| Organization Analysis | Task Analysis | Person Analysis |
|---|---|---|
| Organizational Goals and Objectives | Job Descriptions | Performance Data |
| Manpower Inventories | Job Specifications or Task Analysis | Productivity |
| Skills Inventories | Performance Standards | Absenteeism or tardiness |
| Organizational Climate Indexes | Performing the Job | Accidents |
| Strikes | Observing the Job–Work Sampling | Sicknesses |
| Grievances | Reviewing Literature Concerning the Job | Grievances |
| Absenteeism | Research in other industries | Waste |
| Suggestions | Professional journals | Late deliveries |
| Productivity | Documents | Product quality |
| Accidents | Government sources | Down time |
| Sicknesses | Ph.D. theses | Repairs |
| Observation of employee behavior | Ask Questions About the Job | Equipment utilization |
| Attitude surveys | of the job holder | Customer complaints |
| Customer complaints | of the supervisor | Observation–Work Sampling |
| Efficiency Indexes | of higher management | Interviews |
| Costs of labor | Training Committees | Questionnaires |
| Costs of materials | Analysis of Operating Problems | Tests |

98

Quality of product
Equipment utilization
Costs of distribution
Waste
Down time
Late deliveries
Repairs
Changes in Systems or Subsystems
Management Requests
Exit Interviews
MBO or Work Planning and Review Systems

Down time reports
Waste
Repairs
Late deliveries
Quality control
Card Sorting (Critical Incidents)

Job knowledge
Skills
Achievement
Attitude Surveys
Training Progress Charts
Rating Scales
Critical Incidents
Diaries
Devised Situations
Role playing
Case studies
Conference leadership
  training sessions
Business games
In baskets
Diagnostic Rating
Assessment Centers
Coaching
MBO or Work Planning
  and Review Sessions

*Source:* Adapted from Moore and Dutton (1978) Training needs analysis: Review and Critique. *Academy of Management Review, 3,* 532–45. Used with permission.

Table 9.1. First, some techniques overlap the conceptual distinctions between organizational, task, and person analysis. This follows from propositions made by McGehee and Thayer (1961) suggesting that these investigations be coordinated and interrelated. Second is the apparent lack of direct measurement of work group performance, climate, etc. Major training needs may occur at the group level (such as problem-solving styles, team building, and group processes). Third, considerable data of widely fluctuating quality and quantity are available for training needs analysis. Some data are easier to obtain than others. Fourth, there has been little research on the utility of these techniques for determining training needs. Finally, little research has been directed at improving or developing methods to translate the needs analysis information into specific instructional activities (Goldstein, 1980). The major difficulty in needs analysis becomes how one determines specific problems deemed solvable by training. Many authors (Gilbert, 1967; Mager and Pipe, 1970; Odiorne, 1970; Warren, 1969) suggest that a training need is any discrepancy between present or actual performance and desired performance. Thus, expected levels of performance are specified (from task analysis), current performance is determined (from person analysis), and the two data sets are compared to determine training needs. Organizational analysis is used to determine if the solution of the determined need is consistent with overall organizational strategy, goals, and resources.

Gilbert (1967) and Mager and Pipe (1970) differ from the other authors in suggesting that needs analysis does not end with a discrepancy between actual and desired performance. Mager and Pipe (1970), for example, called the discrepancy a "problem" and suggest that a performance discrepancy should not be automatically interpreted as a training need. This discrepancy is only a symptom, not the problem. Consequently, the analyst must determine whether the discrepancy is a skill deficiency. If the required skill is present and performance is lacking, then the problem may be a motivational problem stemming from lack of relevant rewards, lack of performance feedback, little or no opportunity for practice, or punishment for performing adequately. If the problem is truly a skill deficiency, training may be an appropriate solution; however, if the required skill is present, the problem is one of building a proper motivational system or removing motivational barriers. As can be seen in Figure 9.1, needs assessment starts with a specific group of workers (target population). A major drawback of the way needs analysis is frequently conducted is that it is not typically carried out in a continuing, ongoing manner coordinated with manpower systems of the organization. Needs analysis is often a temporary function (i.e., a survey of a target population) to develop a training program designed to respond to a specific training request. By approaching needs analysis in such a way, many important sources of information and decision points are often missed. Continuing needs assessment is preferable; however, the model presented in Figure

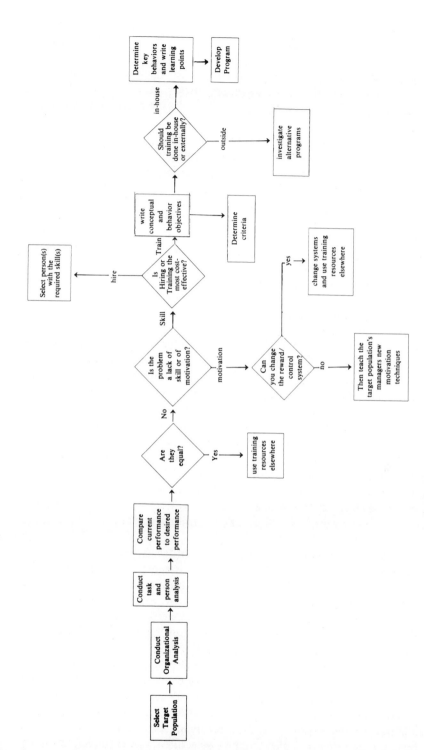

**Figure 9.1** A Model of Training Needs Assessment

101

9.1 can be used in both an on-going needs assessment process or when a training request for a particular target population has been received. Figure 9.1 should be followed to make sure each major decision point is not skipped, even when a training request manifests itself.

Task analysis is done to determine desired performance and the skills, knowledge, and/or abilities necessary to accomplish the performance. Person analysis is done to determine the actual or current performance level of the target population. This analysis may focus on employees currently performing a job, employees who may be performing the job in the future, and/or non-employees who may be hired to perform the job. The data from these analyses are compared to determine if a discrepancy between actual and desired performance exists. The next step in the needs analysis process is essentially the question raised by Mager and Pipe (1970): Is the deficiency a skill deficiency or a motivational barrier? If the questions, "Can the employee perform the task if he/she wanted to?" or "Has the employee done the task in the past?" can both be answered affirmatively, the problem is not a skill deficiency. It then becomes a problem of searching for a motivational barrier such as lack of rewards, punishment, or task interference. If diagnosed, the next decision point is reached: Shall the barrier be removed by changing organizational design, by training another population of employees (i.e., the supervisors of the original target population), by providing training designed to affect trainee motivation, or by some combination of these three? The analyst must decide where the problem originates. If it originates from an organizational barrier such as lack of relevant rewards (merit pay or other work outcomes), then these should be introduced into the organization's reward system. If the motivational barrier is the result of poor supervisory skills on the part of the original target populations' supervisors, then the supervisors become the target population for training. Finally, the problem may be solvable by providing a training program aimed at motivation within the original target population.

Organizational analysis is performed in order to determine if a training solution would conflict with organizational goals and be reasonable considering available resources. Organizational analysis impacts at every point of the model in Figure 9.1. Training programs that are in conflict with organizational goals will not be successful. Many trainers have heard, "I wish my boss had been exposed to this training workshop." This is an indication that the goals of upper-level management and the training program are in conflict. Furthermore, many of the decision points specified in Figure 9.1 require a decision of utility—what is the most economical solution? A prior analysis of resources and priorities is crucial at these decision points.

If a skill deficiency is clearly indicated, the analyst must still face the next decision point; that is, whether the skill deficiency can be best remedied by training the target population or by selecting (or transferring) new employees who will come to the job with the requisite skills. Manpower planning and fiscal resource data are helpful at this point. These data are generated primarily in the organizational analysis.

After this decision is made, a specific training need is established and the analyst can then progress toward program development. Conceptual objectives and key behaviors are developed. Conceptual objectives simply state the training need or needs in a conceptual manner (i.e., increase the selection interviewing skills of a certain group of managers). A final question to be asked is, "Should the training be developed and presented in-house, or should the organization go to an outside consultant/training organization for the program?" This is a question whose answer is heavily dependent upon fiscal and trainer resources and trainer status.

## The Use of Questionnaires in Needs Analysis

In industry, a very common approach to determining training needs is to survey the target population or the supervisors of the target population. These survey techniques range from one-page response sheets to highly sophisticated attitude questionnaires. Whatever their form, the critical assumption made in using survey techniques in needs analysis is that the respondents are able and willing to compare desired and actual performance to determine where deficiencies exist, recognize the difference between motivational and skill problems, and decide between training and selection as solutions. There are two factors which will affect the effectiveness of the needs analysis survey—respondent ability and respondent motivation to answer accurately.

Questionnaires can be subject to a series of response biases. O'Reilly, Parlette, and Bloom (1980) have shown that incumbents' perceptions of job characteristics are associated with perceptual biases reflecting individuals' frames of reference to the job and general job attitudes. It is not clear if, or by how much, respondents may bias needs survey results. To the extent that people differ in these biases, the resulting data will be less reliable and less valid. Regardless of the ability of employees (or supervisors) to make a desired performance actual/performance comparison and the presence or absence of response biases in questionnaires, it is doubtful that employees (or supervisors) can or will always make valid distinctions between skill deficiencies and organizational deficiencies; nor should they be expected to make selection versus training solution decisions.

A final consideration is that attitude surveys, like most psychological measures, provide only relative scores that can be interpreted most effectively through comparisons with previous survey scores or norm data. A frequent mistake in needs analysis survey work is to interpret a relative score in absolute terms. Overall, the trainer should rely on surveys only to give a preliminary indication of training needs areas, not to indicate task areas for behavior modeling training program development.

## Some Definitions

In developing a behavior modeling training program, one must (through needs analysis) determine the *tasks* which are not being performed adequately due to a lack of skill and the *key behaviors* which are required to perform the task(s). One must write a description of these key behaviors. These are called *learning points*. In this section, these terms will be examined.

Task definitions vary greatly with respect to their breadth of coverage. At one end of this continuum are definitions that view the task as the totality of the situation imposed on the worker. This definition would consider the stimuli, responses, and consequences of the task. At the other end of the continuum are definitions that treat a task as a specific performance. This range of definitions also reflects the extent to which tasks are defined as being external to or an intrinsic part of the worker involved (Fleishman, 1975). Miller (1966) suggested that a task is any set of activities occurring about the same time, and sharing common purpose that is recognized by the task performer. At minimum, a task is any set of interrelated activities. Beyond that, one could include the goal or consequence of the task, stimuli which would elicit the task behavior, and instructions to the worker. For our purposes, a task will be any goal-oriented set of interrelated behaviors.

**Figure 9.2**  Behavior Description Learning Points

---

1. Say "Hello" to the applicant.
2. Hold out your right hand for a handshake, shake hands, and say, "Please sit here," as you point to the chair at the side of your desk.
3. Say, "How was the flight to our city?"
4. After the applicant has answered, ask, "Would you like a cup of coffee? Cream or sugar?"
5. Say to your secretary, "Please get us two cups of coffee."
6. After coffee has been received, take out the interview guide and read everything on it to the applicant.

---

Figure 9.3    Summary Label Learning Points

---

1. Greet applicant.
2. Establish rapport.
3. Use the interview guide.

---

A key behavior is a behavior which is necessary to the completion of a task or one of a set of behaviors which must be used to complete a task. Key behaviors are typically required to be in sequential order for a task to be completed.

Learning points are written descriptions of key behaviors. Learning points can take several forms. The most basic is the behavior description format. This form is a simple, specific description of the behavior to be performed. Figure 9.2 shows this kind of learning point. Another type of learning point is the summary label. Summary labels are key words which are used to define or cue certain behaviors or classes of behaviors which are well known to the trainee. An example would be a learning point such as "shake hands." Further explanation of this type of behavior is unnecessary. Figure 9.3 shows summary label learning points. The difference between these types of learning points is basically one of the degree of behavioral specificity.

Learning points can also specify rules underlying sets of behavior which can be used to complete the task. Rule-oriented learning points may or may not include a description of actual behavior. An example of a rule-oriented learning point (used in selection interviewing) would be "establish rapport to get the applicant to talk." To "establish rapport" describes a class of behavior which could be used to complete the task of opening up the candidate in the interview. Figure 9.4 shows some examples of rule-oriented

Figure 9.4    Rule Oriented Learning Points

---

1. Greet applicant warmly and have the applicant sit down so that you can start the interview.
2. Establish rapport with the applicant so that the person will "open up" and tell you about him or herself.
3. Follow the interview guide as you question the applicant so that you do not miss any topics.

---

learning points. Rule-oriented learning points lend themselves well to generalizing learning content to different stimuli in the transfer context. Descriptive learning points lend themselves to simple reproduction.

Where one is teaching a manual skill or a task with a very prescribed set of key behaviors in a behavior modeling training program, descriptive learning points are probably preferable. With most manual skills, there is a given sequence of specified behaviors necessary to complete the task, that will vary little across situations. The sequence of behavior can therefore be exactly described in the training procedure. However, in teaching social skills in a behavior modeling program, one should probably employ rule-oriented or summary label learning points. The trainer would use summary label points for simple or common key behaviors, and rule-oriented points for complex key behaviors. In most social skills, there is more than one way of completing the task. Knowing different possible effective responses to a class of stimuli becomes more important than knowing a specific sequence of behaviors learned without flexibility. In this case, one should attempt to write summary label or rule-oriented learning points (specifying the stimuli and/or consequence), and then use several different modeled performances to present the different key behaviors which might be used to accomplish the labeled class of behavior. Examples of learning points for teaching various skills, such as helping others, answering a complaint, conducting a performance review, and other skills are presented in Appendix C.

In many jobs, tasks (especially "social skill" tasks) include the use of complex cognitive abilities such as problem solving and decision making. When this is the situation, the behavior modeling trainer cannot write learning points which are behavioral or labels. Much of the cognitive ability is not observable. Only the results are. Instead, rule-oriented learning points should be written. Often in using behavior modeling training to teach social skills requiring cognitive ability, it may be useful to express the cognitive skills in a "decision tree" format. One example of a decision tree was seen in Figure 9.1. Each learning point becomes, in essence, a statement of the stimulus (i.e., become cognizant of problem), the behavior (i.e., must decide), and the consequence (i.e., the results of different decision outcomes). The trainer explains the "behavior" element by defining the cognitive process in a decision tree format.

For example, consider the following rule-oriented key behavior: "Whenever you must teach a social skill, consider using behavior modeling because research shows it to be an effective method." "Must teach social skill" is the stimulus, "consider behavior modeling" is the behavior, and "research shows its effectiveness" defines the consequences. The "behavior" or decision process can be further explicated into a decision tree as in Figure 11.1 which outlines the steps for considering behavior modeling.

## Determining Key Behaviors/Learning Points

Once one has done a needs analysis, decided on using behavior modeling, and developed the conceptual objectives for the training program, the next step is to determine the key behaviors and write learning points for the actual content of the behavior modeling training program. Figure 9.5 shows this process. One determines training objectives, and goes through task analysis and person analysis. Task analysis will produce a list of all the tasks required in the focal job. From that data, we can identify the tasks that must be done in order to gain the focal performance/skill. Many organizations already have written job descriptions that can be found in the personnel department. However, these job descriptions are often not comprehensive or detailed enough to determine all of the tasks needed to perform the focal skill. Consequently, the training staff may frequently have to do more analysis in this area. Regardless of how task analysis is done, the result is a list of tasks needed to be performed in order for a skill or a performance to be accomplished. Given this list of tasks we can determine key behaviors.

There are three basic methods for determining key behaviors from task information. They are: 1) observing people who are successful at accomplishing the focal tasks in order to find out what behaviors and sequence of behaviors are required to perform each task; 2) conducting meetings with people who are successful at accomplishing those tasks, and who can identify the most appropriate set of behaviors to accomplish the tasks; or 3) reviewing the research literature for any information that would indicate a set of behaviors required to accomplish the given task. Two of these methods require indentifying persons who are successful at doing the task. They are found through the person analysis resulting from the overall needs analysis. Person analysis focuses on the individual employees' performance and typically includes performance evaluation data. Given this data, one should be able to determine who, of the job incumbents, are successful at completing the tasks required.

Research literature usually offers little to the trainer in the way of identifying key behaviors. We have found the most efficient and effective way of developing key behaviors (if they are not complex) is often by observing successful people performing the tasks identified as being required to meet the training objective. In many cases, with complex behaviors or when tasks include decision making, setting up a meeting with people who are successful at performing the tasks and asking them to list the behaviors they use in performing the task is more efficient than observation of task performance.

Such a meeting is typically conducted by the trainer who may or may not have a list of the tasks needed for proper performance. In other words,

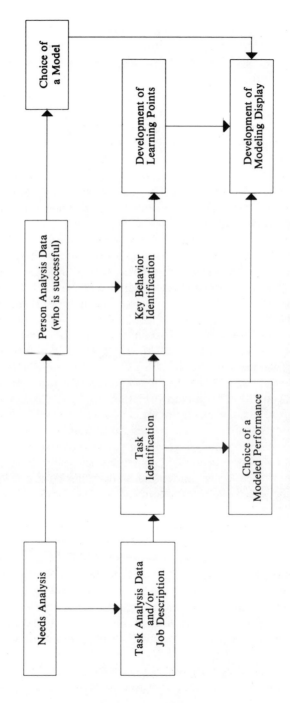

**Figure 9.5** Determining Key Behaviors and Learning Points

the needs analysis may have only identified the objectives of the training program, such as "increasing the interviewing skills of managers" or may have determined some or all of the tasks involved in interviewing, such as establishing rapport with the candidate, asking questions about education, asking questions about work history, asking miscellaneous questions, giving the candidate information about the job and the company, and closing the interview. The above example is a fairly nonspecific listing of the tasks and could come from research literature. One must, in the meeting or by observing, look at each of these tasks and define them behaviorally. For instance, in asking questions about education, there are specific question-asking techniques that can be used or even certain questions that can be asked. The meeting's purpose is to determine what the individual behaviors are and if there is a correct sequence of behaviors.

If the trainer is going to use a meeting of successful interviewers to develop these key behaviors, the trainer should have a list of the tasks photocopied for each person. The trainer will hand out the list of tasks that have been determined as the training content and ask each of the people in the meeting if they do each task. If so, they are asked to write down, in order, the specific behavior involved in completing that task. Discussion may follow. Given this data, the trainer can then determine: 1) the common elements of the behaviors of the people at the meeting, and possibly, 2) different sets of behaviors that successfully complete the task. The trainer, at this point, has a list of key behaviors that would become the core of the behavior modeling training program.

## Summary

Overall, good task analysis will tell us what tasks are required to do a job. Person analysis will tell us which people in a target population are doing each of these tasks well. At the end of this analysis phase, the trainer should have in hand a list of tasks that will make up the training content of the behavior modeling program. These tasks are used to determine a set of key behaviors (very often in a sequence) that are needed to perform each task. The reader interested in a in-depth treatment of job analysis should review McCormick (1970).

# —10—

# Building Behavior Modeling Displays

The key behaviors that are presented live, on film, or on video tape, in what is called the modeling display, show the trainees what they are expected to learn. The modeling display provides the standard performance, which the trainees then practice in order to develop the same or a similar set of behaviors. Unfortunately, the trainer who is developing a behavior modeling workshop will find there is very little research-based guidance for specifying how the development of key behaviors, and of the modeling display which presents those key behaviors to the trainees, is done. Research concerning the development of key behaviors and modeling displays is just beginning. We know some general guidelines, but not very many specifics. Zemke (1982) suggests that we're not even sure, at this time, to what questions the practitioners need answers. He also suggests that the design of modeling displays is more art than scientific engineering, and will remain so until researchers have a chance to catch up with practice. However, some things are known empirically about what works and what does not. In this chapter, we will discuss the different variables involved in developing behavior modeling displays and the mechanics of putting it all together so that there is a quality display of the key behaviors to offer the trainees.

Zemke (1982) has reported that interviews with several experienced modeling display builders have turned up a number of issues and considerations that go into making a film or video tape modeling display. He suggests there are six points of consensus: 1) the key behaviors to be learned must be shown clearly, positively, and correctly; 2) trainees must be able to identify with the person doing the key behaviors; 3) stimuli which could distract trainees from attending to the key behaviors should be shunned; 4) the behavior must be presented in careful steps; it should be programmed from simple to complex situations and from easier to more difficult-to-handle problems; 5) modeling displays should not be confused with information or entertainment films; and 6) trainees expect high quality video comparable to broadcast quality; low quality displays distract. The authors would not argue with anything in this list except for possibly the last issue. There is no evidence that suggests one needs to develop broadcast quality modeling displays to be effective in a behavior modeling program, particularly when effectiveness is determined in a relative sense against other kinds of training. Broadcast quality would be *preferable* if one could develop such films, however, the inability to produce such displays should not deter the potential behavior modeler from beginning.

## The Major Issues in Building Modeling Displays

A modeling display is nothing more than a mechanism for presenting to the trainees the correct key behaviors which they are to learn in the training program. There are three major elements inherent in the modeling display. These elements include: 1) the media technique used to present the modeled performance; 2) the model (person performing the key behaviors); and 3) the modeled key behaviors (the actual training content or behaviors to be taught to the trainees). There is also a set of variables which one could categorize under the heading: the making of the display. These variables include the quality of the display (if it is filmed), titles, inclusion of written learning points, dressing the set, and what kinds of problems are presented which the key behaviors are used to solve. Each of these variables will be discussed in this chapter.

There are a number of variables that affect the efficacy of the behavior modeling training technique. They have been discussed in detail in Section II, but before we go on we need to review the variables that would affect the success of the modeling display. These variables are listed in Table 10.1 under the following categories: 1) the model who performs the key behaviors, 2) the actual key behaviors, 3) the modeling display or scenario, 4) the modeling medium (the method that is used to present the modeling display), and 5) the observer. Each will be summarized in turn.

### Modeling Display Media

The modeling display medium should be one that minimizes any irrelevant distractions so that the observers can observe and hear everything that is in the modeling display. It should also be one that is easy for the trainer to use in the training program. The display medium should allow for the modeling display to be presented in the most vivid and detailed manner. Where desired, it should allow for both live and video presentations to be given together in a modeling display. The medium should not be overly expensive. It should be such that one can present learning points to be used for symbolic coding, and

**Table 10.1  The Variables Affecting the Efficacy of Modeling Displays**

| Display Media | Model | Model's Key Behaviors | Modeling Display | Observer | Observer Continued |
|---|---|---|---|---|---|
| • No Irrelevant Distractions | • Expert/High Status | • Observable | • Key Behaviors Made Distinctive —Labeled —Repeated | • Anticipates Reinforcement | High Ambiguity Tolerance |
| • Can Observe and Hear (Big Screen, etc.) | • Reinforcement for Key Behaviors—Real or Imagined | • Distinctive | • No Irrelevant Material | • Is Aroused | Not Anxious |
| • Easy to Use | Similar to Observers: Age, Sex, Race, Clothes, Speech | • Accurate/Get Job Done | Identical Elements | • Physically Capable of Motor Rehearsal | Receives Instructions |
| Vivid/Detailed | | Identical to Job | Key Behaviors Presented Least to Most Difficult | • Component Responses Available | Has Opportunity to Rewrite Learning Points |
| Live and Video Together | Appears Friendly/Helpful | Not too Complex | Presents Rule-Oriented Learning Points for Generalization | Reinforced for Past Modeling | Has Ability to Image |
| Not Overly Expensive | Informal Leader in Work Group for P.R. | Less than Ten | | Has Sensory Capabilities | Engages in Mental Rehearsal or Covert Rehearsal |
| Can Present Learning Points | Controls Resources Desired by Observers | Realistic | | Instructed to and Allowed to Mentally Code | Is Taught Self-Control Techniques |
| | | Repeated for Generalization and/or Overlearning | | | |
| | | Meaningful to Observer | | | |

Can Show Verbal and Nonverbal Where Both are in Key Behaviors

Coping vs. Mastery

Trainees Can See Applicability in Transfer Context

Can be Described in Learning Points
—Label
—Behavioral
—Rule-oriented

Can be Grouped Organized

Are Psychomotor, Verbal, Social, or Cognitive

Presents Behavioral Learning Points for Reproduction

Learning Points are Superimposed

Positive, Not Negative

Multiple Models for Generalization

Learning Points Organized, Ordered, Grouped, and Understood

Succinct

Simplest Language

Acted vs. Natural

Instructed to and Allowed to Mentally Rehearse

Told to Attend

Told Will Have to Do Key Behaviors

Similar to Model in Relevant Attitudes/Background

Is Attracted to Model

Internal Locus of Control

Independent

Understands the Relapse Process

Is Given "Homework" Skills Practice

it should be able to present both verbal and nonverbal behavior where both are in the key behaviors.

There are many different techniques or media used to present a modeled performance. They include: 1) video tape; 2) film; 3) synchronous filmstrip projector; 4) live presentation; and 5) audio tape. In the implementation of behavior modeling programs, video tape is by far the most common medium used to present the modeled performance. It is easy to use because most organizations have access to video-tape facilities. Even home video-tape outfits can be used to produce behavior modeling programs. Video-tape displays have the benefit of being portable; however, they are limited to presenting the modeled performance on a TV screen. The first author has found that small TV screens are not appropriate for audiences over two or three. A TV screen up to 25 inches would be appropriate for an audience of 10 to 15 people. An audience larger than this would require a larger screen. This is possible with the new large screen TVs, but the clarity of these instruments is not of the highest quality. As the quality of the picture improves in large screen televisions, the possibilities of using video-tape modeling displays with larger groups of trainees will be enhanced. Otherwise, multiple monitors are in order.

Filming is obviously much more difficult and costly than video tape and is rarely used. A syncronous filmstrip projector is also possible. Filmstrip projectors that are self-contained or project onto a wall are available. The advantage of a syncronous filmstrip projector is the portable nature of the equipment. For instance, when the senior author trained gas station employees in suggestive selling, such a projector was a very easy piece of equipment to carry between station locations in order to show the modeling display. The disadvantage is production cost.

It is also possible to use a live presentation of the modeled performance; however, a live presentation requires models who are knowledgeable of and consistent in presenting the key behaviors for every training workshop. The authors have found, however, that live modeling can be beneficial when the trainees can ask questions of the model about why a certain behavior was performed. Also, the trainees can have a chance to critique a live model in an interactive sense and get experience in observing and offering feedback. This is later beneficial in the behavioral rehearsal component.

The last option presented is audio tape which would only be appropriate where the modeled behaviors were exclusively verbal behaviors. Audio tape is very often used in counseling situations where the trainer is teaching primarily verbal skills. Obviously, audio tape is much less costly to use than any of the other possibilities except for live modeling.

There is virtually no research that indicates additional benefits of one media technique over another. Basically, the variables involved in choosing the technique would be: 1) availability of equipment, 2) quality of display, in that, the picture is not snowy (color would be better than black and white), 3) lack of distraction due to the quality of the picture itself, and 4) cost of developing a modeling display. From the authors' experience, the easiest medium to work with typically is video tape. However, a combination of video-tape modeling displays and live modeling is extremely effective, in that it teaches the trainees how to observe and critique a behavioral rehearsal in addition to observing the key behaviors done accurately and consistently on the video tape. It really comes down to cost and efficiency.

The modeling display media enhancers were described in Chapter 4 and are reviewed here. The model performance, as presented in the modeling display, should be vivid and detailed, should have a minimum of irrelevant details or distractions, and should be presented with enough frequency or repetitiveness for learning to occur. An alternative to the latter is to present different modeled performances. More than one model and model performance should be included if it is desirable for the learning to generalize to different stimuli and different contexts. It is also helpful to include a written description (learning points on the screen of the modeling display which describe the key behaviors to be seen in the modeled performance). Whichever medium is chosen to present the modeled performance, it is important to make sure that these modeling display enhancers are available or are possible with the medium chosen.

## Who is the Model?

In producing a modeling display, the trainer must decide who will be the person that performs the key behaviors. This person is called "the model." One has the choice of using an employee from the target population, a trainer, or an actor/actress who will play an employee from the target population. Smith (1982) has used target population persons who have participated in the training as models and has found this to facilitate modeling of subsequent trainees and of the model–trainee. The authors use only employees from the target population in behavior modeling programs. There is virtually no research indicating that one is better than the other. Each type of model has been used in behavior modeling programs and has its own advantages and disadvantages. When dealing with a trainer or an actor/actress as a model, the problem becomes developing realistic problem situations or the scenarios in which the model performance will occur. However, once developed it may be easier to get those individuals to display the key behaviors (especially with a trainer). The problems in developing situations are eliminated when one uses employees from the target population because they know the day-to-day problems and can use one of those problems in the modeled performance. However, employees are not always willing or able actors, and one will have to teach the employee the key behaviors. Overall, there is work involved in using any of these sources of models. The actor/actress has to be taught the scenario and the key behaviors, the trainer has to be taught the scenarios, and the employee has to be taught the key behaviors.

There are several modeling enhancers which relate to the model. Research has indicated that the model should be of similar sex, race, age, speech, and dress to the target population. The model should be perceived as having high competence or expertise by the observers, or should be perceived as having high status. Research has also indicated that, to the extent that the model controls the resources of the observers, modeling will be enhanced. However, this result stems from modeling in a real world context rather than in training programs. Research has shown that, to the extent that the model is friendly or helpful, modeling will be enhanced. Most important is that research has shown that the model must be reinforced for using the key behaviors in order for modeling to be enhanced. This latter issue is an absolute. There must be (in the modeling display) some reinforcement given to the model for performance of the key behaviors. This reinforcement can come from a narrator (or trainer) saying that this is an excellent performance or it can come from solving the problem presented in the display by the use of the key behaviors. From whichever source a model is chosen, these enhancers must be built into the modeling display. It is very difficult to use an actor and satisfy the enhancers of high competence/expertise, status, and/or control resources of observers. To some extent, it is also very difficult to deal with these enhancers using trainers as models. If the trainers are external consultants they may be perceived as having high status. This is not always true with the organization's trainers. Overall, one should aim for the enhancers of high competence and expertness by using successful employees on the job. When one is looking for a model, one should look for people who: 1) are informal leaders in a target population, 2) are fairly verbal, and 3) could easily fall into a role playing situation in filming of the modeled performance. Employees who have previously gone through a behavior modeling program make excellent models. Whichever source one uses, there should be some provision for competence and status and, most importantly, the model should be seen to be reinforced in some manner for the use of the key behaviors.

### The Modeled Performance

The modeled performance (key behaviors) is the most important element of the modeling display because it defines the training content. The key behaviors presented in the modeling display are what the trainees will learn. In a behavior modeling workshop without any lecture/discussion, the trainees will learn no more than these key behaviors. They are extremely important. Given that one has done an adequate analysis, these key behaviors should be the most efficient and effective method to solve the problems for which the key behaviors are presented. The key behaviors are the reason the training program exists.

There are several modeling enhancers which facilitate learning of the key behaviors. The behaviors should be distinctive. They should also be meaningful to the observer. The key behaviors should be neither overly complex nor should there be over nine or ten key behaviors presented within one modeling display. The behaviors must also be observable.

Distinctiveness can be enhanced in several ways: 1) one can display the behaviors out of context, 2) one can exaggerate the behaviors, 3) the behaviors can be repeated frequently, and/or 4) one can include written learning points with the key behaviors in the modeling display. In making a behavior modeling display, one can present the key behaviors against a very bland background totally out of any work context. This will make the key behaviors distinctive, but will possibly detract from their meaningfulness. Also, the model can exaggerate the behaviors. Again, this will make the behaviors distinctive; however, this also distracts from meaningfulness and may be very distracting to the observers who will find fault or humor in the way the key behaviors are carried out by the model.

Some key behaviors readily lend themselves to being repeated frequently. Where this is possible, it should be done. One should always include written learning points with the modeled performance. These learning points can be generated with a character generator (a machine which generates verbal text seen on a video display) and placed on the video tape just before the behavioral sequence, or they can be superimposed on the behavioral sequence (each learning point coming across the bottom of the screen when the key behavior is occurring). However, this takes sophisticated equipment to accomplish. It is possible to put learning points on the modeling display before the performance by simply printing the key behaviors (in fairly large letters) on a large piece of cardboard and then filming it. Another technique is to hand out 3 × 5 cards containing the key behaviors prior to presenting each taped segment. Regardless of which technique is chosen, one of these options should be used.

It is also possible to present more than one scenario showing one or more models displaying the key behaviors. One scenario can present the key behaviors in a very bland situation (to the point of being out of context). The second scenario can present the key behaviors within a job situation. One should still include written learning points either before both scenarios or within one of the scenarios in a superimposed fashion.

The meaningfulness of the key behaviors is also extremely important. Several researchers have suggested that attaching verbal labels which identify the key behaviors in the modeled performance may increase meaningfulness. The obvious way to increase the meaningfulness of the key behaviors is to make those behaviors very specific to the job or task which is to be done by the trainees in the transfer context. Also, using a model from the target population will increase meaningfulness. The problem presented in the modeling display should be one that the target population faces quite often. This will enhance the meaningfulness of the key behaviors for the trainees, and facilitate their using them when facing similar problems back on the job.

The key behaviors should also be few in number and be presented from the simplest to the most complex. If the overall task is fairly complex, it should be divided into its meaningful parts. Teaching interviewing skills is an example. One would not want to present all of the key behaviors inherent in selection interviewing at one time. It would be preferable to break the interview sequence down so that each part could be trained separately with behavior modeling. These parts would probably be: 1) the opening; 2) the questions; 3) the realistic job preview; and 4) the closing. Overall, one should not present more than nine or ten key behaviors in any given modeling display. With more than ten key behaviors, the trainees will simply not be able to pick up all the key behaviors at one time and move them into long-term memory before they practice. Consequently, much of the learning occurs by trial and error during the behavioral rehearsal component. Also, primacy/recency effects occur; that is, trainees will forget the key behaviors in the middle of a sequence and only remember those presented first and last.

Finally, the behavior should be observable. Behavior modeling is not really appropriate for fine-tuned muscular movements found in most athletic performances simply because the fine-tuned muscle coordination required for the performance cannot be observed in a modeling display. A modeling display may help a person with very gross muscular movement. But the fine line between "first" and "placed" in any athletic performance is a tremendous amount of practice to fine-tune those muscular skills. Modeling is not going to enhance the elements that make the difference. Simply drilling in repetitive physical practice or mental practice would be more appropriate.

Besides those variables shown to enhance modeling which are related directly to the key behaviors, there are several other variables which must be considered in choosing key behaviors. Maybe the most important is that it must be apparent to the trainee that the key behaviors will lead to improved efficacy on the job. Some sets of key behaviors lead very readily to such beliefs. If you are presenting key behaviors aimed at giving trainees a way to coach or motivate employees, then those key behaviors should be presented which show how problems are solved (in coaching) or how the employee becomes motivated to do the job. It is critical that the modeling display show a positive solution to the problem through the use of the key behaviors.

There are other situations, however, where it would be very difficult to show that kind of reinforcement on the modeling display. Interviewing skills are such an example. It is very difficult to include any reinforcement for the model for using the key behaviors of effective selection interviewing. It would not make sense to show a successful employee on the job at a later date. The only option one has in this kind of presentation for including reinforcement is for the trainer, either on the tape or live during the workshop, to suggest to the trainees that the modeled key behaviors can result in them hiring more successful employees. A good way to include reinforcement in such a modeling display is to have a VIP introduce the program and help create a perceptual set such that the trainees believe that the model is a very successful person.

Another issue to keep in mind when developing the key behaviors is whether to present perfect behavior or coping behavior. For example, some researchers in behavior modeling say perfect and smooth performances alienate trainees or at least lack meaningfulness for the observers and a coping performance may encourage employees to try out the new key behaviors. Overall, trainees must be able to say, "I think I can do this performance with a little practice." If the model is too perfect, the trainees may not try out the skill in a serious manner. There is no research in the industrial area and very little in the counseling area that gives us guidance here. Overall, it is our opinion that it may be best to show a model in more of a coping situation than a perfect situation. Trainers should be happy to teach trainees to handle situations satisfactorily. It should also be pointed out that if the modeling display presents a situation which is counter to the experience of the trainee audience, the trainees will say, "No, that can't happen in our company," and will not attempt to learn the new key behaviors. Another way to avoid an overperfect performance is to keep it simple. If it is kept simple, it won't seem like something that the trainees cannot do.

Another aspect is negative versus positive examples of behavior. Several behavior modeling trainers suggest that showing negative models before positive models enhances learning. Presenting a situation in which a model fails in a typical situation before performing successfully has the advantage of being realistic and probably familiar to most trainees. In the process, the trainer's creditability may be enhanced because it shows that the trainer knows "how things really work." In response, the trainees may pay more attention to how to avoid the problem by using the key behaviors as presented in the subsequent positive outcome modeling display. However, there is also some evidence that suggests that negative models may be better remembered in the long run than the positive models. Whether the memory of a negative model results in better recall of what *not* to do, or in interference with what should be done, remains to be investigated. It is common in counseling situations to see negative models. It is important to realize that one has only so much time in any behavior modeling workshop for the presentation of modeling displays. To the extent that you are using rule-oriented behavior, you must show several different examples which fall under that rule. When using up the time showing several models, it doesn't make sense to use that time showing negative models which only help gain the trainees' attention and do not help show the trainee what should be done. You should only use negative models to highlight very nondistinctive key behaviors. The senior author has used outtakes from the development of modeling displays as attention-getters during the beginning of some workshops. This has usually been done in workshops with high school and college students, however, in which getting attention is more important than in an adult education workshop where the people are there to solve their day-to-day problems. If one uses a negative model, it should be used as an attention-getter and it should be very clearly a negative model, sometimes to the point of being humorous.

It has already been stated that it is best to present your modeled performances in order from simple to more difficult. This point also has to do with the perfect versus coping issue. It is possible to start with a coping model performance and move up to a perfect model performance. The first author has also used live modeling before video modeling for the same purpose. Overall, one should show a very simple, bland modeled performance first where the behaviors are quite distinctive and the problem is not too difficult. One should then work towards the more difficult problems to solve. Also, one can work from simple to complex in showing the behavior of the other person presented in the model display when the supervisor uses the key behaviors. For instance, if one is doing management training where the key behaviors are designed to be used by supervisors in interactions with employees, the first modeled performance presented should be with an employee who is fairly positive, motivated, etc. Then, in sequence, the different scenarios presented can work up to a situation where a supervisor has to use the same key behaviors to handle a very difficult employee.

Learning points should be included on tape in any modeling display that is developed. There is extensive research, both in the industrial context and the counseling context, that suggests a verbal description of the key behaviors enhances both the attention and retention of the trainees. Behavior modeling done in the counseling context almost always includes written manuals which describe the skills being displayed and where they are appropriately used. The authors have always included learning points in the behavior modeling displays that they have created. Learning points presented at the beginning of the tape cue the trainees to what they should attend to and help them retain what they see. Using learning points is also critical when one is dealing with rule-oriented behavior. The learning points in this situation help guide the trainees through the several models and/or modeled performances that they see. These different modeled performances will be specific ways to handle a specific situation, but they will all fall under the general rule which is presented in the learning points.

Related to this issue is the number of modeled performances that are presented. There is usually only one way to do a performance such as turning on a piece of machinery. One modeled performance would be sufficient. However, in complex social skills, there may be several different ways to handle the situation. In this context, one should include more than one modeled performance. Interviewing is again a good example. One may wish to teach trainees to establish rapport at the first of an interview. There are several ways to establish rapport, such as talking about yourself, talking about something neutral, getting up and getting coffee, etc. The learning points should state the basic rule and several modeled performances should be developed to present the different methods in establishing rapport with an applicant.

Let us emphasize one point again. Remember that the most important objective of behavior modeling is the use of the key behaviors by the trainee on the job (or in the transfer context). To do this, you move the trainee: 1) from bland, simple modeled performances to complex ones, 2) from modeled performances with learning points to those without, 3) from watching a modeled performance to mentally rehearsing his or her own situations, 4) from mentally rehearsing to physically rehearsing, 5) from reproduction of modeled behavior to generalization, 6) from behavioral rehearsals with lots of feedback to behavior rehearsals without any feedback until its completion, 7) from near-continuous reinforcement to variable ratio reinforcement, 8) from practice in training to actual on-the-job use. This is a sequence of events/stimuli for the trainee which should leave the person in the transfer context with new behavior and knowledge about stimuli generalization. *The process is what is important, not any one of its elements.* Too many trainers think the video tape is the key or that the behavioral rehearsal is the key. These opinions are *wrong*. It is the entire process that is important.

## Making the Modeling Display

There are several variables involved in making a modeling display, many of them with little research to indicate which direction to take. Behavior modelers disagree over whether to use real problems for the trainees or neutral issues. Some trainers in industrial training use problems like installing new phones or assigning overtime. They suggest that dealing with company issues turns training into a company meeting and distracts from the process. Too much company content in the modeling display may lead to sessions that are counterproductive to learning. There is, however, important motivation to be gained from viewing people in real settings coping with significant real issues that they have to deal with every day. A good solution is to include a neutral problem *and* a real problem in a modeling display. However, one should stay away from controversial topics that may be a point of contention in the organization. Such topics will lead trainees to attend to the content rather than the process, and in behavior modeling, one is always teaching the process of the key behaviors.

Another issue is dressing the set. There is quite a lot of disagreement among trainers about the visual background in which the model appears while performing the key behaviors. There is also very little research to indicate which direction to take in this regard. What research there is suggests including identical elements and meaningfulness. Consequently, one must do a balancing act between creating a situation that the trainees can identify with and which is credible, but avoiding distractions such as trying to identify whose office the modeling display was filmed in, etc. An example of the worst possible situation would be to have a set with flowers on a desk and have all the trainees say, "When do we get our flowers?" or "I've never seen flowers on a desk in this company."

Obviously, there should be no distraction such as noise in a modeling display. You would not want to film a modeled performance on the job with noisy cash registers or announcements over a P.A. system in the background. Overall, trainees will never be distracted by the lack of relevant but minor details, but will certainly see distractions that occur because of the presence of distracting content. Creating behavior modeling displays having several different scenarios solves many of these problems. One can move from a very stark background to a real on-the-job situation when you are showing more than one modeled performance. When the environment is too close to home and particularly when it is not exactly right, participants seem to nit-pick. When only one modeled performance can be produced, go for a neutral background. When one has the facilities and the time to produce more than one modeled performance showing a set of key behaviors, however, one should start with a bland background and a neutral topic and move up, in the sequence of tapes, to a real background right out of the company and a more difficult situation.

It is seldom that a trainer can make a perfect modeling display. There will be mistakes in the tape. Many of these mistakes will not be seen the first time the tape is viewed, but with repeated viewing, the mistakes become obvious to the trainer. It is always best to let the trainees criticize any mistakes or distractions, but bring them back to the process of the key behaviors through discussion. This, again, points out the importance of having more than one modeled performance. The trainer can show one modeled performance, allow criticism and discussion, and then show one or more modeled performances after that. Someplace in that sequence, the trainees will attend to the set of key behaviors which the trainer would like them to learn.

One should not have too many titles, background music, etc. on the modeling display. It is not a training film, it is a modeling display. It is only presented to show the trainees the proper way to do the key behaviors. Titles and background music only distract from that. It would be acceptable to have a modeling display with nothing on it but the learning points and the different modeled performances. Modeling displays should always be in color, if possible. There is absolutely no research to show that color is better than black and white; however, it has been our experience that use of black and white video leads to the perception of being old and not of high quality. Most people are used to watching color TV and expect color. It is also more realistic.

Any person interested in behavior modeling should purchase a portable video tape outfit for making modeling displays. A half-inch cassette is probably the easiest and the least expensive. This equipment can be taken to any office, work site or into a neutral room to film models. It is also fairly high quality and does not break down with a lot of movement. However, do not copy a half-inch tape onto a three-quarter inch tape because quality is substantially lowered. If your playback facilities are three-quarter inch, tape in three-quarter inch. A major distraction in a modeling display is heavy shadows caused by only one or two lights being used when filming the modeled performance. There are lights on the market that are very soft (but of high intensity) that do not create these kinds of shadows. Purchase that kind of equipment. When filming a modeled performance that includes two people, two cameras can be used. This means filming the modeling displays in a studio having switching equipment (or extensive editing), however. This equipment may not be available and switching camera angles may be distracting when the trainees are trying to learn only one person's behavior. Given a choice between developing your own models and buying those commercially made, you probably should make your own with one camera before you buy a commercial modeling display with which your trainees would not readily identify. If you can only use one camera, and you are dealing with an interaction between two people, that camera should be situated so that it looks over the second person's shoulder and shows the model either facing the camera directly or slightly facing the camera. The camera angle should be such that all relevant verbal and non-verbal behavior of the model is shown on the tape. If possible use a "3-tube" or commercial camera.

Editing video tape is probably one of the most difficult aspects of developing a modeling display. If edits are not done well, one ends up with "bars," or "snow," etc., between sequences of modeled performances or between learning points and modeled performances. Even with a single editing deck this is very likely. If one does not have good editing facilities, it is best to simply film your scenarios and your key behaviors and then have it edited in a studio, so that it is a clear presentation with very little distraction coming from the switch between scenes.

## *Observer*

Finally, let us review the variables which increase the likelihood that the trainee will attend to the modeling display. There are many variables related to the observers that affect whether modeling will be successful. These include their preparation to observe the modeling display, their ability to assimilate what is in the modeling display, and their readiness to move into behavioral rehearsal. The critical elements for the observers are that they anticipate reinforcement (anticipate that learning the key behaviors will lead to some positive consequences), are aroused and able to, at least, attend to the modeling display; are physically capable of motor rehearsal, and have previously learned all component responses required for behavioral rehearsal. The observers should (where possible) receive reinforcement for modeling, and/or have received reinforcement for past modeling. The observers should be instructed to and allowed to mentally code the required behaviors. They should receive instruction and be allowed to mentally rehearse the key behaviors. Finally, the observer should be told to attend to the modeling display and be told that they will be asked to practice the key behaviors in the later behavioral rehearsal component. Other variables include being able to rewrite learning points, receive instructions or coaching, being able and willing to mentally rehearse, and to be exposed to relapse training and/or skills practice homework.

## Some Final Hints in Making a Modeling Display

When we make a modeling display, we determine the key behaviors and who some successful models may be through the needs analysis processes. The next step is to write learning points (descriptions of the key behaviors) and have these reviewed by a group from the target population, who will rewrite them in their own language where necessary. Then, sit down with the persons who have been chosen to become possible models and give them the learning points. The group would discuss the learning points in some detail and different ways to do the learning points, if they are rule-oriented. Then explain to them that you would like to tape them doing the key behaviors and would like them to take the learning points home to study. If a studio is used to develop the modeling display, always have the models practice the key behaviors in a dress rehearsal situation outside of the studio because studio time is expensive. If filming the modeling display on the work site, less practice is necessary and they may be able to simply walk in and do the modeled performance. It has been the author's experience that one should tape every single attempt at doing the modeled performance because many times the first attempt is the most spontaneous and most real, especially when you are using models out of the target population. Simply come in, set up the equipment on location and have the models perform. When in the work situation, ask the models to come up with the problems that will be used to present the key behaviors. The only thing that you should be concerned with is that the problem is not a hot topic in the company that will distract from the learning. In a studio situation, we may have discussed this during the dress rehearsal. Make more tapes than are needed. Tape every single performance and, after thanking the models, review each scenario to choose the two or three best. After the scenarios are chosen, then film the learning points. Most often you will have to go into a studio to have this material edited simply because it will be much clearer and distraction-free. Always order the scenarios from simplest and most bland to most complex and real. Finally, have the final modeling display reviewed by several people in the organization to look for distractions, and issues or content in the background which will distract the trainees.

Given a little care and concern for the many variables involved, a quality modeling display is possible. However, any kind of a modeling display is better than none at all. Behavior modeling training is more effective than virtually any other kind of training in teaching manual or social skills. Given a choice between a training program where one would only use lecture, "round-robin" role playing or something of that sort, or a less than optimal modeling display in a behavior modeling program, the authors would always choose the latter, the modeling display and behavior modeling.

Keep in mind that the modeling display presents the standard of what should be done so the participants can then use behavioral rehearsal and feedback to practice those skills. Without a modeling display, behavioral rehearsal/role play and feedback becomes trial and error learning. It is not as efficient. Appendix D contains the scripts of several modeling displays for the interested reader.

## Summary

There are many complex issues involved in developing a modeling display. There are issues that relate to what media should be chosen for the display, who should be the model, what the modeled key behaviors should be and how they should be presented. Many issues in the development of modeling displays remain unresolved at this point. There is very little research in the technical details of developing modeling displays, dressing the set, the content of the problem being solved, the numbers of scenarios, whether one should use perfect, coping, or negative situations, etc. We have no clear answers from empirical research. Most of the things included in this chapter come from the little available research and the experience of the authors and other trainers. There simply is no one right answer in most of the issues to clearly define the technology of developing behavior modeling displays. One has to "wing it" to a certain extent. However, many issues are outlined here and should be considered in developing a modeling display. Only by considering all of these issues and how they affect a given training application will one be able to develop a quality of modeling display.

# —11—

## Putting It All Together

Once one has developed a modeling display, the only issues left to consider before conducting a behavior modeling program are how to implement the behavioral rehearsal and the overall format of the program. Issues related to behavior rehearsal will be reviewed and some hints relative to implementing skills practice will be offered. A decision tree concerning when to use behavior modeling will be examined and different workshop formats will be discussed.

In behavior modeling training, the trainees are exposed to four major activities: modeling, retention, practice, and feedback. After the trainees have seen the modeling display and have performed activities to help them retain that visual image, they go through what is called skills practice which involves the practice of the key behaviors seen in the modeling display and the receiving of feedback about that practice.

### The Enhancers of Behavioral Rehearsal Feedback

There are a number of critical elements in behavioral rehearsal. (See Table 11.1.) The trainees should have a choice to rehearse the key behaviors. The rehearsal should be public or the trainee should otherwise commit himself or herself to the new key behaviors. The key behaviors should have instrumentality to the trainee; that is, using the key behaviors should be seen as leading to some reward or reinforcement. Over and above these critical elements, there should be as many chances to rehearse the key behaviors as is possible during skills practice. In behavioral rehearsal, it is important to eliminate evaluation apprehension by rehearsing in small groups rather than in front of a large training group. The behavioral rehearsal should be seen as

**Table 11.1   The Variables Effecting the Effectiveness of Skills Practice**

| Skills Practice | |
| --- | --- |
| *Behavioral Rehearsal* | *Feedback* |
| • Choice to Rehearse or Not | • Constructive/Informative |
| • Public (At Least One Observer) | • Includes Knowledge of Results |
| • Leads to Reward for Effective Use of Key Behaviors | • On Job for Transfer—Especially from Supervisor |
| As Many Chances to Rehearse as Possible | From All Sources —Trainer —Trainees —Self —Video/Audio Tape |
| No Evaluation Apprehension (In Small Groups) | |
| Spaced Learning vs. Massed | Live Model Helps Observers Learn How to Give Feedback |
| Allows for Reward to Observer for Rehearsing | Both Positive and Negative —Mostly Positive |
| Can Experiment and Improvise During Rehearsal | Immediate |
| Structured Only by Key Behaviors | Proper Type |
| Overlearning Occurs | Continuous Schedule at First, But Move to Variable Ratio |
| Coaching is Used with Poorer Trainees | Not Too Much at One Time, Yet Sufficient |
| | Should Not be Overly Prescriptive and Judgmental |

rewarding to the trainee. It should be relatively unstructured by scripts or instructions; only a requirement to use the key behaviors is necessary. Finally, the behavioral rehearsal should provide a variety of stimulus situations so that the key behaviors can be practiced in response to all or most stimuli that would occur in the transfer contexts that would require use of the key behaviors.

The final major element of the skills practice activity in behavior modeling training is the feedback component. This component is important because, after the observer observes the key behaviors in the modeling display, takes them into memory, and practices them in the behavioral rehearsal component, the observer must receive some kind of feedback for the behavioral rehearsal. The feedback component is extremely important for a number of reasons. First, it is the first opportunity for the trainee to find out if he or she has in fact understood how to use the key behaviors. Second, it is an opportunity for the trainee to fine-tune the behavior within a supportive environment. Finally, when superiors are included in the training program, there is a greater likelihood that the trainee will receive the same reinforcement on the job, thus increasing the trainee's motivation to transfer the new skills to the job context.

## Other Issues in Behavioral Rehearsal

An individual's practice in behavior modeling is guided by the trainee's exposure to the modeling display and any learning points that the participant may have in his/her hand when coming to the skills practice room. Skills practice can still be structured or unstructured, the practice can be conducted in different size groups with different participant make-ups, the trainee may practice with another trainee or with a trainer, and the trainee may practice in front of the whole training group or just in front of one or two trainees. Each of these variations will be explored.

We know that behavioral rehearsal is facilitated as long as: 1) a person has the choice to participate, 2) it is public, 3) and the person can improvise and be rewarded for it. The authors have rarely seen a trainee refuse to participate in skills practice, though many are at first reluctant. Some trainees have refused to appear in front of a video tape camera which is being used to facilitate feedback, but the authors have never had anyone refuse to actually role play. Therefore, the variable of choice is not of great concern. Most trainees come to a training program to learn and will not refuse to be a part of a major element of that learning. However, no one should be forced to behaviorally rehearse. Keeping the behavioral rehearsal fairly unstructured should give the trainees the feeling of being able to choose.

In skills practice, there are many different ways to bring the trainees into a practice situation. Some trainers divide the entire group of trainees into groups of three and have them do "round-robin" role playing. However, where there is only one trainer for several groups, the amount of feedback the trainees can receive from the trainer becomes limited. Alternatively, one or two large groups could be used, which allows the trainer to observe and give feedback to all role plays, but because of time constraints may result in not all trainees having an opportunity to rehearse. The authors have found that small groups are preferable. The real issue in training is the level of commitment of the trainee to the new behavior. When the trainee practices the new behavior in public, even if in front of only one other trainee, the level of commitment is raised. Furthermore, the smaller the group, the less anxious the trainee will be. We all feel evaluation apprehension to a certain degree when we are practicing something new, and keeping the practice group smaller should lessen evaluation apprehension. Finally, practicing in front of the entire training group has, in some cases, not been found to be productive (Decker, 1983). One thing that is extremely important to remember is that in the group (and it is typically a group of three people: one to play a supervisor, one to play a subordinate, and one to act as an observer) there should *not* be actual supervisor/subordinate pairs, or any people that work directly together. If this is the case, trainees' performances tend to become very constrained, and learning will not occur as readily as if they were dealing with people they did not have to go back to work with the next day.

In most behavior modeling situations, we are teaching social skills where the trainee interacts with another person to practice the key behaviors. (This is not always the case, of course. Where one is teaching manual skills, the trainee may interact with a piece of equipment.) In the skills practice component, the trainee must practice the key behaviors, usually with another person taking the role of a customer or subordinate. The other person can be a trainee or a trainer. We have done behavior modeling workshops in both ways and have found it much easier for the trainees to practice among themselves. However, if the trainees are not truly committed to the learning, and just go through the motions of practice, or worse, do not give valid feedback to others in the group, it may be better to use a trainer in the practice. But, for the most part, using trainers is not advisable because they typically do not know the jargon or vocabulary of the job, nor are they familiar enough with actual situations to make the role play real for the trainee. (In addition, the trainers get very worn out doing a continuous round of behavioral rehearsals with different trainees.) In counseling situations, we see no problem with trainers being the second role player because they will understand the content.

### Some Hints Concerning Feedback

One must practice a behavior and receive some feedback about the accuracy of that practice in order to learn and change behavior. In a behavior modeling program, this feedback comes from the trainees themselves, other trainees, the trainer or trainers, and/or from any video or audio recordings made of the practice sessions. It is not unusual for trainees to critique themselves after completing a role play, often quite critically, as they compare their own role played behaviors with the desired key behaviors, and their own performances overall with that of the modeling display. In three-person groups, both the other role player, and in particular the non-role playing observer, provide valuable feedback to the trainee. By rotating roles within these groups, each person gets a chance both to practice and observe. There is also the trainer who walks around from group to group and adds to the feedback or is assigned to one group. Of course, it is better if there is a trainer for every group of three individuals practicing, and in many programs this is done. Finally, feedback can come from an audio or video recording of the practice attempts. If the key behaviors are primarily verbal in nature, audio recordings may be sufficient; however, if the key behaviors concern a social interaction, then video-tape recording is better, because all verbal and non-verbal behaviors are captured on the recording.

The optimum skills practice session is a situation where the trainee has the opportunity to practice the key behaviors more than one time, preferably in a small group where any anxiety or evaluation apprehension is reduced, with people the trainee does not work with daily on the job and probably with other trainees who understand the company (and maybe the job). Most importantly, however, the trainee should be in a situation where he/she gets immediate detailed behavioral feedback that comes from all the sources that are available (other trainees, a skilled trainer, the person himself or herself, and audio or video recording equipment). The importance of detailed feedback from both trainer and tape recordings cannot be stressed enough; however, it does make the process very trainer and equipment intensive, especially when using video-tape equipment in groups of three or four people. If you do not have sufficient video equipment to equip all groups, consider using both audio and video recording, so all get to review their exact performance in some fashion. The video is spread more thinly, but everyone gets at least one chance to practice in front of the video-tape equipment.

## Some Final Hints About Skills Practice

Behavioral rehearsal can be conducted in a wide variety of settings. The effect of rehearsal in any of these settings depends upon adequate preparation. Shaw et al. (1980) have indicated there are three major areas in which preparation is essential: the people, the situation, and the trainer.

Whenever a new training session is designed and implemented within a group, the training process is an intervention in the life of that group. It introduces new conditions that affect group members. If supervisors are given training on how to handle disciplinary problems, complaints, etc., employees may find themselves dealing with supervisors who are more knowledgeable and skillful in handling those situations. Thus, the training process influences, and may restructure, the way in which people in the organization interact. Participants in a behavior modeling training program need to be prepared for this, especially if the training is to adequately transfer onto the job. Furthermore, the participants in the training program need to know what to expect in the behavioral rehearsal component. The trainer in charge of the behavior modeling program should also know what the organizational structure is in the training group. In other words, the trainer should know if there are supervisor/subordinate pairs in the training group because these people should not be together in a small group to behaviorally rehearse.

The behavior modeling trainer must also be aware that the training sessions are designed as learning experiences in which people are encouraged to experiment with new behavior. Problem situations may be dealt with out of context, some issues may be magnified for experimentation, and there may be distortion in some behavioral rehearsals because they are spontaneous and participants improvise as the scenario develops. It is advisable for the trainer to make the trainees aware that their actions in role playing are confidential. Role playing often involves ventilation of feelings, tension, and previously unexpressed thoughts or ideas. Participants need to know that trial and error, open/expressive behavior, and spontaneity are desirable so that they can experiment with the new behavior in a neutral situation before they go back on the job. Furthermore, the trainees should be informed that the role playing component of behavior modeling will be of much more benefit to them if they attempt to take on their own role or the role of a subordinate in as realistic a manner as possible. Participants should not "rub each other's backs" or make a joke out of the role playing sessions by coming across as an employee that would probably get fired if it were a real situation.

The trainer must deal with these issues in preparing the participants for the training workshop. Trainees must be aware that skills practice is an opening-up process, a process to experiment with new behaviors, and as such, should be confidential and will not include supervisor/subordinate pairs. Also, it is important to make the participants aware, in behavioral rehearsal, that they should attempt to practice the new behaviors for situations that they have had a difficult time handling in the past. Participants have data that no one else possesses; they know how they feel, what they want, and the kinds of problems they encounter.

There are two basic designs for a role playing/behavioral rehearsal experience: structured and unstructured. Role play is structured when the trainer provides the participants with instructions that point out the relationship between the characters, and include background information about the situation in the role play. In other words, all aspects of the role play are structured by the trainer. Within this structure, however, there is still flexibility and ample room for participants to experiment with new behavior and try out a variety of new approaches. In unstructured role play situations, the relationships between key role players and among the various elements of the situation are developed by the group members. Participants are not supplied with detailed instructions, written role instructions, key behaviors, etc. The role play facilitator encourages trainees to define the critical elements of the situation, and to develop the interactions or role plays that will help explore and expand these situations.

Obviously, it is possible to have varying degrees of structure in the behavioral rehearsal. One could go so far as to give the participants scripts to follow in practicing or one could give the trainees absolutely nothing to structure the behavioral rehearsal. There is very little research to guide us in this area. In some of the behavior modeling programs which the authors have developed to teach social skills, behavioral rehearsal has been structured only to the degree that the trainees have the learning points on paper or on $3 \times 5$ cards, and are instructed to follow those learning points. The trainees come up with the problems and situations in which they use the key behaviors. The trainees are asked to practice a situation they have dealt with unsuccessfully in the past or a situation they will have to deal with in the next two days. (We would call this semistructured and would argue that semistructured probably is better than either structured or unstructured. Unstructured behavioral rehearsal may be nothing more than trial and error, and structured behavioral rehearsal removes any possibility of the trainees improvising and learning to generalize key behaviors across situations. (Of course, in teaching manual skills, the behavioral rehearsal is necessarily structured by the single set of skills or equipment used, in most cases.)

Much of the success of behavioral rehearsal depends upon the physical location and surroundings in which it takes place. The room should have a minimum of about 25 square feet per participant; very small or very large rooms are not suitable. If one had to choose between two unsuitable situations, however, the smaller room would be preferred because of its intimacy. Second, the location should be private and have no distractions. No outside person should be able to enter the room, be able to look into it, or overhear what is happening. Participants should not be interrupted by phone calls or other distractions. The room should be quiet and extraneous noises should be at a minimum. Finally, the room should have no fixed furniture. A classroom or auditorium with fixed seats is, consequently, a poor location. Behavioral rehearsal of different modules (especially in supervisory training) may include situations where participants are sitting down, standing up, moving or walking down a hallway, etc. all in one workshop. The behavioral rehearsal room should be able to accommodate these different situations.

## When to Use Behavior Modeling

Figure 11.1 is a decision tree with a series of seven questions to ask yourself before you attempt to develop and use your behavior modeling program. It starts out with the possibility that a training need exists (the given). The first question is, "Does the employee already possess the skills to be presented in the training program?" If the answer is "yes," you may want to seek an alter-

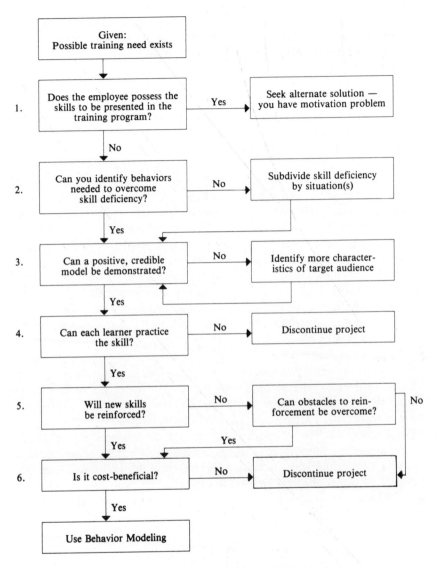

**Figure 11.1**  Behavior Modeling Decision Flow Chart

*Source:* Adapted from Robinson, J. C. and Gaines, D. L. "Seven questions to ask your-self before using behavior modeling," *Training*, 1980, Dec. *17*(12), 60–69.

nate solution to training because you probably have a motivation problem. If the answer is "no," you have a skill deficiency. If there is a skill deficiency, you have to ask yourself if you can identify the behaviors needed to overcome the deficiency. If you cannot, you need to subdivide the skills so that you can identify the individual behaviors. The next question concerns whether a positive credible model can be demonstrated. If "no," you may have to go back and reexamine the behavior or the target audience. However, once you have identified the behavior and narrowed the target audience, you should be able to choose a positive credible model to use in the modeling display. The next question is, "Can the learner practice the skill?" If the answer is absolutely no, then discontinue the project because you can't properly learn a behavior without practicing it. In most cases, the learner can practice the skill in some manner. The next question is, "Will the new skill be reinforced?" Obviously, if it cannot be, there is probably an obstacle to reinforcement and that obstacle has to be overcome. Finally, "Is the training cost-beneficial?" That may be the most important question. It may be possible to develop a behavior modeling program but it may not be cost-efficient. It is easy to say training is costly because of high up-front costs without measuring the benefit in long-term productivity increase. When these long-term benefits are considered, the utility of implementing a behavioral modeling program will, in most cases, be worth the investment.

Overall, Figure 11.1 gives you six questions to ask yourself before you attempt to develop and implement a behavior modeling program. The questions should be examined in every situation before you attempt to put a behavior modeling program together because behavior modeling is time consuming and expensive.

## Different Formats

Behavior modeling can be offered in two basic formats, which can be referred to as "skills practice format" and "workshop format." The former is pure behavior modeling. The only activities that go on in this format are modeling, retention aids, behavioral rehearsal, and feedback. The workshop format includes both lecture/discussion and behavioral modeling components. Three different methods of using behavior modeling will be described: one example of pure behavior modeling, one example of a workshop with lecture first, and one example of a workshop with lecture and behavior modeling interspersed.

### The Skills Practice Format

The different formats that one can use in a behavior modeling program obviously have varying costs. With the skills practice format, one trainer (in one room) can train three or four participants per two hour session resulting in 12 participants trained in one module (or one set of key behaviors) per day. This requires one set of video-tape equipment if one is using video-tape feedback. Using the same number of trainers and facilities as in a typical workshop format (i.e., three trainers, three rooms, three video-tape outfits), 36

**Table 11.2  Skills Practice Schedule**

SCHEDULE

| | | |
|---|---|---|
| 08:00 | Welcome | Skills Practice Trainer(s) |
| | Introduction of Topic and Staff | Skills Practice Trainer(s) |
| | Key Behaviors: Coaching | Skills Practice Trainer(s) |
| | Training Tape Coaching | Skills Practice Trainer(s) |
| 08:30 | Skills Practice | Skills Practice Trainer(s) |
| | 1. Acquaintance with video equipment and taping procedure | |
| | 2. Practice: Coaching | |
| 10:00 | Wrap-up | Skills Practice Trainer(s) |

| | |
|---|---|
| 10:00–12:00 | |
| 01:00–03:00 | Repeat above with different participants or different module. |
| 03:00–05:00 | |

participants can be trained in one set of key behaviors per day in the skills practice format. Table 11.2 presents a schedule that could be used in a skills practice format to teach coaching. The coaching key behaviors and the behavioral rehearsal instructions for this skills practice format are presented in Table 11.3. In this format, the trainer simply introduces the topic, hands out a schedule of the program (such as that presented in Table 11.2), describes the key behaviors, makes sure that the three to four trainees understand the key behaviors, and shows the modeling display in the first half-hour. For the next hour and a half, the three to four participants behaviorally rehearse the key behaviors with one person role playing supervisor, one person role playing subordinate, and the third (and fourth if there is a fourth) person observing. The skills practice trainer video-tapes each practice attempt, after each role play helps the observers give feedback as well as gives his or her own, plays the video back after each role play, and controls the time so that everyone is done at the same time. Then, any questions or concerns are cleared up and the participants are free to go. The key behaviors of the skills practice trainer in this format are listed below. [Goldstein et al. (1980) provide a list of trainer key behaviors for trainers in counseling/clinical settings.]

1. Greet the three participants and introduce yourself.
2. Show them the equipment and room (stress confidentiality).
3. Seat them and explain roles (their seats will determine their roles—the supervisor will be the person seated facing the camera, etc.).
4. Explain the steps of the training (i.e., modeling, retention, practice, and feedback).

**Table 11.3   Skills Practice Instructions**

KEY BEHAVIORS: COACHING

If you are role playing:

Use your own job title and position.

The employee's work is acceptable in every respect, except one, where performance is inferior and improvement is needed.

Use these Key Behaviors:

1. State the problem in behavioral terms and then focus on the problem, not the person. Tie the problem to consequences for the person.

2. Try to bring the reasons for the problem out into the open.

3. Ask for the employee's suggestions and discuss the employee's ideas on how to solve the problem.

4. Listen openly.

5. Agree on steps each of you will take to solve the problem.

6. Plan and record a specific follow-up date, if appropriate.

If you are observing:

Watch to see how the Key Behaviors affect the employee.

Be ready to discuss how you would handle this situation.

---

5. Explain that attention to the modeling display is critical.
6. Hand out the key behaviors, discuss them, and ask them to memorize them—symbolic coding. (Use a form such as that shown in Table 11.3).
7. Show the modeling display tape.
8. If there is a second modeling display tape, show it.
9. Ask the participants to close their eyes and picture themselves doing the performance with one of their subordinates (mental rehearsal). Any discussion should occur after mental rehearsal.
10. Ask supervisor/subordinates to agree on a problem for the behavior rehearsal (make sure to rewind the modeling display tape, take it out of the VTR, and put the recording tape in the VTR while they do this).
11. Hand observation instructions to observer and give him or her instructions.
12. Ask participants if they are ready and record first role play.
13. Ask for observer feedback (rewind the video tape while the observer is giving feedback).
14. Replay the tape and give your feedback. (You can give feedback in the middle of the tape if you put the VTR on "pause" or you can wait until the tape is replayed completely. It is best to stop the tape.)

15. Repeat steps 10–14 for each participant as the person role plays one or more times.
16. Answer any questions.
17. Pair up trainees for on-the-job feedback (when appropriate). (This is so they can get together and reinforce each other for the use of the key behaviors on the job).
18. Wrap up.

Figure 11.2 provides an example of the trainer's position during the actual behavior rehearsal (i.e., key behaviors #9 through #13). Figure 11.3 is an example of the trainer giving feedback as the tape is replayed (i.e., key behaviors #14–#16). It is best to stand next to the equipment during role playing and feedback, but not during modeling.

The trainer who uses the skills practice format must be skilled in using behavior modeling methods and the video-tape equipment. The room to be used in this format should be large enough to accommodate four to five people (including the trainer), equipment, and furniture. The skills practice room should have absolutely no distractions. No outside person should be able to enter the room, look into it, or be able to overhear what is going on in it. Participants should not be interrupted by phone calls or visitors of any kind. The room should be quiet with minimal outside noise. The room should not have a window in it and should not have any fixed furniture. The lower portion of Figure 11.4 shows the typical setup for a skills practice room.

The TV monitor should be either on a trolley that can be turned away from the participants, can be shut off, or have some dark covering that can be draped over it. This prevents the participants from watching the TV monitor while they are role playing. (One of the hints in any skills practice setting is that if you turn off the TV monitor while the participants are role playing, turn the volume down so that you don't get feedback screech through the TV monitor when you turn it back on.)

The only equipment needed for the skills practice format, besides the room and the furniture, is the video-tape equipment. As we discussed earlier, one can use audio, rather than video, equipment to provide feedback in behavior modeling although this is not as desirable. The video equipment needed for one group of trainees in a single skills practice format is one video camera (black and white will do, but color is better), one VTR (cassette VTRs are much easier and better to use than reel-to-reel, but whatever you have will do—remember that reel-to-reel is black and white only), one TV monitor (preferably a 19-inch screen or larger) and one microphone.

## The Lecture-First Format

The lecture-first workshop format can be done with two or more trainers. It is typically used to accommodate more participants while keeping the trainer man-hours down. An advantage is that there is a need for only

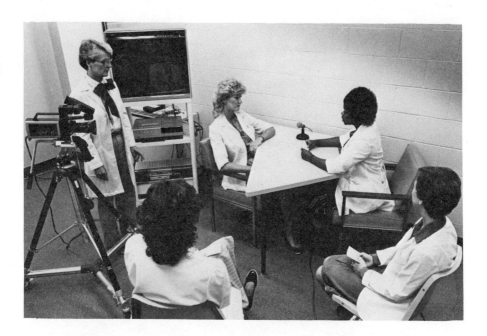

**Figure 11.2**   A behavioral rehearsal session

one trainer in the first (or morning) session for lecture/discussion; extra trainers can be brought in for the behavior modeling sessions in the second (or afternoon) session. If you do not have the trainers and the equipment for each group, a "round-robin" role playing approach may be substituted in which the trainers can rotate around to the different groups to give feedback where necessary. That is why the lecture-first option is important. You can present the lecture to all trainees, and then later schedule people in for different behavior modeling skills practice sessions using only one trainer, one room, and one set of equipment. The key behaviors for the trainer are not different from those used in the skills practice format. The morning schedule can be done virtually any way the trainer normally conducts a lecture/discussion session. The afternoon (or later) behavior modeling format should follow the key behaviors that were presented for the skills practice format. The lecture-first workshop format requires two different room set-ups, one for the lecture and the other for the behavior modeling. The upper portion of Figure 11.4 presents one possible set-up for the lecture portion of this workshop.

    With the lecture-first workshop format, it is possible to train six to nine people in one day using one trainer and one or two rooms (one lecture room to be converted or one lecture and one skills practice room). The six to eight people are in a lecture discussion session in the morning and in two two-hour

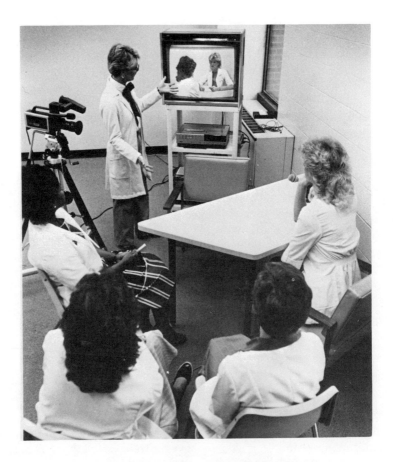

**Figure 11.3**   Trainer giving feedback

behavior modeling sessions in the afternoon. (See Skills Practice Schedule, Table 11.2.) With one trainer in the morning and two in the afternoon, it is possible to train 12 to 16 people in one module with a lecture-first workshop format. This entails the use of two skills practice rooms in the afternoon with two trainers and two sets of video-tape equipment.

## Interspersed Workshop Format

This format is considerably more complex than either the skills practice format or the lecture-first workshop format. The basic outline for the workshop is presented in Table 11.4. Two groups of trainees participate, simultaneously, one each in the lecture and the skills practice activities.

In this workshop, it is possible to train 12 participants in two modules with three trainers, three rooms, and two complete sets of video-tape equipment (including camera, microphone, etc.) and one playback VTR and mon-

**Lecture Room**

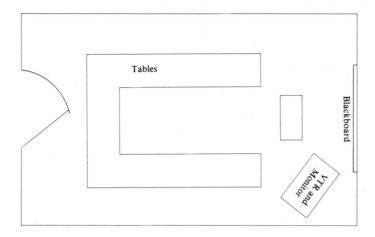

**Skills Practice Room**

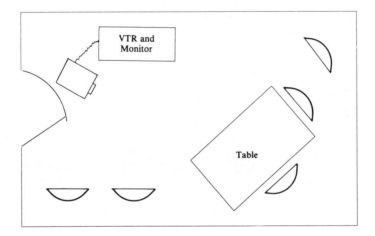

**Figure 11.4** Physical Setting for Workshop Format

itor. If four participants are put in a skills practice session, the participation level would increase to 16. With four trainers, this workshop can train 24 participants in a day. You can see by referring to Table 11.5 that half the participants are in the lecture/discussion session with a lead trainer while the other half of the participants are in two or more skills practice rooms, with skills practice trainers, doing behavioral rehearsal. The skills practice sessions of the workshop format are the same as those described in the previous section on the skills practice format except, in some cases, the modeling display tape is not shown in the skills practice room. The schedules presented in Tables 11.4 and 11.5 are designed with the assumption that the modeling tape is not shown in the skills practice room, but is shown in the lecture room to all trainees before they go on to their respective skills practice rooms; however, this is not required. The modeling tape can be shown in the skills practice room if there is a copy of the modeling display tape for every room. However, if there is any discussion about the modeling tapes of the key behaviors, some of the participants will miss it simply because there will be different amounts of discussion in different skills practice rooms.

In the interspersed format, the modeling tape is shown at the beginning of the workshop and then the participants are divided: half going immediately to the skills practice rooms to practice what they have seen on the modeling tape and the other half sitting in the lecture room and dealing with other topics. Those participants in the lecture room must be shown the modeling display tape again immediately before they break up and go to the skills practice rooms. This is extremely important because the modeling tape is most effective when it is seen just prior to the skills practice component. Also, mental rehearsal should be encouraged again before skills practice.

Here are the key behaviors of introduction for the lead trainer in the lecture format:

1. (08:00) Welcome participants (sign up, if appropriate).
2. Introduce: (1) yourself, (2) the skills practice trainers.
3. Have participants introduce themselves.
4. State workshop objectives and explain the behavior modeling process.
5. Explain schedules (Tables 11.4 and 11.5). Explain where restrooms are, etc.
6. Handout *and discuss* key behaviors. (See Table 11.3 for an example.) Have participants memorize key behaviors.
7. Show modeling display.
8. Ask participants to close their eyes and picture themselves doing the performance with one of their subordinates.
9. Divide group and send the appropriate participants to skills practice rooms.
10. (09:00) Establish rapport with remaining trainees—answer questions.
11. Do lecture/discussion segment. (This can be anything of the trainer's choosing.)
12. (10:15) Repeat steps 7–9.
13. (10:35) Repeat steps 10 and 11.
14. (01:00) Start all over again with a new module.

You can see in Table 11.4 that the second module in this example workshop deals with an employee-initiated complaint. Table 11.6 presents the key behaviors and role playing instructions for this module.

**Table 11.4   Interspersed Workshop Format for Supervisor Interpersonal Skills Training**

MORNING SCHEDULE

| | | |
|---|---|---|
| 0:800 | Welcome | VIP or Lead Trainer |
| | Introduction | VIP or Lead Trainer |
| | Introduction of Participants and Staff | Lead Trainer |
| | Workshop Objectives | Lead Trainer |
| | Schedule of Day's Events | Lead Trainer |
| | Key Behaviors: Coaching Situations | Lead Trainer |
| | Training Tape: Coaching Situation | Lead Trainer |
| 09:00 | GROUP A: LECTURE AND DISCUSSION | Lead Trainer |
| | GROUP B: SKILLS PRACTICE | Skills Practice Trainer A and B |
| | 1. Acquaintance with video equipment and taping procedure. | |
| | 2. Review of key behaviors: Coaching. | |
| | 3. Practice: Coaching Situations. | |
| 10:25 | Break | |
| 10:35 | GROUP A: SKILLS PRACTICE | Skills Practice Trainer A and B |
| | GROUP B: LECTURE AND DISCUSSION | Lead Trainer |
| 12:00 | Lunch | |

AFTERNOON SCHEDULE

| | | |
|---|---|---|
| 01:00 | Review of Afternoon Schedule | Lead Trainer |
| | Key Behaviors: | |
| | Employee-Initiated Complaint | Lead Trainer |
| | Training Tape: | |
| | Employee-Initiated Complaint | Lead Trainer |
| 01:30 | GROUP A: SKILLS PRACTICE | Skills Practice Trainer A and B |
| | 1. Review of key behaviors: Employee-Initiated Complaint | |
| | 2. Practice: Employee-Initiated Complaint | |
| | GROUP B: LECTURE AND DISCUSSION | Lead Trainer |
| 02:45 | Break | |
| 03:05 | GROUP A: LECTURE AND DISCUSSION | Lead Trainer |
| | GROUP B: SKILLS PRACTICE | Skills Practice Trainer A and B |
| 04:30 | Wrap-up and Evaluation of Workshop | Lead Trainer |

**Table 11.5 Interspersed Workshop Format for Supervisor Interpersonal Skills Training**

SKILLS PRACTICE SCHEDULE
*Time*

| Name | 08:00 | 09:00 | 10:35 | 01:00 | 01:30 | 03:05 |
|---|---|---|---|---|---|---|
| **Group A** | | | | | | |
| Participant 1 | Room A (I) | Room A (L) | Room B (SP) | Room A (I) | Room C (SP) | Room A (L) |
| Participant 2 | Room A (I) | Room A (L) | Room B (SP) | Room A (I) | Room C (SP) | Room A (L) |
| Participant 3 | Room A (I) | Room A (L) | Room B (SP) | Room A (I) | Room C (SP) | Room A (L) |
| Participant 4 | Room A (I) | Room A (L) | Room C (SP) | Room A (I) | Room B (SP) | Room A (L) |
| Participant 5 | Room A (I) | Room A (L) | Room C (SP) | Room A (I) | Room B (SP) | Room A (L) |
| Participant 6 | Room A (I) | Room A (L) | Room C (SP) | Room A (I) | Room B (SP) | Room A (L) |
| **Group B** | | | | | | |
| Participant 7 | Room A (I) | Room B (SP) | Room A (L) | Room A (I) | Room A (L) | Room C (SP) |
| Participant 8 | Room A (I) | Room B (SP) | Room A (L) | Room A (I) | Room A (L) | Room C (SP) |
| Participant 9 | Room A (I) | Room B (SP) | Room A (L) | Room A (I) | Room A (L) | Room C (SP) |
| Participant 10 | Room A (I) | Room C (SP) | Room A (L) | Room A (I) | Room A (L) | Room B (SP) |
| Participant 11 | Room A (I) | Room C (SP) | Room A (L) | Room A (I) | Room A (L) | Room B (SP) |
| Participant 12 | Room A (I) | Room C (SP) | Room A (L) | Room A (I) | Room A (L) | Room B (SP) |

I = Introduction and Key Behaviors
L = Lecture
SP = Skills Practice

**Table 11.6   Skills Practice Instructions**

---

KEY BEHAVIORS: EMPLOYEE-INITIATED COMPLAINT

If you are role playing:

Use your own job title and position.

You are not expecting the discussion.

*Use these Key Behaviors:*

1. Listen openly.

2. Do not speak until the employee has had his or her say.

3. Avoid reacting emotionally. (Don't get defensive.)

4. Ask for the employee's expectations about a solution to the problem.

5. Agree on specific steps to be taken and specific deadlines.

If you are observing:

Watch to see how the Key Behaviors affect the employee.

Be ready to discuss how you would handle this situation.

---

With the interspersed workshop format, three rooms will be needed: one lecture room and two skills practice rooms (See Figure 11.4). At least three video-tape outfits will be needed: one for each skills practice room, as explained in the skills practical format discussion. In the lecture room, a playback VTR and monitor to show the modeling tape will be needed. The monitor in the lecture room should be as large as possible or two monitors connected to the same VTR should be used, so that when the modeling tape is shown each participant sees it clearly. If there are questions, show it again. It is imperative that all the participants see the tape clearly.

## Which Is Best?

The skills practice workshop is pure behavior modeling, it does not allow for any lecture or discussion. Many of the sets of key behaviors taught are simple and may not need lecture/discussion; but in other cases, key behaviors may become very complex or fit into a larger situation so that some kind of understanding or discussion should accompany that behavioral learning. One example of this would be assertiveness. Assertive key behaviors are very difficult and not very distinctive. Lecture/discussion should accompany such behavior modeling learning. Another example is performance appraisal. The key behaviors of the annual performance appraisal interview are fairly straightforward and distinctive. However, the key behaviors of the performance appraisal interview fit into a larger scheme where the participant may have to learn something about the organization's appraisal policy and/or learn something about rating or writing appraisals, etc. This learning would be in a lecture/discussion format. Given these situations, a workshop format would be more appropriate than a skills practice format.

The major decision point between the lecture-first and the interspersed workshop formats concerns the facilities available for the training. The lecture-first format can be accomplished using only one trainer in the morning and one to two in the afternoon, depending on the number of participants, while the interspersed format needs at least three trainers all day. More participants can be trained in more content faster, however, with the interspersed format. With the lecture-first format, 12 participants can be trained in one module in one day with 12 trainer hours. All 12 people would be brought in for the morning lecture/discussion component and in the afternoon two trainers would be used in two skills practice rooms. They would each have two groups of three in the afternoon following the regular skills practice schedules for a half-day. If the interspersed format (with three rooms, two sets of video-tape equipment, a playback unit and three trainers) is used, 12 participants in two modules can be trained in a day. This entails 24 trainer hours. Overall, the trainer hours stay the same for the same amount of material but the interspersed workshop is more efficient. With the lecture first format it takes 12 trainer hours to train 12 participants in one module. If two modules were done in two days, 24 trainer hours would be needed. The difference is that you need fewer trainers at any given time. However, participant time is increased. In general, therefore, either workshop format is more complete than the simpler skills practice format, and the interspersed format is probably the easiest and the best to use in almost all cases where you have the equipment, facilities, and trainers available to use that format.

## Participants

The participants coming into a behavior modeling program should be made aware that role playing is involved. If video-tape equipment is being used to enhance feedback, they should also be told of this. The participants should be made aware that role playing is often an opening-up process where they can try out new types of behavior in nonthreatening situations. Also, the participants must be told that any video-taped recordings made are erased and not retained. The easiest way to do this is to explain to the participants that you simply record over and over on the same place in the tape when recording each role play and that they all get erased as the next role play is recorded. (At the end of the workshop, make sure that the skills practice trainer shows the participants that the tapes are indeed erased.)

One of the things that you can do when participants are uncomfortable with being video-taped is to allow them to experiment with the equipment and see themselves on TV before any role playing starts. Also, ask the participants who have been on video tape previously to role play first.

One thing that may happen in a behavior modeling program where participants from different areas of the organization are brought together is that the participants interact very closely in a role playing situation and they begin to understand that other people in the organization have exactly the same problems that they do. Sometimes the participants (in listening to each other) will come up with very unique solutions to problems. This interaction between participants may be just as valuable as the entire workshop. Participants will interact in a more realistic manner in the role playing when the participants come from different areas. When participants come from the same small unit, they tend to "rub each others' backs" and not take the role playing as seriously as they could.

Sometimes, trainees will "break role" and explain their behavior or make other comments. They should be urged to get back into the "role" and comment after it is done. If the practice is obviously going astray, it can be stopped and restarted. One method that has been used to keep such trainees "in role" is to write the learning points on a flip chart or blackboard and have the trainer point to each as the trainee does it in the practice attempt. This helps the practicing trainee as well as observers follow each of the steps in order. [For more information on management of problem behavior in skills practice, particularly with adolescents, see Goldstein et al. (1980).]

## Timing

There are many different ways to run behavior modeling programs. Some organizations tend to schedule training programs across long sessions one or two times a week, with many modules covered in each session. This usually can be done with no disadvantage as long as there is sufficient time for the participants to complete each session without taking away significantly from their job performance. Some trainers believe that this kind of training lends itself to more direct and intensive examination of participants' behavior and the learning of new behavior. The severe disadvantage, however, is the conflict that may arise with work schedules. Additionally, participants do not have an opportunity to try out new behaviors between sessions. If you are using behavior modeling to teach several different sets of key behaviors, it is our suggestion that each training module (performance, appraisal, feedback, disciplining, etc.) be separated by one or two weeks so the participants get a chance to try out the new behaviors and gain reinforcement and feedback on the job. If you go through module after module and the participants do not get a chance to really practice on the job, much of the training will be lost because the long-term reinforcement for successful use of the behavior will not occur, and participants will forget many key behaviors before they get a chance to use them.

## Homework

Many trainers may wish to use homework skills practice to enhance transfer. In this procedure, trainees are encouraged to use the key behaviors in their own real-life settings (e.g., job) and take notes about their successes and failures. This technique is often very useful when behavior modeling is used to teach a series of modules (one per set of key behaviors) over a number of weeks. The homework form (provided in Figure 11.5) can be used to facilitate not only homework practice, but discussion of that practice in the following program in the series.

**Figure 11.5**   Homework Report

Name _____ Date _____
Group Leaders _____

FILL IN DURING CLASS
1.   What skill will you use?

2.   What are the steps for the skill?

3.   Where will you try the skill?

4.   With whom will you try the skill?

5.   When will you try the skill?

FILL IN AFTER DOING YOUR HOMEWORK
1.   What happened when you did the homework?

2.   Which steps did you really follow?

3.   How good a job did you do in using the skill? (Circle one.)
     Excellent            Good            Fair            Poor

4.   What do you think should be your next homework assignment?

*Source:* Taken from Goldstein et al. (1980). *Skill-Streaming the Adolescent.* Champaign, IL: Research Press.

## Ethics

You as a lead trainer or skills practice trainer, and any other skills practice trainers involved in behavior modeling, will be exposed to many criticisms, perspectives about the organization, and other proprietary information. It is important that the group of participants feel secure in the knowledge that you and the other trainers will not in any way violate the confidentiality of the training sessions. It is important that they can experiment with ideas and different behaviors without the feeling that their comments or abilities at picking up new behavior will be transmitted to top management or any other individuals in the organization. You need to tell the participants explicitly that what is said in the discussion and in skills practice sessions is strictly confidential and that what is video-taped will be erased—and then *make sure that this is the case.*

## The Trainer's Role

As a behavior modeling trainer you will be coordinating one of the most sophisticated programs available. Possibly the only training programs more complex than behavior modeling are computer-assisted training programs. Behavior modeling provides participants with the opportunity to learn, to grow, and to obtain new effective behavior to apply in day-to-day situations.

The behavior modeling trainer is not necessarily a subject matter expert. More than anything else the trainer should be an individual who has a real interest and personal commitment to the improvement of trainees in the organization and some familiarity in speaking to and dealing with trainees. The lead trainer in behavior modeling coordinates and schedules the activities of the program. He or she is the one who has to perform the mechanical aspects of the program, such as arranging the rooms and having all of the necessary materials and video-tape equipment which is required. Also, if the lead trainer chooses to run the behavior modeling program in one of the workshop formats, he or she would be there to guide the discussion, facilitate the analysis of the program material, and lead the participants through any of the discussion sessions.

One of the most important points is that the process of running behavior modeling sessions means that the lead trainer and the skills practice trainers will soon develop, perhaps more than anyone else in the organization, an understanding of the organizational problems as seen by the participants of the workshops. Given that a supervisory program is run two or three times, trainers will be able to learn of the problems and suggested solutions in their organization, and as a result, develop many pat answers to problems that are raised in future training sessions. However, behavior modeling is designed to teach process skills, not content. The participants in any program must develop their own solutions to day-to-day situations. The trainers are not there to give the trainees the one best way to handle any situation they may encounter. The behavior modeling trainers are there to coordinate a program which is designed to give each of the participants some process skills in handling different problems in different contexts. It is the process skill which is taught in behavior modeling and which can then be applied across different situations.

As a lead trainer in behavior modeling training, you will need three things: 1) a complete understanding of the training method (which this book will give you), 2) an understanding of the basic content of the training program (you must develop key behaviors and understand them), and 3) a fairly intimate knowledge of video-tape equipment (or have an audio-visual expert on your staff). This book supplies all of the procedural aspects for behavior modeling and also tells you how to develop key behaviors. Many key behaviors for management training are provided as examples. Behavior modeling is an extremely popular training technique and we believe it will continue to be popular as more research continues to show its efficacy, and how it can be improved.

The skills practice trainers are the core of any behavior modeling program. They interact on a one-to-one basis with the participants, they control the role playing and they are the ones who give feedback and social reinforcement for the participant's behavioral rehearsal performance. Their selection and training is critical.

The skills practice trainers need several skills or qualities. They need to be fairly energetic, enthusiastic, and have good oral communication skills. They need to be interested in people. They also need to understand what the key behaviors are and what they mean behaviorally. Skills practice trainers need to know how to run video-tape equipment. They need to be the type of people who refrain from offering solutions to the participants' problems, and to be the type of people who will not repeat what they have heard in the training room. They also need to be able to work under pressure. Finally, the skills practice trainers need to have some skills in giving feedback to participants. This feedback needs to be specific and behavioral in nature.

Overall, the trainers in behavior modeling do not have to have extensive training to start out because they do not need to be content experts. After a few workshops, however, they may become knowledgeable in many content areas and the training will become quite easy. It can be a very frustrating activity and it takes a great deal of energy (and sometimes large amounts of willpower) to refrain from simply solving problems. Nevertheless, it is a very rewarding job for trainers because they know that the trainees will be walking out of the training room with new skills.

## Some Final Hints

Finally, all behavior modeling trainers must realize that there is a definite learning transition that the trainee goes through in a behavior modeling program. The trainee sees the learning points first, and the key behaviors are discussed. The trainee then sees the modeling display. A high quality modeling display will contain the learning points, a modeled performance with the learning points superimposed when the key behavior occurs, and lastly a modeled performance without learning points. At this point, the trainee mentally rehearses the key behaviors in one of his or her own situations. The participant then physically reproduces the behavior. So far, the trainee has made the transition from a written description of the key behaviors, to a combination written and video image of the key behaviors, to a video-only image, to a mental image, and finally to a physical enactment of that mental image or one very similar to it. *Then*, the trainee should be allowed to practice several different situations using the key behaviors with different people. During the early portions of the practice, the trainee will receive frequent, immediate feedback. The trainer should move the feedback from social, immediate, continuous, and frequent to feedback which is more self-originated, not always immediate, and less frequent. This type of feedback more closely resembles that received on the job. Consequently, as a trainee moves from practicing skills in the neutral training setting to using those skills in the "life-or-death" real world, the person also moves to being less reliant on external feedback for initiating and maintaining the behavior.

This transition is extremely important. It is fostered and ushered by the trainer. If it breaks down in any way, the transfer of learning will also break down and there will be no new behavior evidenced on the job. It must be understood, or illustrated, and if necessary, explained to the trainee!

# IV

## The Future of
## Behavior Modeling

# —12—

# EVALUATION OF BEHAVIOR
# MODELING TRAINING PROGRAMS

Few things in the training field create as much controversy or discussion as the word "evaluation." Trainers will always agree on the *need* for sound appraisal of training programs; however, trainers rarely agree on the best *method* of evaluation, and rarely do empirical evaluation. A typical approach in training is to review a program at the corporate level, and if the program looks good, the organization uses it. Programs are used again and again. Sometimes the trainees are asked how they liked it, but the program continues in the organization until someone in a position of authority decides that it is no longer useful or working. All of this is done on the basis of people's opinions and judgments. Rarely is it based on an empirical evaluation of causal relationships (did the training cause any changes in the organization?). Often, the result is an effective program used in the wrong place, dropped altogether, or an ineffective program being used. Rational decisions related to the adoption of, or methodological changes in, various training technologies require some empirical basis for determining that the training was or was not responsible for whatever changes occurred. This is the aim of training evaluation. It consists of procedures designed to collect the information necessary to make effective programming decisions.

Most of the evaluation that is conducted is done with questionnaires at the end of the training program. This kind of evaluation does not tell us whether the trainees learned anything or if they will use new behavior on the job. Rather, it simply indicates whether the trainees enjoyed the experience or whether they *believe* it will be useful. Whether or not it actually does result in changes in behavior remains unknown. The whole essence of using a complex training method like behavior modeling is to ensure that there is new behavior on the job or new skills being used in the transfer context. If one is going to put the money and time into developing a behavior modeling training program, then one should also be willing to put the money and time into evaluation to determine whether that training program is actually doing what it was intended to do.

There are times when evaluation is not done and there are many reasons for this; but, let us look at the basic question of why one *would* evaluate in the first place. One reason is that it is mandated. If someone in authority—the training director or above—says, "You shall evaluate your training," then you will evaluate your training. You may not evaluate it well, but some kind of evaluation will get done because someone in authority has mandated it. The second reason is for the improvement of a training program. One should always strive to make tomorrow's training program better than today's. Certainly in most organizations we would like to continually improve training programs so that the participants continue to get more out of them and they are more effective. Certain kinds of evaluation can be done to look at the content of a training program in order to identify elements of it that need to be improved. The third reason one would evaluate a training program is justification. There are many times when we are called upon to defend or justify the continuation of a certain training program or even the training department itself. If you can produce objective data that proves a training program does have an effect on day-to-day operating problems of the company, rarely will money for that training program be cut from the budget. With many such programs operating, the department will continue to be funded.

Given these reasons for evaluating training, why don't trainers do it? One of the major reasons evaluation is not done is that it is very difficult and costly to do. Another reason is that trainers may not consider it necessary. Finally, many trainers do not have the skills to do empirical evaluation. A well thought-out procedure that can assess the true impact of a training program on job performance and ultimately on organizational productivity is neither an easy nor inexpensive undertaking. Unless an organization is truly committed to finding out whether their training programs work or do not work, evaluation is not going to be done.

One evaluation study will not solve all training problems or determine the efficacy of one particular training technology; however, each study is an important step forward. Campbell (1971) suggested that the training literature is faddish to an extreme. Training fads center around the introduction of new techniques and follow characteristic patterns. A new technique appears and develops a group of advocates who first describe its successful use in a number of situations. Then, advocates busy themselves trying out numerous modifications of the basic technique. A few empirical studies may be carried out to demonstrate that the method works. Finally, the inevitable backlash sets in. A few vocal opponents begin to criticize the usefulness of the technique, most often in the absence of data. Such criticism typically has little effect until the appearance of a new technique and the repetition of the same cycle. Goldstein (1980), in a more recent review, found much of the same trend.

Many organizational trainers have simply not been trained in evaluation methods and designs. This is, overall, one of the greatest needs in training today. People going into organizational training should be trained in field experimentation so that they can evaluate their training adequately. Paper and pencil testing and questionnaires do not measure actual learning or behavior change. Evaluation done at the end of training does not capture whether transfer occurred and, therefore, does not indicate training's worth to an organization.

This chapter is designed to be a general introduction to training evaluation (especially of behavior modeling). The different levels of criteria, different training designs, judging the adequacy of those experimental designs, and hints about evaluating behavior modeling will be presented. The sections concerning types of criteria and experimental designs will stress those criteria and designs appropriate for behavior modeling. Empirical evaluation of behavior change is fairly easy to accomplish in behavior modeling training. Behavior modeling is a very trainer- and equipment-intensive training method. Therefore, it is expensive and, in most cases, needs to be justified. This alone should be enough reason to evaluate behavior modeling, over and above all the other reasons. The final section of the chapter will examine methods to determine dollar costs of training results.

## Measures of Training Effectiveness

### Trainee Reaction

The effectiveness of a training program can be evaluated in terms of four criteria: trainee reaction, learning, behavior change, and organizational results (Kirkpatrick, 1967). Trainee reaction measures how the trainees liked the training program. It is typically done using a questionnaire that is completed by the trainees at the end of a program. The questionnaire may contain questions concerning the program's content, the trainer, the trainer's objectives, the methods used, physical facilities, and even, in some cases, quality of meals. So that irrelevent data is not gathered, the specific trainee reactions that the organization is interested in should be decided upon before training and included in the questionnaire that is to be filled out.

Figure 12.1 is an example of a trainee reaction questionnaire. Such a questionnaire should: 1) elicit reactions to as many of the training objectives as are measurable by questionnaire, 2) permit open-ended and anonymous answers, and 3) allow trainees to write additional comments, if desired. Wexley and Latham (1981) suggest that two or three items having no relationship to the training program be included on the reaction questionnaire to determine whether the trainees are responding thoughtfully or not to the questionnaire. Rating everything either excellent or poor, especially on the two or three nonrelated items, is an indication that the trainees probably are blindly answering the questionnaire. Such a questionnaire should be distributed at

**Figure 12.1**  Continuing Education Program Evaluation Form

NAME OF PROGRAM: _____ DATE: _____

An important part of any educational program is its evaluation. Your help in assisting the Extension Division to improve its programs will be of great help in planning similar programs. We are not searching for compliments; we need your honest opinion about the program you have just completed.

1.  How would you rate the overall program as an educational experience?

    ☐ Excellent     ☐ Very good     ☐ Good     ☐ Fair     ☐ Poor

2.  To what extent did the program content meet your needs and interests?

    ☐ Very well     ☐ To some extent     ☐ Very little

3.  What would you have added to the program?

4.  What would you have deleted from the program?

5.  What benefits (if any) did you receive from participating in the program?

6.  How would you rate the following?

|                       | Excellent | Very Good | Good | Fair | Poor |
|-----------------------|-----------|-----------|------|------|------|
| Facilities            | ☐         | ☐         | ☐    | ☐    | ☐    |
| Meals                 | ☐         | ☐         | ☐    | ☐    | ☐    |
| Helpfulness of staff  | ☐         | ☐         | ☐    | ☐    | ☐    |

7.  Please comment *critically* on any or all of the presentations:

8.  Will your job or personal behavior change as a result of this continuing education program?

    ☐ Definitely   ☐ Probably   ☐ Undecided   ☐ Probably Not   ☐ Definitely
                                                                    Not

    If yes, how?

9.  OTHER COMMENTS:

                              Name: _____
                                              (optional)

                              Date: _____

_____

*Source*: University of Missouri-St. Louis Business-Continuing Education-Extension Division.

the beginning of a program so participants can see what dimensions are to be measured and have adequate time to complete it.

Trainee reaction is an appropriate criterion when one is interested in how well the trainees like the program and/or if you are looking to improve the day-to-day presentation of the training program. This is appropriate where you are in the business of selling training (assuming that trainees will be drawn to a training program that is liked); but, the more appropriate use of trainee-reaction criteria is to guide the day-to-day improvement of the operation of the program by changing such things as facilities, the placement of breaks, the inclusion of more practice/less practice, or things the trainer says or does. The trainees' perceptions about these kinds of items can be measured on a questionnaire and the program mechanics can be improved based on those results. Most trainers know you cannot please everyone all the time and, of course, this should be kept in mind. However, trainee reaction questionnaires should be completed at the end of every behavior modeling training program to check the day-to-day mechanics of the training program.

A somewhat different approach for collecting trainee reactions is shown in Figure 12.2. By using this type of form, trainees have an opportunity at the beginning of a program to select the course objectives that specifically apply to them, are given a means of expressing the relative importance of each objective selected and can then express how well, in their opinion, each objective has been fulfilled (Fast, 1974).

As Wexley and Latham (1981) point out, favorable trainee reactions to any training program do not guarantee that learning has taken place or that the behavior(s) of the trainee has changed as a result of the training program. Nevertheless, trainee reactions are important for several reasons: 1) reports of positive reactions help insure organizational support for a program; 2) trainee reactions help the training staff assess the success of the program's implementation, and 3) reaction data indicates whether or not the trainees like the program.

It is sometimes useful to look at the reactions of different groups of trainees and to analyze them separately. Also, it might be important to collect reaction measures several months after the training program has taken place. Doing this allows the trainee to realistically assess the effectiveness of the training content on his or her job. This may be very important with behavior modeling training since, at the end of training, most trainees' reactions are inflated because of enthusiasm. Most trainees enjoy the role playing and learning of very specific behaviors which they think they can use almost immediately on the job. Consequently, the reaction measures taken immediately after the training may be higher than would be expected over time.

## Learning Criteria

Learning criteria assess the knowledge that was learned by trainees in the training program. Knowledge is memory for facts and figures presented in the training program, or in the case of behavior modeling, identifying on paper the key behaviors. Knowledge is typically measured by paper and pencil tests much like those used in high school or college courses. Paper and pencil tests can include true–false, multiple-choice, fill-in-the-blank, matching, and essay-type questions. Quite often, true–false or multiple-choice

**Figure 12.2**  A Reaction Form Used by the Life Office Management Association (LOMA)

Systems Design Workshop

| | ✔ | DEGREE OF IMPORTANCE x | DEGREE OF FULFILLMENT = | INDEX OF OBJECTIVE FULFILLMENT |
|---|---|---|---|---|
| Your Name _____ | | | | |
| OBJECTIVES | | | | |
| Check those that are important to you. (Ignore those that are not.) | | *Weight each checked objective for its importance to you, allocating exactly 100 points among all of those checked. A total of 100 points must be assigned. | **Rate each objective you checked (from 0-10) to indicate how well it was fulfilled. | |
| Be able to: | | | | |
| 1. Identify and describe the various elements in the systems development process and understand their significance. | | | | |
| 2. Understand the use and value of systems feasibility studies. | | | | |
| 3. Identify essential considerations (critical factors in a systems design problem). | | | | |
| 4. Design a management report. | | | | |
| 5. Design an input form. | | | | |
| 6. Develop an overall systems flow. | | | | |
| 7. Understand the objectives and techniques of designing input/output controls. | | | | |
| 8. Select among and be able to use basic data base structures. | | | | |
| 9. Prepare an oral presentation of design recommendations for management. | | | | |
| 10. Exchange ideas with other participants. | | | | |
| | | 100 | TOTAL = | |

*If you checked only one objective, assign all 100 points to it; if you checked two objectives, spread the 100 points between them, etc.

**0 is unsatisfactory; 1–2 poor; 3–4 below average; 5 average; 6 above average; 7 good; 8 very good; 9–10 excellent.

*Source*: Fast, D. "A New Approach to Quantifying Training Program Effectiveness," *Training and Development Journal* 28:9 (1974), 8–14. Reproduced by special permission from the September, 1974 *Training and Development Journal*. Copyright © 1974 by the American Society for Training and Development, Inc.

questions are used because they are relatively easy for the trainee to complete, and very easy for the trainer to score. Fill-in and essay-type questions are easier to develop than true–false or multiple-choice questions, but are much more difficult (and less objective) to score. It is important, however, to realize that true–false and multiple-choice questions only assess trainees' ability to recognize the correct information when it is put before them, rather than using their memory to recall or reproduce the correct answer. Consequently, if one is interested in recall or reconstruction of correct answers, fill-in and essay-type questions would be more appropriate. Fill-in items can be designed to allow objective scoring. Figure 12.3 shows examples of fill-in items.

Essay questions not only can measure a person's memory for facts and figures, but also can assess cognitive skills such as problem solving, integration, and conceptual thinking (and writing skills). Similar to essay questions are performance test items which are used to determine if trainees have mastered a *particular* skill. Figure 12.4 illustrates performance test items. Performance test items and essay items are usually used to assess some kind of cognitive skill, but the scoring is very difficult because it is not objective.

**Figure 12.3**  An Example of a Completion or Fill-in Item

Instructions: Notice that there are seven circles on the print. Notice that there is a list of answers numbered 1 through 12 on the right-hand side of the print. Seven answers are correct, five answers are wrong and do not apply. Write one of these seven correct answers in each of these seven white circles. Use the numbers. Use each number only once.

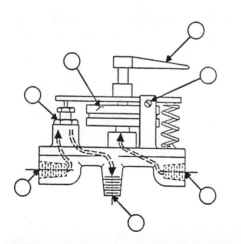

1.  Instrument Air Connection

2.  Pressure Capsule

3.  Set Pointer

4.  Metering Needle Valve

5.  Orifice

6.  Capillary Tube

7.  Connection to Control Valve

8.  Pilot Valve

9.  Chart Plate

10.  Nozzle

11.  Pressure Connection

12.  Fulcrum

*Source*: Wexley, K. N. and Latham, G. P. (1981) *Developing and Training Human Resources in Organizations*. Glenview, IL: Scott Foresman. Reproduced by permission.

**Figure 12.4**   Instructions to Performance Tests

---

Mechanics: "You have in front of you a gear reducer, a lone shaft, bearings, and coupling. I want you to assemble and adjust the proper alignment so that the finished assembly is a right-hand (or left-hand) driven assembly. Set the coupling gap 1/8″ apart. You do not have to put the grid member in place or fasten the coupling covers. After you are finished, I will ask you where and how the grid member should go in. You will have 45 minutes to complete this job."

Painters: "I want you to boost yourself up about 10 feet off the floor using this boatsman chair, and then tie yourself off so that you don't fall. After that, I would like you to hook this spraygun to the air supply, set the regulator to the correct pressure, and then spray this wall."

---

*Source*: Wexley, K. N. and Latham, G. P. (1981) *Developing and Training Human Resources in Organizations*. Glenview, IL: Scott Foresman. Reproduced by permission.

The learning criterion test items cover whatever knowledge and skills have been determined through needs analysis to be part of the training content. Consequently, in order to construct a paper and pencil test, one must be concerned that the items: 1) representatively sample the content of the training program, 2) measure recognition or recall of information as is appropriately required on the job (in most cases this would be recall), and 3) do not require ability levels (for example, reading or writing ability) beyond that necessary on the job. These issues also fall under the broader heading of content validity. A fuller treatment of developing content valid tests can be found in Adkins (1974), Ebel (1972), and Gronlund (1976).

In most behavior modeling programs, where you are teaching a manual or social skill rather than factual material, the learning criterion is not used. The only cases where learning criteria would be used are in those situations where one has offered a workshop format with a substantial amount of factual material. In this case, the paper and pencil test assessing learning criteria would address itself only to the content of the lecture/discussion portion of the workshop. Another way in which the learning criterion has been used in behavior modeling is through the trainees' role playing. For example, the last one or two role plays could be evaluated by the trainer(s) to see if, in fact, the trainees knew which key behaviors to use in each simulated situation. Of course, learning to recall new skills in a training situation, and transferring the use of the skills to the actual job situation, are very different evaluation considerations.

## Behavior Change

One of the biggest problems in the training field is that some training techniques do not facilitate transfer of the training content from the classroom to the job. In organizational training, transfer is a critical element.

Many times we do not get transfer in organizational training because a trainee was taught the theory and principles of the technique, but the person never learned how to translate this into behavior on the job. There is a big difference between knowing principles and using them on the job. This is evident in many training programs that teach factual material through lecture. A person going through such a training program may remember the material, but not know how to use the new behavior on the job. A test at the end of such a training program may prove that the training does, in fact, increase learning; however, if behavior is not measured after the program (i.e., on the job), one does not know if the effect of the training program will transfer to the job. Consequently, measuring behavioral criteria is important if you are in the business of teaching new skills to be used on the job. Since this is the primary purpose of behavior modeling training, it is absolutely critical that behavioral measures be gathered on the job.

The objectives of behavior change criteria are to measure the change in the use of a particular behavior by the trainee before and after the training program. There are three basic questions here. First, how do you measure the behavior change? You can observe the actual behavior or you can measure a result of that behavior. In the case where you measure a result of the behavior, however, you must make sure that it is a situation where the result can only come from the new behavior (and there are no other alternate behaviors that may give the same result). The second question is, who observes? There are, in any given situation, a number of sources for appraisal of behavior. There are several groups of people who would be in a situation to know the behavior when they see it, to observe it, and to rate it. These include the trainee's superiors, subordinates, co-workers or peers, and/or the customers of the trainee.

When using ratings or observations as the criterion to evaluate the effectiveness of a training program one should consider factors associated with the rating process such as the use of different rating formats, rating errors, and the cognitive processes of the rater. These issues are covered in depth in many performance appraisal books (see, for example, Bernardin and Beatty, 1983; and Latham and Wexley, 1981). The third consideration when developing behavior change criteria is when the data should be gathered. The appraisal can take place soon after the training or it can be done several months later. In most situations, it should be done both immediately after the training, and at some later date so that the trainee can be given an adequate opportunity to put the new behavior into practice on the job. Quite often, there is a "sleeper effect," where it takes time for trainees to exhibit, on the job, what they have acquired from the training. This is very common in behavior modeling training.

The form that is used to record ratings, how many raters should be used, and what kind of training they should receive before observing and rating behavior should also be considered. Another issue to consider is whether you are going to collect observations of behavior as they occur or as retrospective appraisal. In other words, are the raters recording events immediately as they take place or are they remembering past behavior to be recorded at the time of performance appraisal. Performance appraisal data used as behavior change criteria is, in almost all cases, retrospective appraisal.

Figure 12.5 is an example of a rating form used to appraise a behavior modeling program. This form could be completed at the end of training in a final behavioral test, or on-the-job, when the behavior occurs. Figure 12.6 is an example of a behavioral observation scale (BOS scale) (Latham and Wexley, 1981) which can be used to judge retrospective on-the-job performance as behavior change criteria. This form may also represent a portion of a performance appraisal system, but can be used for appraising behavior change because it is very behaviorally specific.

When one is attempting to collect criteria data through observation and rating, one must determine whether the behavior can be observed and rated on the job, or whether it is necessary to take the trainee population off the job into a contrived situation so that their behavior can be observed and rated. In many situations, the behavior will occur frequently enough on the job so that the key behaviors can be observed and rated. However, in many situations this will not be the case and it may be that you will have to arrange a contrived situation where the new behavior is used. One way to do this is to schedule what could be called a "booster session"; that is, bring the trainees back into the training room, about a month after the training, for one quick role play as a practice situation. In this case, the trainees come back to the training room, talk to the trainer about any problems they have had or any situations that have arisen concerning the key behaviors, practice one or more role play with the trainer (they can bring one of their subordinates) and the trainer records it on video tape. When the session is over, and with the consent of the trainees, the trainer does not erase the tape. The trainer keeps the tape and it can be observed and rated at a later date to yield the criterion data.

## Organizational Results

The objectives of many industrial training programs can be expressed in terms of some end result for the organization such as reduced turnover, fewer grievances, reduced absenteeism, less scrap, increased sales or productivity, or fewer accidents. These are usually expressed in quantifiable data which usually can be tied to a monetary cost or benefit.

It is often difficult to determine whether changes in result criteria can be unequivocally attributed to the training program or to other changes in the organization such as market competitiveness changes, changes in management, increased pay, new equipment, better selection, or seasonal

**Figure 12.5**   Behavior Modeling Criteria Rating Form

Ratee Name _____ I.D. #_____
Rater Name _____
Condition _____

Please circle the number that comes closest to your opinion.

### COACHING

The Supervisor/Trainee:

| | | |
|---|---|---|
| Focused on the problem. | 1  2  3  4  5  6  7 | Did not focus on the problem. |
| Did not attack the subordinate or did not put him/her on the spot. | 1  2  3  4  5  6  7 | Attacked subordinate or put him/her on the spot. |
| Asked for the subordinate's suggestions for solutions to the problem. | 1  2  3  4  5  6  7 | Did not ask for the subordinate's suggestions for solutions to the problem. |
| Got the subordinate committed to one or more solutions to the problem. | 1  2  3  4  5  6  7 | Did not get the subordinate committed to one or more solutions to the problem. |
| Listened openly after asking for solutions. | 1  2  3  4  5  6  7 | Did not listen openly after asking for solutions. |
| Agreed on specific steps the subordinate would take to help solve the problem. | 1  2  3  4  5  6  7 | Did not agree on specific steps the subordinate would take to help solve the problem. |
| Set a specific follow-up date with the subordinate. | 1  2  3  4  5  6  7 | Did not set a specific follow-up date with the subordinate. |
| Did not get defensive. | 1  2  3  4  5  6  7 | Got defensive. |
| Used nonverbal behaviors that were appropriate. | 1  2  3  4  5  6  7 | Did not use nonverbal behaviors that were appropriate. |

**Figure 12.5**   Behavior Modeling Criteria Rating Form (cont.)

## EMPLOYEE COMPLAINT

The Supervisor/Trainee:

| | | |
|---|---|---|
| Listened openly to the complaint. | 1  2  3  4  5  6  7 | Did not listen openly to the complaint. |
| Did not speak until the employee had had his/her say. | 1  2  3  4  5  6  7 | Did speak (interrupt) before the employee had had his/her say. |
| Did not get defensive. | 1  2  3  4  5  6  7 | Got defensive. |
| Did not react emotionally (other than defensively). | 1  2  3  4  5  6  7 | Did react emotionally (other than defensively). |
| Used nonverbal behaviors that were appropriate. | 1  2  3  4  5  6  7 | Did not use nonverbal behaviors that were appropriate. |
| Asked for the employee's expectations about a solution to the problem. | 1  2  3  4  5  6  7 | Did not ask for the employee's expectations about a solution to the problem. |
| Listened openly as the employee suggested solutions. | 1  2  3  4  5  6  7 | Did not listen openly as the employee suggested solutions. |
| Agreed with the subordinate on specific plans he/she would take to solve the problem. | 1  2  3  4  5  6  7 | Did not agree with the subordinate on a specific plan he/she would take to solve the problem. |
| Agreed on a specific deadline for solving the problem. | 1  2  3  4  5  6  7 | Did not agree on a specific deadline for solving the problem. |
| Got the subordinate committed to a solution to the problem. | 1  2  3  4  5  6  7 | Did not get the subordinate committed to a solution to the problem. |

**Figure 12.6**   Example Behavior Observation Rating Scale

Instructor _____

Student _____

Date _____

INSTRUCTIONS: Please consider the above-named individual's behavior in the classroom for the past four months. Read each statement carefully, and on the basis of your actual observation or on dependable knowledge, circle the number that best indicates the extent to which this particular instructor actually demonstrated each of the following behaviors. For each behavior, a "5" represents "Almost Always" or 95 to 100 percent of the time. A "4" represents "Frequently" or 85 to 94 percent of the time. A "3" represents "Sometimes" or 75 to 84 percent of the time. A "2" represents "Seldom" or 65 to 74 percent of the time. A "1" represents "Almost Never" or 0 to 64 percent of the time.

I. *Lecturing/Teaching Style*

1. Instructor talks about himself/herself only during first class period.

   Almost never     1   2   3   4   5     Almost always

2. Instructor clearly states goals at beginning of each class and attempts to meet them.

   Almost never     1   2   3   4   5     Almost always

3. Instructor dedicates class time to subject material (does not sell magazines and newspapers in class.)

   Almost never     1   2   3   4   5     Almost always

4. Instructor finds multiple ways to make the same point until all students understand.

   Almost never     1   2   3   4   5     Almost always

5. Teacher presents concepts clearly and understandably.

   Almost never     1   2   3   4   5     Almost always

6. Instructor uses different teaching techniques.

   Almost never     1   2   3   4   5     Almost always

7. Instructor acts like all questions are relevant in front of class.

   Almost never     1   2   3   4   5     Almost always

8. Teacher is on time for class and does not run class over end of period.

   Almost never     1   2   3   4   5     Almost always

**Figure 12.6** Example Behavior Observation Rating Scale (cont.)

9. Instructor demonstrates expertise in the field by being able to answer student questions which are applicable to the subject.

Almost never    1   2   3   4   5    Almost always

10. Instructor repeatedly (three to four times) asks if there are any questions.

Almost never    1   2   3   4   5    Almost always

*Source:* Hoffman, C. C. (1981) *Behavioral observation versus behavioral expectation scales: Developmental and psychometric properties.* Unpublished master's thesis, University of Nebraska at Omaha. Advisor: Dennis Dossett.

changes of some kind. One must be especially careful in deciding the length of data collection, the unit of analysis, how subjects were assigned to training, and other experimental design issues, if one is to be able to rule out all of the numerous alternate explanations for the criteria data changes. Thus, results criteria should be closely tied to the training key behaviors. Despite all of the difficulties in collecting and analyzing such data, the trainer should attempt to collect cost-related measures. Such measures give management evidence that training efforts impact on organization effectiveness.

In behavior modeling training, one could possibly use all of the different types of training evaluation criteria. One would use trainee reaction to determine how well trainees liked the program and what one could do to change the day-to-day operation of a program (such as facilities, rooms, snacks, etc.); use learning criteria if one wanted to evaluate the results of the lecture/discussion portion of a workshop; and use behavioral criteria to assess whether the training program did, in fact, change behavior at the end of training (and possibly on the job). One would be interested in organizational results criteria in conjunction with the behavior change criteria so that one could show that training is a viable solution to organizational problems. All criteria have value. At a minimum, trainee reaction should be positive, or else it is unlikely that the program, regardless of how effective, will be continued. Likewise, measures of behavior change criteria should be implemented, as this is the level of criteria which is most closely associated with behavior modeling training, that is, changing behavior on the job.

## Experimental Designs

The basic issue in the design of training evaluation research is whether one can set up experimental conditions so as to be able to say that changes in the criterion were indeed the result of training. Most experimental designs leave us with an equivocal answer to this question. Since the fundamental purpose of training is to bring about a *systematic* change in behavior, a simple "after training measure" only, often used in case studies, cannot document such effects. A "before training measure" is essential for comparison. In other words, is the "after" measure higher than the "before" measure? However, the demonstration of a change from before to after measures for a training group does not unequivocally show that the change was due to the training only. Since there was a time interlude between the before and after measures, only some of which was taken up by the training, the behavior change may have resulted from other experiences or events. Thus, a control group that receives the before and after measures but not the training is also needed. The training and control groups should be comparable on the before measure; that is, they should be essentially equivalent groups. If the after measure is higher for the training group, then one can suggest the training program has caused the change in the criterion. Unfortunately, the case study method, as well as simple before training–after training (also referred to as a pretest–posttest) design are probably the designs most frequently used in training evaluation.

Before we proceed much further, we need to have some scheme for judging the adequacy of research designs. Cook and Campbell (1979) have written a book about judging the usefulness of research designs and the extent to which research designs do, in fact, help determine causality. For our purposes, research designs should be judged on at least two variables: internal and external validity. The term validity means the truth or falsity of propositions, including propositions about cause and effect. Internal validity refers to the validity with which one can infer that a relationship between a training program and criteria measure is causal; that is, the training program has caused the differences in the criterion scores. This involves eliminating all possible alternative explanations for why, after training, criterion performance has improved. External validity refers to whether or not we can infer that the causal relationship itself can be generalized to different populations, settings, and times. In other words, if the training worked once, can we assume it will work again for a different sample of trainees.

### Internal Validity

There are situations which would cause one to believe a causal relationship exists between the training program and a measure of some training criteria when, in fact, such an inference would be false. The following is a discussion of some of those situations, called "threats to validity," which one would see in training evaluation. Cook and Campbell (1979) discuss a number of possible threats to internal validity. Also, it should be pointed out that although our discussion will be largely in terms of threats taken singularly, there is a possibility that multiple threats to internal validity can operate in a cumulative or interactive fashion in a single research study. These threats can lead to either falsely assuming that training did or did not cause criteria score differences. Keeping this in mind, the following definitions of specific threats are offered:

*History* is when an observed criteria score might be due to an event other than the training program which takes place between the pretest and posttest. For example, a new management team is brought into the company in the interim between the pretest and the posttest.

*Maturation* is when a criterion score might be due to the trainee learning new skills or behaviors between the pretest and posttest simply as a result of greater tenure or experience on the job.

*Testing* is when an effect might be due to the number of times particular responses are measured. Familiarity with a test can sometimes enhance performance because answers are remembered between testing sessions.

*Instrumentation* is a threat that is due to a change in the measuring instrument between pretest and posttest. For example, one would expect improvement in test scores if the pretest required sentence completion (recall), while the post training test was multiple choice (recognition).

*Selection* is when an effect may be due to a difference between the kinds of people or their skills/abilities in the experimental group as opposed to the control group. Selection is always involved in research where the experimental and the control group are not equivalent. For example, administering training only to those individuals most in need of training.

*Mortality* is when an effect may be due to the different kinds of persons who dropped out of one group during the course of an experiment. The groups will end up significantly different, either from each other, or from the pretest group, or both, because persons dropped out of either the experimental or the control group in a systematic way.

*Statistical regression* occurs when subjects are selected on the basis of their scoring extremely high or extremely low on the pretest compared to others. Posttest scores would be expected to be less extreme not just because of training, but because of a degree of unreliability in the pretest measure, scores can only vary in one direction, toward the center. This "change" is due to the regression of scores to the mean of the overall population.

*Interactions with selection* occurs when any of the other threats interacts with selection effects. For example, if training is purposely conducted on the youngest, least-tenured employees, then change is likely to be observed if for no other reason then the selection of these less experienced performers, a selection-maturation effect.

As noted by Cook and Campbell (1979), randomly assigning subjects to both training and control groups will generally safeguard against the above threats to internal validity. However, there are a number of threats which can threaten the conclusive determination of the effectiveness of a training program regardless of randomization.

*Diffusion of treatment* is when the experimental and control groups can communicate with each other and individuals in the training group give the training content to those in the control group. The experiment may, therefore, become invalid because there are no differences between the experimental and control groups. This occurs commonly in training research because training is usually a valued commodity which the control group subjects would like to learn. Diffusion of treatment can be eliminated by keeping the control group and the experimental groups separated either spatially or temporally.

*Compensatory equalization of treatment* occurs when administrators or managers try to compensate those not undergoing training. For example, those not yet participating in training could be rated higher in their performance appraisal because they feel the comparison between those in each group is no longer fair.

*Compensatory rivalry*, sometimes referred to as the "John Henry Effect," occurs when members of the control group become motivated to compete out of feelings of being the underdog.

*Resentful demoralization of respondents receiving less desirable treatments* is the opposite of compensatory rivalry. Rather than being motivated to work harder, the nontreatment control group members become demoralized. Thus differences in groups' posttest measures occur not because training improved performance, but because lack of training caused less motivation to perform.

*Local history* occurs if a unique event is not shared by both training and control groups. For example, if members of one group were told that a reduction in workforce would occur and it would not effect members of the other group. Local history effects could also be considered as a selection-history interaction effect.

In the simplest form, assigning individuals to conditions on a random or chance basis means that the idiosyncrasies of persons assigned to one group will, on the average, be counterbalanced by individuals with comparable but not necessarily identical idiosyncrasies in the other group (Cook and Campbell, 1979). Given that each group is large enough, the average scores on a pretest should be the same for both the experimental and control group. The equivalence achieved by random assignment is a matter of probability; it is not inevitable. Consequently, groups in an experiment should remain large and, where possible, pretests should be used to actually measure comparability of groups.

## External Validity

As noted earlier, external validity has to do with whether the effect of training found in a particular sample can be generalized to others in the relevant population. Cook and Campbell describe several threats to external validity.

*Interaction of selection and treatment* is a situation where only a narrow class of individuals is selected for the study, for example restricting participation in an assertiveness training program to women only. Consequently, the results of the study cannot be generalized beyond the group used to establish the initial relationship. One way to deal with this threat is to make involvement in the experiment as convenient as possible so that a wider variety of possible trainees participates in the study.

*Interaction of setting and treatment* occurs when the treatment is tested in only one particular type of setting. In other words, a program effective in corporate offices may not generalize to a factory training program. The solution here is to vary settings across several studies when evaluating each training technique or program.

*Interaction of history and treatment* is when some unique event happens at the same time as the training. For example, a program that takes place on a very special day, such as when bonuses are announced, could result in inflated trainee reactions, and the researcher is left wondering whether the training program would in fact obtain the same results at another time. The solution is to try to avoid holding training programs at these unique or special times.

*Interaction of treatment and treatment* is when two treatments are implemented simultaneously, making generalizations about one treatment, without the other, questionable. Such a situation could arise if a behavior modeling training was implemented at the same time as a management by objectives (MBO) program was instituted for members of the training group. Later changes in job performance measures could be attributed to one or the other or both programs.

The last threat to external validity is *pretest sensitization*. In this threat, the pretest and the training program combine to become the actual treatment that the trainees are receiving. An example is a training program designed to teach mathematics skills. Most people have learned mathematics skills in high school, but probably have forgotten many of them. The pretest would help them remember many of those basic skills and, therefore, their performance in the training program would be enhanced. Consequently, the pretest becomes part of the actual training intervention and the training program would not be as effective in another situation without the pretest. This threat occurs in situations with learning criteria, where the pretest may enhance performance in the training program. The only sure ways to rule out this threat to external validity is to use an unobtrusive pretest or collect criterion data that would not be susceptible to this threat. An example would be behavior change criteria.

## More Experimental Designs

Given what we now know about analyzing experimental designs, it is easy to eliminate the preexperimental research designs: i.e. the case study, the pretest/posttest design, and the pretest/posttest control group without randomization design. The latter is diagramed below:*

Pretest/posttest with control but without randomization design

$$O_1 \quad X \quad O_2$$
$$O_1 \qquad O_2$$

The case study design does not rule out any threats to internal or external validity. The pretest/posttest design rules out selection and mortality, but none of the other threats to internal or external validity. The pretest/posttest control group without randomization design rules out several threats to internal validity (those not involving *selection*) and some threats to external validity.

There are two designs which permit a rigorous evaluation of training. They are the pretest/posttest design with control group and random selection, and the after-only design with control group and randomization. These are considered true experimental designs. These two designs are shown below:

Pretest/posttest with control and randomization

$$R \, O_1 \quad X \quad O_2$$
$$R \, O_1 \qquad O_2$$

After test only with control and randomization

$$R \quad X \quad O_1$$
$$R \qquad O_1$$

Unfortunately, for training evaluation, randomization is rarely possible. Typically, training is conducted with intact groups, all supervisors at a particular plant or all managers in a particular office. Even if you did assign people truly randomly (by flipping a coin or using a "random numbers" table), people will get sick or go on vacation and other people will be assigned

---

* X = intervention (training program),
  O = observation/measurement, numbers represent different times,
  R = randomized assignment, throughout.

**Figure 12.7**   Using Several Groups to Establish Experimental Conditions

*Training*
*Groups*

1                              R $O_1$ X $O_2$

2                              R            $O_1$ X $O_2$

*Weeks*                        1   2   3   4   5

to take their place in the training program. This destroys the effects of random assignment. Random assignment is fairly easy, however, where you have more trainees than you have training slots in a program because then you can randomly assign part of your trainees to the first training program and part of them to the second program and use these people in a sequential manner for your experimental and control group. This design shown in Figure 12.7 and was used by Latham and Saari (1979) very effectively.

In the pretest/posttest control group design, individuals are randomly assigned to both groups. This random assignment ensures that an increase in performance in an experimental group relative to the control group cannot be attributed to the fact that the experimental group was more intelligent, experienced, motivated, etc. The pretest/posttest control group design controls for all threats to internal validity except for diffusion of treatment. This can be taken care of simply by keeping the experimental and control groups separated either temporally or spatially.

In the after-only control group design, individuals are again randomly assigned to either the training group or the control group. No measures are necessary prior to training because random assignment *and large cell sizes* insure that the two groups can be considered similar. One can also use matching, where pairs of workers who are found alike on variables such as age, sex, experience, prior training, ability, etc. are matched and then assigned as pairs to the control and experimental group. One member of each pair is randomly assigned to the training group while the other is assigned to the control group. This design is particularly useful when the time required to collect pretest measures is not available or it is believed that the pretesting of trainees may in some way cause a testing/training interaction (pretest sensitization) and severely threaten external validity. This design controls for all threats to internal validity.

The two designs described above are very useful and not too difficult to use. There is one other true experimental design proposed by Solomon (1949), which is shown below:

$$\begin{array}{lll} R\ O_1 & X_1 & O_2 \\ R\ O_1 & & O_2 \\ R & X_2 & O_2 \\ R & & O_2 \end{array}$$

The Solomon Four Square Design probably represents the ultimate in experimental control for training research. Unfortunately, it has some very practical limitations. Only one-fourth of the appropriate group can be trained in the evaluation period and the target group must be large enough to divide into four large subgroups. Also, you must be able to randomly assign to four different groups and one group must receive "placebo" training. This design is very impractical to implement and, consequently, is rarely used. However, it does eliminate virtually all threats to internal and external validity. If a trainer is interested in it, the trainer should review Solomon (1949) or Cook and Campbell (1979).

There are other alternative research designs available. These research designs are incomplete and not considered true experimental designs, unlike those previously discussed. Consequently, they are called quasi-experimental designs. They are also reviewed in Cook and Campbell (1979). There are many quasi-experimental designs but only three designs will be covered here because they are simple and can be often used without significant expertise.

The first, called the Time Series Design, is diagramed below:

$$O_1 \quad O_2 \quad O_3 \quad O_4 \quad X \quad O_5 \quad O_6 \quad O_7 \quad O_8$$

In this design, a series of measures is taken prior and subsequent to training. The logic behind this training evaluation design is that if a performance was *consistently* hovering at a given level before training was introduced and performance suddenly increased and remained *consistently* high following training, then it can be concluded that the training program brought about the increase in performance. An important feature of this design is that there must be a large number of pretest data points covering a sufficiently extended period of time so that all possible patterns or variations of behavior can be measured. One difficult element about this kind of training design is that one must have a criterion that can be measured sequentially before and after training without affecting training or causing the scores to increase. For example, it would be inappropriate to use a paper and pencil test since the scores would increase simply by the experience of the trainees completing the test time and time again. On the other hand, measuring attendance could be possible within a time series design. A major drawback to the design is the chance that some unique (history) event will occur at the same time the training is initiated that would cause the later increase in performance.

Wexley and Latham (1981) give an example of history affecting a time series design. Five monthly measures of production were taken on several logging operations. Loggers were then given training in goal setting and five more monthly production measures were taken after training. The results indicated absolutely no change in production across the ten months. It could be concluded that training neither helped nor hurt production. However, there was heavy rainfall in the five months after training. It may have been that without goal setting training, performance would have drastically decreased because of the heavy rainfall. The point is that we do not know the answer because there was no control group against which to compare and rule out the threat of history.

The time series design can be vastly improved by adding a control group, referred to as a multiple time series design. This design is shown below:

$$O_1 \quad O_2 \quad O_3 \quad O_4 \quad X \quad O_5 \quad O_6 \quad O_7 \quad O_8$$
$$O_1 \quad O_2 \quad O_3 \quad O_4 \quad \phantom{X} \quad O_5 \quad O_6 \quad O_7 \quad O_8$$

The multiple time series design rules out all threats to internal validity regardless of whether or not subjects are randomly assigned to condition. Given the example from Wexley and Latham mentioned above, a multiple time series design would allow one to compare the premeasures of control group and the experimental group to determine the effect of rain on performance and then compare the two groups' after measures to determine if the experimental group was significantly higher. With this design, one could determine if the training maintained production by counteracting the negative effects of heavy rainfall.

The third design is called a multiple baseline design (Komaki, 1977; see also Wexley and Latham, 1981). This design does not require having more than one group; rather, comparisons are made within individuals or groups of individuals. Each person or group serves as his or her own control. The second group is still the control group for the first group. Therefore, you do not need to have a separate control group to infer cause and effect relationships between training and the criteria measure. The design is basically one where baseline data are taken over a period of time and then the training is introduced with one behavior or with one group of people. After some predetermined number of training sessions, the treatment is then introduced with a second behavior or group of people. Again, following an observed change, training is introduced with the next behavior or the next group of people, and so on until the training has been introduced with all the behaviors or groups.

To evaluate the effect of the training, comparisons are made between the baseline and intervention data to determine whether the effects of training are replicated at different times. If performance improves after but not before the training phase and this happens each time the training is introduced in a staggered fashion, then we can conclude that the training is responsible for the positive results. This design controls all threats to internal validity, but it is rather difficult to use.

## A Sample Behavior Modeling Evaluation

Latham and Saari (1979) present probably the best example of an evaluation of a behavior modeling training program. This study was done to examine the effects of a behavior modeling program to increase the effectiveness of first-line supervisors in dealing with their employees. The program contained nine training modules. One hundred first-line supervisors in an organization were to be trained; but since it was impossible to train all 100 individuals simultaneously, the researchers randomly selected 40 supervisors and then randomly assigned them to either the training or control group. The people assigned to these two groups did not know that they had been labeled a control group or an experimental group, and they assumed that, for logistical reasons, they were either among the first or the last to receive the training. The training group was divided into two groups of ten to facilitate the behavior modeling instruction. Each group met for two hours each week for nine weeks to cover the nine modules. Each training session followed a typical behavior modeling format. The numbers of people in this study allowed a design where the control group received the training, but after the experimental group, much like that described in Figure 12.7.

The dependent variables included trainee reaction, learning, behavior change, and performance measures. Trainee reactions to the program were collected immediately and again eight months after the training. Learning measures were collected six months after training. The behavior criteria were collected three months after training and the performance appraisal data were collected one year after the training.

The reaction data were from five questions collected on a questionnaire immediately after the final training session and again eight months later. The learning measures consisted of a test containing 85 situational questions. The questions were developed from critical incidents obtained in job analysis. They were turned into questions by asking, "How would you handle the following situation?" The test was completed on the job under uniform conditions. Code numbers were used for identification purposes so that superintendents who scored each test could not be biased by knowledge of a respondent's identity or whether the person had received the training or not.

The behavioral measures consisted of tape-recorded role plays of supervisors resolving supervisor–employee problems. For these role plays, brief scripts were developed about each of the nine training topics. The scripts were randomly assigned to the supervisors and none of the situations had been previously described during training nor were they the same as those depicted on the modeling displays. The individuals who played the role of the employee in the role play were people who had been through the training program; however, they did not role play with supervisors from their own training class. This was done to prevent them from knowing whether the person in the role as supervisor was from another training class or had yet to receive training. The pairing of role players was randomly determined. These tape-recordings were evaluated by 15 superintendents who worked in groups of three. Superintendents were blind as to the identity of the supervisor and whether the supervisor had received training or not. Superintendents from one area of the company evaluated the tape-recordings of supervisors from another area of the company. The rating scale consisted of the learning points taught in the class, each with a five point scale, on which the superintendents rated the quality of the performance. Superintendents evaluated the supervisors on behavioral observation scales one month before and one year after the training for the behavioral criteria. This was part of a normal performance evaluation. Because the superintendents knew who had received training when completing this measure, they received intensive instruction on minimizing rating errors when appraising the study participants.

The results of this study are reviewed in Chapter 1. They show that the behavior modeling was very successful. One year after the training had taken place, the 20 foremen in the control group received the same training as the original training group and in the later tests performed as well as the original training group.

## Some Hints About Evaluating Behavior Modeling

We have looked at experimental design issues briefly. You have some knowledge about judging the use of different criteria and different research designs for use in training evaluation; however, a coverage like this cannot truly teach all of the techniques of experimental design. The reader is encouraged to examine Cook and Campbell (1979) or other sources for further discussion about research design. Evaluating training is not an easy undertaking, but it should almost always be done to improve training, to insure that it is, in fact, affecting trainees positively, and to help justify the use of training or the particular training program. Some experimental designs are very difficult to use, like the pretest/posttest control design with random selection. Others such as the posttest-only are easier. The time series is easy in some situations. If you cannot randomize or you have small groups of people, but you do have a criterion measure where the scores will not increase as people repeatedly are measured on it, then the time series is an excellent procedure. It gives nearly unequivocal support to any inference one would make about a causal relationship between training and the criteria measure. This is what evaluation is all about. If you can't clearly say that the training caused (or did not cause) a change in learning, a behavior, or some organizational result through a proper research design, then the evaluation was not worth the effort.

Some of the suggestions that we can give about evaluating behavior modeling have already been seen in one form or another in this book. For instance, in the Latham and Saari article (1979), it can be seen that the researchers had more people to be trained than they could put in any one training program so they staggered the training groups temporally such that a future training group became the control group for the present experimental group. Some hints about using performance appraisal instruments as criteria and data can be seen in Latham and Saari (1979); however, one should insure the accuracy of any performance appraisal system before that data is used as training criteria. Obviously, one of the ways to do that for behavior modeling is to insure that any performance data is as behaviorally based as possible. If it is not, the results of your evaluation study may be suspect.

One of the easiest ways to collect behavior change and performance data in a behavior modeling program is to call the trainees back for what they think is a "booster session." One or two months after training, trainees return to practice one or two role plays with the trainer. This could even be done in half an hour in most situations. Those role plays are taped and the tape is shown back to the trainee; *and with the permission of the trainee*, the tape is saved and later rated by trained raters. The rating form is nothing more than the key behaviors put into a rating scale format (see Figure 12.5). Performance ratings of this group are compared to that of an untrained control group. Where a true control group is not available, role plays right at the beginning of a later training group could be used, again with the consent of the participants. Later trainees are thus the control group for a previous training group. The booster session is also useful when you are trying to compare two different behavior modeling training programs where you have changed one element within one training program (which is then considered the experimental program). The old method is the control group. You then can compare two different ways of doing the training.

There is a quantum leap when moving from an attempt to measure behavior to trying to measure organizational results. It is much easier to measure behavior change at the end of the training, or one month later, than it is to measure any organizational result. By measuring organization results, you are attempting to prove that: 1) the behavior modeling program was effective in changing behavior, 2) that changed behavior did, in fact, transfer onto the job or into the transfer context, 3) that behavior did affect an organizational result criteria, and 4) that no other variable affected the organizational result criteria. That is very tough to prove, even with proper experimental design. It is very difficult to rule out all of the alternative explanations for any relationship between training and a criterion variable such that you can say that training has caused a change in the organizational result criteria. Behavior change criteria are easier; they show that the trainee is effective in changing behavior. However, organizational result criteria will indicate the connection between the training and solving operating problems in the organization. Stated another way, consequently, behavioral change criteria are probably sufficient if you want to show that training works, but if you need to justify the use of behavior modeling or any other kind of training in an organization, organizational result criteria are in order and evaluation will become significantly more difficult.

There is often a sizable gap between the practice of training evaluation and the science of training evaluation. Organizational constraints often preclude the use of the most sophisticated designs, but this does not mean that trainers should simply skip evaluation; it simply means that less than ideal designs will have to be used. This is better than not doing evaluation at all or just using trainee reaction to justify programs. The authors feel strongly that training evaluation should be done, and it should be done in at least a minimally acceptable empirical method.

## Estimating Costs of Behavior Modeling Programs

Cascio (1982) describes methods of trying to determine the financial impact of human resource development programs. Once one has developed an experimental design for evaluating a training program to see if it does in fact change some criterion measure in a positive way, what is then left is to express this consequence in economic or financial terms.

One consideration is determining meeting costs, especially off-site meetings, if these are necessary. Methods of calculating these costs can be found in both Cascio (1982) and McKeon (1981). Figure 12.8 is an example of a form which can be used to calculate the cost of off-site versus on-site training programs. This form can also be used to determine how time should be spent during the training days and whether increasing or shortening training hours will, in fact, change the dollars paid out for the training program.

Trainers can, by the use of cost-effectiveness models, do what other areas of businesses have done for years: that is, justify the allocation of organizational resources on the basis of empirical evidence as to its actual impact rather than on the basis of the beliefs or opinions of individuals. Unfortunately, most training programs are based on opinions or beliefs rather than empirical data showing the value of the program in dollars or in solving operating problems. We encourage all trainers to investigate evaluation further and develop evaluation systems when behavior modeling training is used.

**Figure 12.8**   Cost Breakdown for an Off-Site Management Meeting

| | Total Costs (In dollars) | Cost Per Participant Per Day (In dollars) |
|---|---|---|
| A. Development of programs (figured on an annual basis) | | |
| 1. Training department overhead | | |
| 2. Training staff salaries | | |
| 3. Use of outside consultants | | |
| 4. Equipment and materials for meeting (films, supplies, workbooks) | 100,000 | 100.00[1] |
| B. Participant cost (figured on an annual basis) | | |
| 1. Salaries and benefits of participants (figured for average participant)   $20,000 | | |
| 2. Capital investment in participants (based on an average of various industries from *Fortune* magazine)   $25,000 | 45,000 | 190.68[2] |
| C. Delivery of one meeting of 20 persons | | |
| 1. Facility costs | | |
| a. Sleeping rooms   1,000 | | |
| b. Three meals daily   800 | | |
| c. Coffee breaks   60 | | |
| d. Misc. tips, telephone   200 | | |
| e. Reception   200 | 2,260 | 56.50[3] |
| 2. Meeting charges | | |
| a. Room rental | | |
| b. A/V rental | | |
| c. Secretarial services | | |
| 3. Transportation to the meeting | 2,500 | 62.50[4] |

Summary: Total Per Day Per Person Cost

| | | |
|---|---|---|
| A. Development of programs | $ 100 | |
| B. Participant cost | 190 | |
| C. Delivery of one meeting (hotel and transportation) | 119 | |
| | Total $ 409 | |

*Note*: Meeting duration: two full days. Number of attendees: 20 people. These costs do not reflect a figure for the productive time lost of the people in the program. If that cost were added—and it would be realistic to do so—the above cost would increase dramatically.

[1]To determine per day cost, divide $100,000 by number of meeting days held per year (10). Then divide answer ($10,000) by total number of management people (100) attending all programs = $100 per day of a meeting.

[2]To determine per day cost, divide total of $45,000 by 236 (average number of working days in a year) = $190.68 per day of work year.

[3]To determine per day, per person cost, divide group total ($2,260) by number of participants (20) and then divide resulting figure ($113) by number of meeting days (2) = $56.50 per day.

[4]To determine per day, per person cost, divide group total ($2,500) by number of people and then divide resulting figure ($125) by number of meeting days (2) = $62.50 per day.

*Source*: Adapted from W. J. McKeon. "How to Determine Off-Site Meeting Costs." *Training and Development Journal*, May 1981, p. 117, by Cascio, W. F. (1982). Used by permission.

# —13—

# Final Thoughts on Behavior
# Modeling Training

There is nothing particularly unique about the "monkey see, monkey do" principle of learning; yet, that is what behavior modeling is basically all about. We know that, at minimum, people must practice and receive feedback (about that practice) in order to learn. We also know that if they are shown an example before the practice, the learning becomes more efficient and moves away from the trial and error variety of learning. Yet, at the same time, behavior modeling is much more than a simple principle of watch an example, practice an example, and receive feedback about that practice. We have a simple concept with a systematic training technique built around it. There are many variables involved in designing a behavior modeling program and enhancing all of the elements which, in the end, create learning and/or behavior change. Yet, behavior modeling is easy to do.

We know that behavior modeling is an effective training program for changing manual and social skills. We would expect that the future of behavior modeling will be one where we see it being used more often. We may see the behavior modeling technique described by different terms, but the principle of showing an example, practicing, and getting feedback is consistent. If it is put into a formal workshop, we will see more than one trainer, video tape used for feedback, and all of the other aspects that add to the cost and effectiveness of behavior modeling. Much of what we see will be determined by the degree to which trainers wish to adhere to their understanding of the technique in their training efforts. With this book, there is understanding of the process as far as we know it. More research will add to that understanding.

As we see behavior modeling used extensively in the future, several things will accompany that use. Obviously, other training programs will not be used as much, particularly lecture and other types of workshops which are designed to change behavior. Generalized human relations training will be relied upon to a lesser extent if trainers attempt to directly change behavior. We may see an increasing sophistication in equipment such as large-screen televisions in the training room. (Let us remember that video tape is there only for feedback. It is not some new method within itself; it simply gives the trainee better feedback about behavioral practice than any other method, including anything the trainer can say.)

It is hoped that what we know about behavior modeling training will also filter down to on-the-job training. On-the-job training, as done by supervisors, should incorporate the principles of behavior modeling. Figure 13.1 shows key behaviors for doing on-the-job training. They are an adaptation of key behaviors that were developed during World War II by the Training Within Industry group; these key behaviors are nothing more than behavior modeling without video tape, workshops, several trainers, rooms, coffee, etc. There is no reason why we cannot use the principles of social learning in a one-to-one training situation on the job.

It is hoped that the future of behavior modeling will move in this direction—closer to the job (or the transfer context). Appendix E is a set of instructions for an exercise to teach individuals the on-the-job training key behaviors (described above). If trainers use behavior modeling more often, we should see more empirical evaluation of training, using behavior-change and organizational result criteria. Behavior modeling is not that difficult to evaluate. In 1945, Training Within Industry, a group formed to assist industrial training efforts during World War II, said that there were two reasons for the failure of training: 1) There is a history of training departments promoting generalized training programs, unrelated to the problems of the organization, and management fails to see training as an effective tool. 2) Training staffs are preoccupied with means—how the program is to operate and the methodology to be used—rather than with results, so management fails to see a relationship between training and its ability to solve operating problems

**Figure 13.1**   On-the-Job Training Key Behaviors

1. In writing, outline each step of the task to be taught.
2. Explain the objective of the task to the employee.
3. Show the employee how to do it.
4. Explain key points (write them down for the employee if they are complex).
5. Let the employee watch you do it again.
6. Let the employee do the simple parts of the task.
7. Help the employee do the whole task (watch and give feedback).
8. Let the employee do the whole task.
9. Praise the employee for doing the task correctly.

(Training Within Industry Report, 1945). Since behavior modeling is focused on learning behavior, it is easy to evaluate by measuring resultant behavior change. It may also be seen as being directly applicable to daily operating programs since the participants practice using the key behaviors to solve their own day-to-day problems. Evaluation of behavior modeling is not an overwhelming task, and it can and should be done. Finally, one thing the authors would like to see in the future of behavior modeling is more trainers attempting the technology by themselves, creating their own programs.

# Appendixes

# —A—

# Counseling/Clinical Evaluation Research

## Counseling Research

Besides those evaluation studies done in the industrial context, there are numerous studies that have examined the efficacy of behavior modeling techniques in counseling situations. Behavior modeling has been examined in programs designed to teach counseling strategies, interviewing skills, and decision making strategies to graduate students. It has also been used to change counseling client behavior. The use of behavior modeling techniques in counseling is reviewed by Ivey (1971) and Ivey and Authier (1978). The name typically used in the counseling area to describe these techniques is microtraining or micro-counseling.

The applications of behavior modeling in the industrial and counseling contexts are essentially the same. Both are used to teach manual and social skills to adult trainees. The counseling studies to be discussed in this appendix uniformly applied all of the components of the behavior modeling technique as described in Chapter 1. Furthermore, studies looking at the training of counseling skills can include all the levels of training evaluation: trainee reaction, learning, behavior change, and transfer criteria. It is possible to use an organizational result criterion in counseling contexts if the goal of the skills being learned is to improve the social functioning of the client being counseled. Therefore, these studies add to our knowledge about behavior modeling.

## *Training Counseling Students*

There are more studies examining the effectiveness of behavior modeling in the counseling literature than in the industrial literature. The following studies compared behavior modeling to no training. The early studies of Ivey

(Ivey and Authier, 1978) demonstrated that micro-counseling can be a powerful and efficient technique for teaching counseling interview skills (attending behavior in students was significantly improved in these studies). The studies were not true experimental designs, however, and could be questioned because only one of the studies employed a control group.

In a true experimental design, Kerrebrock (1971) trained high school academic advisors in attending behavior, reflection of feelings, and expression of feeling skills. In later counseling sessions, the trained group used the latter two skills significantly more frequently than did the untrained control group. Haase and DiMattia (1970) effectively taught paraprofessionals attending behavior and expression of feeling skills. In a one-year follow-up (Haase, DiMattia, and Guttman, 1972) with the same subjects, it was found that the trained subjects still used the behaviors significantly more than the untrained control group. Ronnestadt (1977) looked at the effect of the micro-counseling technique on increasing the communication of empathic understanding of beginning counseling students. He found that the training significantly increased these skills more than training programs which included feedback only and modeling only. Futhermore, Erdman (1974) has looked at the effect of using behavior modeling to train counseling skills and found positive results.

The following studies have examined behavior modeling in comparison to other training techniques. Moreland, Ivey, and Phillips (1973) compared 12 subjects who received traditional interview training with 12 subjects receiving behavior modeling. On several of the behaviors of the training, the micro-counseling subjects were rated significantly greater in improvement than the comparison subjects. In two studies (Toukmanian and Rennie, 1975; Gustafson, 1975), a training program, called Human Relations Training, was compared to micro-counseling. The HRT subjects received training through lecture and reading in seven core counselor skills. Both of these studies showed the superior efficacy of micro-counseling using dependent variables that related to both HRT training and the micro-counseling training.

In a significant study, Wallace et al. (1975) examined the effectiveness of micro-counseling techniques to teach decision making in counseling situations in comparison with traditional lecture method and modeling only. Fifty-four graduate students were assigned to a lecture condition, a modeling condition, and a micro-counseling condition. In the micro-counseling condition, subjects were exposed to written descriptions of decision-making counseling and a twenty-minute modeling tape depicting the counseling behaviors. Each subject had the opportunity to counsel a roleplaying client to at least one stage of the decision-making process. Each subject received performance feedback (positive reinforcement) from the group leader whenever the counseling behavior had approximated the standard. Wallace et al. (1975) found that the traditional approach to teaching decision making (lecture, assigned readings), even when fortified with a filmed instructional model, was apparently inferior to the teaching method incorporating micro-training. The experimental teaching method employed in the study differed somewhat from the micro-counseling technique in that the students each practiced only part rather than the complete decision-making model. It was, however, a true experimental design.

Dunn (1975) compared a behavior modeling program with an empathy group training program, self-instruction training, a placebo training group, and a no-treatment control group. Each trainee underwent three hours of training and conducted four ten-minute taped interviews. Tapes of the interviews were rated by three trained judges. The behavior modeling group and the empathy trainees evidenced the most rapid rate and the highest level of skill acquisition. Angelone (1983) also found behavior modeling to be an effective technique to increase empathy.

Evans, Uhlemann, and Hearn (1975) compared micro-counseling with sensitivity training and a no-treatment control group using perspective "hotline" workers. Students in the micro-counseling program used more of the trained responses and were rated as more empathetic than the other training groups. This was a well-controlled true experimental design. Hearn (1976) compared the efficacy of micro-counseling, sensitivity training, and programmed learning for teaching counseling skills. Again the micro-counseling condition proved more effective on several measures. This was also a true experimental design.

Furthermore, micro-counseling has been found to be effective in teaching empathic communication (Stone and Vance, 1976), skills associated with the termination of a counseling contract (Leonard, 1977), general counseling skills (Teevan and Gabel, 1978; Fyffe and Oei, 1979; O'Toole, 1979), reducing reticence of college students for participation in classroom discussions (Phelps, 1979), reducing the anxiety of counselors in training (Murphy, 1979), and the acquisition of group leadership skills (Charonko, 1979). Overall, there are ample studies to show that behavior modeling is an extremely effective training technique for teaching counseling students the complex social skills required in the counseling interview.

### Studies of Counseling Client Outcome

The first published data relating to the efficacy of behavior modeling to affect client behavior was conducted by Gluckstern (1972). She found that clients of micro-training workshop participants moved from talking about external topics into talking about themselves faster than with untrained counselors. This study did not contain a formal control group, however. More recently, Hearn (1976) obtained results similar to those of Gluckstern (1972) and included a control group in her study.

Goldstein (1973) developed Structured Learning Therapy for teaching counseling clients. Structured Learning Therapy is simply the behavior modeling (or micro-training) technique applied to teaching new skills to counseling clients and includes modeling, role play, social reinforcement, and transfer of training. In fact, Goldstein was one of the originators of what is called behavior modeling training in the industrial context. Structured Learning Therapy has been found to be an effective technique for patients who were recalcitrant. Gutride, Goldstein, and Hunter (1972) studied 106 psychiatric patients; these subjects were randomly assigned to Structured Learning Therapy, social companionship therapy, or a no-treatment control group. The goal of the training was to increase meal-time social behavior. Results show that Structured Learning Therapy patients improved more than the social comparison or no-training groups. Structured Learning Therapy has also been found to be a reliable treatment for asocial psychiatric patients (Gutride, Goldstein, and Hunter, 1973), for increasing accurate expression of feelings (Haase et al., 1971), and for increasing generalization of skills from training sessions to later behavior (Donk, 1972; Orlando, 1974; and Petrick, 1976).

Micro-training techniques have also been shown to increase assertive behavior (McFall and Twentyman, 1973) and prosocial behavior in institutionalized children (Zashin, 1981) and goal setting behavior in counseling clients (Eoyang, 1979). Overall, there is rather impressive evidence that behavior modeling is an effective technique for teaching counseling skills to students and for changing client behavior. Most of the studies discussed here used sound experimental designs such that internal validity cannot be questioned.

Fox (1983) has extensively reviewed behavior modeling evaluation reports. He lists the following articles which have not been previously mentioned in this text. In all of the studies cited below, statistically significant gains were produced by the basic Behavior Modeling approach, for trainees in comparison with controls and/or pre-training trainee behavior scores. Though, for the most part, these studies are well-designed, internal validity problems are present, and most do not deal effectively with testing for the transferability of results to non-training settings.

## Assertiveness Training Studies

### With College Students

Significant gains were associated with the use of the basic model of Behavior Modeling in the studies reported by Boland (1974), Bouffard (1973), Buttrum (1974), Manderino (1974), McFall and Galbraith (two studies) (1977), Mehnert (1974), Paulson (1974), and Thorpe (1973).

## With Psychiatric Patients

Argyle, Trower, and Bryant (1974), Doty (1975), Goldsmith and Mc-Fall (1975), Hersen, Eisler, and Miller (1974), Hersen et al. (1974), Lomont et al. (1962), and Loogin and Rooney (1973).

## With Children and Young People

Morrill (1973), Parr (1974), Schinke and Rose (1976), and Wolfe and Fodor (1977).

## Job Interviewing Training Studies

### With Youth and Young Adults

Braukmann et al. (predelinquents) (1974), Heimberg et al. (disadvantaged youth) (1982), and Schinke et al. (teenage mothers) (1978).

### Subjects with Psychiatric Histories

Hollandsworth, Glazeski, and Dressel (1978), Kelly et al. (1979), and Twentyman, Jensen, and Kloss (complex offenders) (1978).

## Other Social Skills

Cobb (cooperative behavior in young boys) (1974), Holstein (1974) and Twentyman and Martin (1978) (modification of maladaptive mother–child interaction), La Greca and Santogrossi (social skills for elementary school children) (1980), Melnick (modification of minimal dating behavior of male undergraduates) (1973), Sarason and Ganzer (rehabilitation of juvenile delinquents) (1973), Tofte-Tipps, Mendonca, and Peach (social skills for two developmentally handicapped, socially isolated children) (1982), and Werner et al. (preparation of juvenile delinquents for encounters with police officers) (1975).

# —B—

# The Concepts of Reinforcement

The principles of reinforcement describe the relationship between behavior and environmental events that influence behavior. Developing effective reinforcement programs depends upon understanding the types of consequences that influence behavior and how they influence behavior. This section is designed to produce that understanding.

## Reinforcement and Punishment

Positive and negative reinforcement constitute two kinds of events which can be used to increase the frequency of a response (Skinner, 1953). Punishment is an event that decreases behaviors preceding the punishment. Positive reinforcement refers to an increase in the frequency of a behavior when it is followed by a favorable event. Positive or favorable events are frequently referred to as rewards in everyday language. It is desirable, however, to distinguish the term "positive reinforcer" from "reward." A positive reinforcer is defined by its effect on behavior. If an event follows behavior and the frequency of the behavior increases, the event is a reinforcer. Conversely, any event which does not increase the behavior it follows is not a positive reinforcer. In contrast, rewards are defined merely as something given or received (in return for doing something) that is usually valued by the individual. But they do not necessarily increase the probability of the behavior they follow. Positive reinforcers include any events which, when presented, increase the frequency of the behavior they follow.

There are two categories of positive reinforcers: primary (or unconditioned) and secondary (or conditioned) reinforcers. Events which serve as primary reinforcers do not depend upon any training or previous experience to have acquired their reinforcing value, for example, food to a hungry person or water to a thirsty person. Conditioned reinforcers are not automatically reinforcing. Stimuli or events which once were neutral in value may require reinforcing properties as a result of being paired with events that are already reinforcing. Conditioned reinforcers include events such as praise, grades, money, the completion of a goal, etc.

Negative reinforcement refers to an increase in the frequency of a behavior by removing an aversive event immediately after the response is performed. Removal of the aversive event is contingent upon an avoidance or escape response. It is important to know that reinforcement (positive or negative) always refers to an increase in behavior. Examples of negative reinforcement are evident in everyday experience such as putting on a coat while standing outside on a cold day. Putting on a coat (the behavior) usually removes an aversive state (being cold). The probability of wearing a coat in cold weather is increased. Taking medicine to relieve a headache may be negatively reinforced by the elimination of pain, etc.

Punishment is the presentation of aversive events or removal of a positive event following a response. This decreases the frequency of that response. Punishment, as ordinarily defined, refers to a penalty imposed for performing a particular act. The definition used here includes an additional requirement: that the frequency of the response is decreased (Kazdin, 1980). Punishment does not necessarily entail pain or physical coercion. In addition, punishment does not mean retribution for misbehaving. Numerous examples of punishment pervade everyday life, such as being reprimanded or slapped after engaging in some behavior, being burned after touching a hot stove, or losing privileges after staying out late. Punishment and negative reinforcement are often confused, even though they are very different. The key difference is that reinforcement, whether negative or positive, always refers to procedures that increase the response; punishment always refers to procedures that decrease a response.

## Shaping

Frequently, the development of new behavior cannot be achieved by reinforcing the response when it occurs. In many situations, the response may never occur as you would like it. The desired behavior may be so complex that elements that make up the response are not in the repertoire of the individual. For example, developing the use of words requires the use of sounds, syllables, and their combinations. In shaping, the terminal behavior is achieved by reinforcing small steps or approximations towards the final response rather than reinforcing the final response itself (which is not yet evident). Responses are reinforced which either resemble the final response or which include components of that response.

Shaping requires reinforcing behaviors already in the repertoire of the individuals which resemble the terminal response. As the initial approximation is performed consistently, the criterion for reinforcement is altered slightly so that the response which is to be reinforced resembles the final goal more closely than the previous response. By reinforcement of responses which approach the terminal goal successively, the terminal response is finally developed.

## Chaining

A method similar to shaping is chaining. Most behaviors consist of a sequence of several responses; this is almost always the case in behavior modeling training. The component parts of a chain may represent individual responses already in the repertoire of the learner, or they may not. Yet, a chain represents a combination of responses ordered in a particular sequence. If the responses in a chain (or sequence) are not in the repertoire of the individual, modeling and/or reinforcement will have to be applied so that the person learns the individual responses. If the responses in the chain are in the repertoire of the person, successive reinforcement will have to be applied for subsections of that chain. As more and more individual responses are added to the chain, reinforcement is only given for the correct enactment of the chain. Through this process, the final sequence of behavior is obtained.

## Prompting

Developing new behavior is facilitated by using cues, instructions, gestures, directions, examples, and models to initiate a response. We have already discussed the use of models for the initiation of a response. However, events which help initiate a response are called prompts. Prompts precede a response. When a prompt results in a response being initiated, it is useful as an inclusion in training. The use of prompts increases the likelihood of responses. Mahoney (1971) used a variety of prompts to train normal and retarded children to walk to the lavatory as part of toilet training. For example, toys were placed near the entrance to the lavatory to increase the likelihood of the child approaching (visual prompts), the experimenter led the child by the hand (physical prompt), and instructions ("let's go potty") were used (verbal prompt) to initiate walking. The use of prompts in this study increased the likelihood of the response. For example, walking to the lavatory was more likely to occur when the experimenter actually guided the child than when the child was left to respond on his or her own. Whenever responses are being shaped, prompts may be used frequently to facilitate this process. This is also true in chaining. In behavior modeling training, we are provided with an excellent prompt, in that learning points are used to describe key behaviors presented in the modeling display. As described earlier, learning points are a written description of the key behaviors. These learning points or labels can also be used as prompts in giving feedback to trainees.

## Delay of Reinforcement

The effectiveness of reinforcement depends upon several factors. One of them is the delay between performance of a response and delivery of reinforcement. Responses which occur in close proximity to reinforcement are learned better than responses remote from reinforcement (Kimble, 1961; Skinner, 1953). Thus, a reinforcer should be delivered immediately after the occurrence of an accurate response to maximize the effect of reinforcement. It must be noted that the bulk of the laboratory research from which this finding stems was conducted with animal subjects. It is likely, however, that the finding still applies to humans. Reinforcement should occur as quickly as possible after the response so the desired response is reinforced, rather than other unintended behavior which occurred during the delay period. Delay of reinforcement may lead to strengthening of inappropriate or ineffective behaviors (which is not the intent of training). With adult human subjects, however, it is likely that cognitive processes take over and as long as one explains why the reinforcement is provided, the trainee makes the contingent connection between the response and the reinforcement. The immediate reinforcement is probably very important in the early stages of training when the target response is developing. After a response is performed consistently, the amount of time between the response and reinforcement can be increased, especially when cognitive explanation is provided. It is also desirable to change from an immediate to a delayed reinforcement (if possible) after the behavior is well developed so that the behavior is not dependent upon immediate consequences. In a great many situations in everyday life, reinforcement is not given immediately after behavior. For example, wages, grades, and fame fall long after responses are completed.

## Magnitude of Reinforcement

The amount of reinforcement delivered also determines the extent to which a response will be performed. Generally, the greater the amount of reinforcement delivered for a response, the more frequent will be the response in the future (Kimble, 1961). Although the magnitude of reinforcement is directly related to performance, there are limits to this relationship. An unlimited amount of reinforcement will not necessarily maintain a high rate of performance. A reinforcer such as food may lose its effect when given in excessive amounts. This is referred to as "satiation." The effect of magnitude of reinforcement is limited by the point at which the individual becomes satiated, and this is especially evident with primary reinforcers. There are differences in the effect of the magnitude of reinforcement on learning vs. performance. Magnitude of reinforcement does not have a great effect on learning, where it does on performance. In the laboratory, subjects appear to learn no more rapidly for large rewards than for small ones; however, once learning has taken place, performance will be more consistent if large rewards are provided (Kazdin, 1980).

## Quality or Type of Reinforcer

Quality of reinforcement is determined by the preference of the trainee. Reinforcers that are highly preferred by the trainee lead to greater performance. Obviously, there are certain reinforcers that are preferred by most people in training programs, such as praise from a person perceived to have high status. Also, reinforcement from other trainees can be highly reinforcing in behavior modeling training programs. This reinforcement should be encouraged. At one point in time, a reinforcer may be more effective in changing behavior than another because the trainee is satiated with one and deprived of another (Premack, 1965). Consequently, these questions should be attended to by the trainer on an individual basis, where possible.

## Schedule of Reinforcement

Schedule of reinforcement refers to the rule denoting how many responses or which specific responses will be reinforced. While reinforcing every correct response during training or acquisition is the most efficient way to initially obtain correct performance, partial reinforcement after acquisition is the most efficient means of obtaining that performance over any extended period of time. Reinforcers must always be administered in some schedule, however. In the simplest schedule, responses are reinforced each time they occur. This is a continuous schedule of reinforcement. On the other hand, reinforcement may be delivered after some number of responses rather than for all of them. This is referred to as an intermittent or variable schedule of reinforcement.

One common response which is continuously reinforced is putting coins into a soda or cigarette machine and pressing the appropriate lever. The product is almost always delivered. The only thing that keeps this from being continuous reinforcement is mechanical failure. An example of intermittent reinforcement is placing coins in a slot machine. One is not reinforced every time one puts a coin in the slot machine and pulls the handle down. Slot machines are on a variable ratio schedule of reinforcement. A ratio schedule of reinforcement is where reinforcement occurs after a given number of responses have been performed. Variable means that the number of responses between reinforcement varies. Intermittent reinforcement can be given on the basis of the amount of time that passes before the responses are reinforced or the number of responses. As mentioned earlier, in the beginning of a behavior change program, behavior should be reinforced continuously.

In practice, it is virtually impossible to survey behavior consistently to ensure that each performance is reinforced. On the job (or in the transfer context) the behavior is almost impossible to reinforce continuously. So, during training, as quickly as is possible, one should move trainees from a continuous schedule of reinforcement to an intermittent schedule of reinforcement. This should be accomplished not only in training but on the job. As soon as a person goes back to the transfer context or the job, the behavior should be reinforced as often as possible. Then this schedule should be stretched out and become intermittent for long-term maintenance of the behavior.

## Stimulus Generalization

Behavior occurs in specific situations. A response which is repeatedly reinforced in a particular situation is likely to be repeated only in that situation. Situations often share common properties, however, such as different brand soda machines which still operate in a similar manner for so many coins. If a response which is reinforced in one situation or setting also increases in other settings (even though it is not reinforced in these other settings), stimulus generalization has occurred. Stimulus generalization refers to the transfer of responses to situations other than those in which training takes place. Stimulus generalization is an important consideration in behavior modeling training. Typically, we are teaching skills in behavior modeling training which will be used across contexts or situations. Stimulus generalization can be increased by: 1) showing the key behaviors used in different situations in several modeling displays, and 2) in reinforcing the skills across different practice situations. Each of these should be done. Several modeled performances should be shown and training participants should be encouraged to practice the skills across different role play situations (different problems and/or people).

# —C—

# More Sets of Learning Points

**Figure C.1  Giving Instructions**

| STEPS | TRAINER NOTES |
|---|---|
| 1. Decide what needs to be done. | It might be a chore or a favor. |
| 2. Think about the different people who could do it and choose one. | |
| 3. Ask that person to do what you want done in specific terms. | Tell the person how to do it when the task is complex. |
| 4. Ask the other person if he or she understands what to do. | |
| 5. Change or repeat your instructions if you need to. | This step is optional. |

SUGGESTED CONTENT FOR MODELING DISPLAYS:

A. School or neighborhood: Main actor divides chores for decorating gym for school party.

B. Home: Main actor tells little sister how to put records away correctly.

C. Peer group: Main actor instructs friends on how to care for pets.

COMMENTS:

This skill refers to the enlistment of others to carry out a task and thus requires youngsters to think about division of responsibility.

*Source*: Goldstein, A.P. et al. (1980) *Skill-Streaming the Adolescent*. Champaign, IL: Research Press.

**Figure C.2  Helping Others**

| STEPS | TRAINER NOTES |
|---|---|
| 1. Decide if the other person might need and want your help. | Think about the needs of the other person; observe. |
| 2. Think of the ways you could be helpful. | You could be doing something, giving encouragement, or getting help from someone else. |
| 3. Ask the other person if he or she needs and wants your help. | Make the offer sincere, allowing the other to decline if he or she wishes. |
| 4. Help the other person. | |

SUGGESTED CONTENT FOR MODELING DISPLAYS:

A. School or neighborhood: Main actor offers to help teacher arrange chairs in classroom.
B. Home: Main actor offers to prepare dinner.
C. Peer group: Main actor offers to bring class assignments home for sick friend.

*Source*: Goldstein, A.P. et al. (1980) *Skill-Streaming the Adolescent*. Champaign, IL: Research Press.

**Figure C.3  Answering a Complaint**

| STEPS | TRAINER NOTES |
|---|---|
| 1. Listen to the complaint. | Listen openly. |
| 2. Ask the person to explain anything you don't understand. | |
| 3. Tell the person that you understand the complaint. | Rephrase; acknowledge the content and feeling. |
| 4. State your ideas about the complaint, accepting the blame if appropriate. | |
| 5. Suggest what each of you could do about the complaint. | You might compromise, defend your position, or apologize. |

SUGGESTED CONTENT FOR MODELING DISPLAYS:

A. School or neighborhood: Main actor responds to neighbor's complaint about noisy party.
B. Home: Main actor responds to parent's complaint about selection of friends.
C. Peer group: Main actor responds to friend's complaint about returning sporting equipment in poor condition.

*Source*: Goldstein, A.P. et al. (1980) *Skill-Streaming the Adolescent*. Champaign, IL: Research Press.

**Figure C.4   Getting Ready for a Difficult Conversation**

| STEPS | TRAINER NOTES |
|---|---|
| 1. Think about how you will feel during the conversation. | You might be tense, anxious, or impatient. |
| 2. Think about how the other person will feel. | He or she may feel anxious, bored, or angry. |
| 3. Think about different ways you could say what you want to say. | |
| 4. Think about what the other person might say back to you. | |
| 5. Think about any other things that might happen during the conversation. | Repeat Steps 1–5 at least twice, using different approaches to the situation. |
| 6. Choose the best approach you can think of and try it. | |

SUGGESTED CONTENT FOR MODELING DISPLAYS:

A. School or neighborhood: Main actor prepares to talk with teacher about dropping subject.
B. Home: Main actor prepares to tell parent about school failure.
C. Peer group: Main actor prepares to ask for first date.

COMMENTS:

In preparing for difficult or stressful conversations, it is useful for youngsters to see that the way they approach the situation can influence the final outcome. This skill involves rehearsing a variety of approaches and then reflecting upon which approach produces the best results. Feedback from group members on the effectiveness of each approach can be particularly useful in this regard.

*Source*: Goldstein, A.P. et al. (1980) *Skill-Streaming the Adolescent*. Champaign, IL: Research Press.

**Figure C.5   Key Behaviors: Talking to the Boss About a Work-Related Problem**

1. State your desire to talk about a work-related problem.
2. If it is not a convenient time, ask when and where it would be convenient.
3. State the problem and explain its effect on work activities.
4. Listen for a restatement of problem or for indication that problem has been understood.
5. State your willingness to cooperate in any solution to the problem and listen openly to supervisor's comments.
6. (IF NECESSARY)
   a. State alternative or your preferred solution.
   b. Agree on the steps that each of you will take to solve the problem.
7. Ask if there is a need to follow-up the problem. If so, plan and record a specific follow-up date.

### Figure C.6   Key Behaviors: Performance Review

1. Put the employee at ease.
2. Make it clear that the purpose for the performance review is to help the employee to do the best possible job and to see if there is anything you can do to help him or her.
3. Review the ratings with the employee, citing specific examples of behavior that resulted.
4. Ask for the employee's feelings about the ratings and his or her suggestions for changes. Listen openly.
5. Discuss salary in another meeting (if possible). State this desire to the employee.
6. Together, decide on specific ways in which performance areas can be strengthened. Write the resulting plans on paper.
7. Express your confidence in the employee.
8. Set a follow-up date.

### Figure C.7   Key Behaviors: Discipline

1. Define the problem in terms of lack of improvement since the previous discussion.
2. Ask for and openly listen to reasons for the continued behavior. Respond with empathy.
3. Explain why the behavior cannot continue.
4. If disciplinary action is called for, indicate what action you must take and why.
5. Agree on specific action to be taken to solve the problem.
6. Set a follow-up date and outline further steps to be taken if the problem is not corrected.
7. Assure the employee of your interest in helping him or her to succeed.

### Figure C.8   Selection Interviewing

KEY BEHAVIORS IN PLANNING FOR AN INTERVIEW
1. Construct and use an interview guide
2. Review the job requirements
3. Write down the realistic job information you will tell the applicant
4. Review the application/resume of the applicant
5. Write specific questions for each applicant on the interview guide.

KEY BEHAVIORS IN OPENING THE INTERVIEW
1. Warm, friendly welcome—relax and smile
2. Talk about yourself to put person at ease
3. Tell person what you will cover during the interview

KEY BEHAVIORS IN PROBING FOR INFORMATION
1. Probe for unfavorable information.
2. Seek information to refute your first impression.
3. Don't ask leading questions.
4. Ask only one question at a time.
5. Use words such as *how, what, why,* and *tell me.*
6. Take notes.

**Figure C.8    Selection Interviewing (cont.)**

KEY BEHAVIORS IN GIVING REALISTIC JOB INFORMATION
1. Tell the applicant you will now tell him or her some things about the job and that he or she can ask questions at any time.
2. Tell the applicant what you have in your job preview notes.
3. Ask the applicant for any questions.

KEY BEHAVIORS IN CLOSING THE INTERVIEW
1. Summarize applicant's strengths and weaknesses
2. Ask if he has anything to add
3. Tell him what the next steps in the employment process are
4. Thank the applicant
5. Complete interview notes after interview

# —D—

## Scripts for Behavior Modeling Films

**Figure D.1  Key Behaviors for "Coaching"**

1. State the problem in behavioral terms, and immediately focus on the problem, not the person (tie problem to functioning of the organization).
2. Try to bring the reasons for the problem into the open.
3. Ask for the person's suggestions and discuss his or her ideas on how to solve the problem.
4. Listen openly.
5. Agree on the steps that each of you will take to solve the problem.
6. Plan and record a specific follow-up date.

*"Initial Coaching" Modeling Display Script Number 1*
(employee is a hospital transport employee who moves patients from area to area)

(Supr) Model–Hi, _____ . I'd like to discuss a problem we're having with an excessive amount of time unaccounted for on assignment. I noticed on the biweekly report that last week you came up late on your assignments and I would like to know if there is any particular reason why this problem is occurring. You know there is a policy that all patients should be transported within a time-limit of 20 minutes.

Sub–I've been having a hard time finding wheelchairs.

Supr–Wheelchairs? Do you have any suggestions to eliminate the excessive time?

Sub–I thought we were going to order some more, but I've been having a really hard time, and I think everybody else has too. A lot of times the nurses take a really long time to get these patients and we have to wait and wait. We wait our five minutes and then they tell us that we have to wait a couple more and thats what's making us fall behind. And, I think I might be talking a little too much also. How much was I late, I mean how many minutes?

Supr–Okay, my record shows that you were 180 minutes late on your assignments.

Sub–For a pay period?

Supr–For a pay period.

Sub–Alright.

Supr–One of the reasons is that you have a problem locating wheelchairs, and reason number two is you have a waiting period on the divisions waiting for the nurses to respond to your own request for patients.

Sub–We wait a really long time.

Supr–Okay. I'll go over these two factors with the nurses at our next head nurses meeting and I'll discuss this problem of waiting a long time for patients along with the divisions. We also have ordered an addition of 60 wheelchairs which might eliminate the long period that it takes them to locate a wheelchair.

Sub–That will probably help.

Supr–Why don't we set up a date of, say, August 25 at 10:00 in my office to discuss the problem. See if it still persists. You realize that I want to eliminate the excessive time?

Sub–Okay.

Supr–Okay, thank you.

### "Coaching" Modeling Display Script Number 2
(employee is a nurse)

(Supr) Model:   I asked you to come into the office today because I noticed there was a problem yesterday. The orders on Mrs. Jones in 16 were not taken off until the evening people discovered it at 6:00, and they were written at 1:00. You did have that patient yesterday. Can you tell me why they weren't taken off?

Sub–Well, you know how understaffed we are. I just didn't have the time. I have a lot of patients and I could barely get my care done. I knew that you had pulled help from another floor and I figured that anything that I had left hanging they could probably pick up.

Supr–You're saying that you did not have time to take the orders off?

Sub–I just didn't get around to it.

Supr–Okay. The problem is, when one does not take the orders off on a patient and leaves it for the next shift, two things may happen: First, the next shift may not find the order and it doesn't get done at all; or second, if they do find the order, as was in this case, they end up having to do extra work and they can't get their own work done. Can you think of some suggestion that you could offer perhaps so that this will not happen again?

Sub–Maybe you could have somebody in charge to do strictly all of the orders so that we . . . that takes a lot of time to do all the orders on everyone.

Supr–That's true. Orders do take a lot of time to take off. Are you suggesting then that one individual be assigned to each shift to take off the orders or to monitor that they are being taken off?

Sub–To take them off for us and inform us of the new order but not to be in charge of taking them off. Somebody at least on the day shift, the day shift is awful busy.

Supr–That sounds reasonable to me. Why don't you and I bring that up at the next staff meeting, which is next Monday at 9:00 and we'll see if the other nurses like that idea. If they do, then we'll go ahead and implement it. How long do you think we should do that before we check to see if it's working?

Sub–I think if we'd give it a couple weeks.

Supr–So, two weeks from the time we start that?

Sub–Right.

Supr–I would be willing to go ahead and try that, if the other nurses agree and we can reevaluate that within two weeks time. If the other staff does not agree that that is a viable solution to the problem, then you and I should get together to discuss it again after the staff meeting.

Sub–Okay.

Supr–Is that alright?

Sub–Alright.

Supr–Okay, let's do that.

**Figure D.2 "Refusing Unreasonable Request" (Assertiveness) Modeling Display Learning Points**

1. Use assertive nonverbal behavior.
      —look directly at focal person when speaking
      —use gestures which are appropriate to verbal messages
      —use facial expressions which match the verbal message

2. Avoid adversive reactions.
      —such as: aggression
                  slander (criticism of focal person)
                  sarcasm
                  over-apologizing
                  threats

**Figure D.2   "Refusing Unreasonable Request" (Assertiveness) Modeling Display
Learning Points (cont.)**

3. Use appropriate verbal behavior.
  —accept manipulative criticism yet maintain
   responsibility for your decision
  —calmly repeat a negative reply without justifying it
  —be honest about your feelings, needs, etc.
   (use "I" statements)
  —accept your faults calmly without apology

## *"Refusing Unreasonable Request" (Assertiveness)*
## *Modeling Display Script*

 –Boy Maryellen! Am I glad to see you! But I've got a problem and I was
afraid I couldn't get anyone to help me out.
Model–Oh, yeah? What's the problem?
 –Well, I'd like to borrow your car this afternoon.
Model–Hum, that is a problem. I don't think I want to lend my car today.
 –Well, why not?
Model–I understand that you need it. I just don't want to lend my car today.
 –Well, do you have someplace to go?
Model–I might want to use it later.
 –You could just say when and I could bring it back to you on time.
Model–I know that you would. I just don't want to lend my car today.
 –I don't understand. You know whenever I've asked to borrow your car
before you've always lent it to me.
Model–I know I did.
 –So what's the difference? Why won't you lend it to me today? I wouldn't
do anything to your car.
Model–Oh, I know, Paul; and I can see that you're in a jam. But I just don't
want to lend my car.
 –Come on Maryellen! I'm a good driver.
Model–I know, that's true; but when I lend my car I worry, and I just don't
need that hassle today.
 –But I'm not going to wreck it or anything!
Model–I know, and it's probably dumb to feel this way, but I do.
 –Well, Maryellen, if it's so dumb, why won't you lend me your car?
Model–Because I just don't want to have to worry!
 –But, I wouldn't do anything wrong.
Model–I know, Paul. It's not you that's the problem, it's me; but I just don't
want to lend my car because I worry—so I'm not going to lend it.

–Okay, I can understand how you feel. If I had a car I probably wouldn't want to lend it out either . . . to have the worry and everything.
Model–Oh . . . well, thanks for understanding.
 –Oh, that's all right. Maybe I'll see you later, if I can find a car from some-one else. Um . . . maybe at Phil's party?
Model–Okay. . . I'll see you then . . . bye-bye.
 –Okay . . . Bye, Maryellen.

**Figure D.3   Key Behaviors for "Handling an Employee-Initiated Complaint"**

1. Listen openly.
2. Do not speak until the employee has had his/her say.
3. Avoid reacting emotionally. (Don't Get Defensive).
4. Ask for his/her expectations about a solution to the problem.
5. Agree on specific steps to be taken and specific deadlines.

### *"Handling an Employee Complaint" Modeling Display Script* (employee is a hospital technician)

Sub–By the way, Jim, there is a problem over there at the blood desk. It's too heavy, the work load is way too heavy. Is there something we can do about it?
Supr–Have you thought of any solutions?
Sub–Yes, I noticed that within the last couple months, on Tuesdays and Thursdays, there are two people on Anarobes. On Tuesdays and Thursdays, there's not that much work back there. Maybe we can pull a person on Tues-days and Thursdays.
Supr–Okay, that's a good solution.
Sub–We can try it out, and we can even start it tomorrow.
Supr–We can go ahead and have the second person in the Anarobic Labora-tory, they can rotate on the blood desk on Tuesday and Thursday afternoon and that will help temporarily. Now, there is a problem in that that is only a temporary solution. Do you have any ideas for a permanent solution?
Sub–I do, I'd like to have two people over there, permanently. Is that possi-ble?
Supr–That's possible. This is the time of the year when we put in for our budgets, and this would be the time when we want to put in for it. Now, in order to get it passed through the budget committee we're going to have to have good justification. Can you give me good justification for having that second person on the blood desk?
Sub–Yes, I can.
Supr–Okay, what you're going to need to do then is sit down and write me out a proposal, write down the reasons why you think we need another per-

**Figure D.3   Key Behaviors for "Handling an Employee-Initiated Complaint"**
**(cont.)**

son on that desk and hand it to me. Why don't we set up an appointment and we can talk about it. Are you available next Tuesday?

Sub–I sure am and I'll write up all the proposals and justifications and bring them to you on Tuesday.

Supr–We'll sit down next Tuesday at 2:00.

Sub–Okay that's fine.

Supr–But as a temporary measure we'll go ahead and tomorrow we'll start sending a second person from Anarobes to rotate on the blood desk.

Sub–Okay, fine.

# —E—

# An Exercise to Teach On-The-Job Training Key Behaviors

## (Student Instructions) Using On-The-Job Training

### Overview

There is much to know about training and developing employees. The training process includes training needs analysis, development of behavioral objectives, developing the training program, and evaluating the program. Many of these functions will be (or should be) performed by a training specialist. However, every manager will be involved in training his or her employees on the job. Very seldom, if ever, do employees have all the knowledge that will be necessary to successfully perform all of the tasks required in a new job. If they do not, training can be the answer. This will usually take the form of on-the-job training. In this exercise, you will learn to use an effective on-the-job training technique.

### Objectives

1. To build skill in training employees using an on-the-job training technique.
2. To become familiar with some of the strengths and weaknesses associated with on-the-job training.

### Premeeting Assignment

NONE. *Do not read ahead.*

### Procedure

1. The class will be split into two even groups. Group 1 will become trainers and Group 2 will become trainees. Group 2 leaves the classroom.

## Instructions for Group 1

2. Look at Figure E.1 and learn how to perform this operation. Your instructor will give you all the needed materials. Make sure you can perform the operation by practicing it several times. This is "overlearning."
3. Read and memorize the On-The-Job Training Key Behaviors presented in Figure E.2. You will use these key behaviors to teach a "trainee" how to produce the paper cup.
   TIME: About 15 minutes.
4. When the "trainees" come back into the room, choose one. Using the On-The-Job Training Key Behaviors, teach him or her to produce the paper cup. Remember that trainers create a proper training climate by being serious.
   TIME: About 15 minutes.
5. You have just learned how to train an employee in a manual (psychomotor) skill. Now you must leave the room and become a "trainee."

## Instructions for Group 2

5. Now you have become a "trainer." Read and memorize the On-The-Job Training Key Behaviors in Figure E.2. These are the behaviors the Group 1 "trainers" used to train you to fold the paper cup. You are going to use these key behaviors to teach a "trainee" to perform a social skill: giving recognition to an employee for good performance.
6. Read and memorize the steps of giving recognition for good performance presented in Figure E.3.
7. Choose another "trainer" and practice the steps of giving recognition on each other. You must be able to do a task before you attempt to train an employee to do it.
   TIME: About 15 minutes.
8. When the "trainees" come back into the room, choose one. You will use the On-The-Job Training Key Behaviors to train this trainee in the three steps of giving an employee recognition for good performance.
   IMPORTANT: In Key Behaviors 2 and 4, you must show the "trainee" how to do the steps of the task; and in Key Behaviors 5, 6, and 7, the "trainee" must do the steps. Since this task requires two people, you and the trainee must give recognition to each other. Consequently, when you show the trainee how to do it (2 and 4) you must ask the "trainee" what he or she has done that deserves recognition and do the steps of the task to the "trainee." When the "trainee" does the task, you must tell the "trainee" something you have done recently which deserves recognition, so that the "trainee" can do the steps of the task for you.
   OPTIONAL METHOD: You choose two trainees. Teach one using the On-The-Job Training Key Behaviors to give recognition to the second "trainee." In Key Behaviors 2 and 4, you do the three steps of giving recognition to the second trainee, and during Key Behaviors 5, 6, and 7, the first "trainee" does the three steps of giving recognition to the second "trainee." Then the two trainees switch roles and you teach again.
   TIME: About 15 minutes.

**Figure E.1   Steps of the Task: Folding a Paper Cup**

| STEPS IN THE OPERATION | KEY POINTS |
|---|---|
| Step: A logical segment of the operation in which something is done to advance the work. | Key point: Any directions or bits of information that help to perform the step correctly, safely, and easily. |
| Place 8″ × 10½″ sheet of paper in front of you on flat surface. | 1. Be sure surface is flat—free of interfering objects. |
| Fold lower left hand corner up. | 2a. Line up the right hand edges.<br>b. Make a sharp crease. |
| Turn paper over. | 3a. Pick up lower right hand corner with right hand and place it at the top.<br>b. Folded flap should not be underneath. |
| Fold excess lower edge up. | 4a. Line up right hand edges.<br>b. Fold should line up with bottom edge.<br>c. Make sharp crease. |
| Fold lower left hand corner flush with edge "A." | 5a. Keep edges "B" and "C" parallel.<br>b. Hold bottom edge in the center with finger while making fold. |
| Fold upper corner to point "D." | 6a. Hold cup firmly with left hand.<br>b. Bring upper corner down with right hand. |
| Separate lower right hand corner and fold back. | 7a. Hold cup with left hand.<br>b. Fold back with right hand.<br>c. Make sharp creases. |
| Turn cup over and fold remaining flap back. | 8. Make sharp creases. |
| Check cup to be sure it will hold water. | 9. Open cup and look inside. |

**Figure E.2    On-The-Job Training Key Behaviors**

1. Tell the trainee the objective of the task and ask him or her to watch you demonstrate it.
2. Show the trainee how to do it without saying anything.
3. Explain the key points or behaviors (give the trainee the key points written out, if possible).
4. Show the trainee how to do it again.
5. Have the trainee do one or more single parts of the task and praise him or her for correct reproduction (optional).
6. Have the trainee do the entire task and praise him or her for correct reproduction.
7. If mistakes are made, have the trainee practice until accurate reproduction is achieved.
8. Praise the trainee for his or her success in learning the task.

**Figure E.3    Steps of the Task: Giving Recognition for Good Performance**

1. State clearly what the employee did which deserves recognition.
2. Express your personal satisfaction with the employee and his or her performance. Be sincere.
3. Explain why it is important to continue in this manner.

## Exercise 2 (Instructor's Instructions) Using On-The-Job Training

### Purpose and Introduction

This exercise is designed to give your students experience in using on-the-job training skills to teach employees manual and social skills. Any training process should include training needs analysis, development of behavioral objectives, developing the training program, and evaluating the program. Many of these functions will be (or should be) performed by a training specialist. However, every manager will be involved in training his or her employees on the job. Very seldom, if ever, do employees have all of the knowledge that will be necessary to successfully perform all of the tasks required in a new job. If they do not, training can be the answer. This usually will take the form of on-the-job training. The training method used in this exercise is based on a Training Within Industry program of World War II: Job Instruction Training. However, the best introduction to this exercise is to discuss the implications of social learning theory for on-the-job training.

### Objectives For Students

1. To build skill in training employees using an on-the-job training technique.
2. To become familiar with some of the strengths and weaknesses associated with on-the-job training.

## Time Suggested

One class period (or 1 hour).

## Procedure

### Premeeting assignment

None. Do not tell your students you will be doing this exercise because they should not read through it.

*NOTE*: You must bring to class 5 sheets of 8" × 10½" paper for each student. You must also learn to fold the cup presented in Figure E.1 of the student workbook.

### In class

1. Split the class into two even groups (½ class). Group 1 will become trainers and Group 2 will become trainees. If you have an odd number, make Group 2 larger. Have Group 2 leave the room (for about 10–15 minutes). Tell them to stay close and you will tell them when to return.
2. Have group 1 read the instructions (for Group 1).
3. Have the students learn to do the task outlined (Figure E.1) without any help from you. If it takes more time than allowed, suggest you will show them how to do it if they all agree that learning something from written instructions (i.e., technical manual) is very difficult.
4. Have them memorize the Key Behaviors for On-The-Job Training presented in Figure E.2.
   TIME: 15 minutes.
5. Bring Group 2 back into the room and have the trainers (Group 1) teach the trainees (Group 2) how to fold the cup using the On-The-Job Training Key Behaviors. (The trainers may keep Figures E.1 and E.2 in front of them while they train).
6. When all trainees have learned the task, ask the trainers to have the trainees fold one or two more cups. This is overlearning. You should then explain the importance of practice beyond the point of first accurate reproduction (overlearning). For more information, see Goldstein, I. *Training: Program Development and Evaluation*. Monterey, Ca.: Brooks Cole, 1974 or Wexley, K. N. and G. P. Latham. *Developing and Training Human Resources in Organizations*. Glenview, Ill.: Scott, Foresman, 1981.
7. Ask the trainers by which training method they would have preferred to learn this task (hopefully, they will say O.J.T.). Have the trainers show the trainees how they learned the task.
   TIME: 15 minutes.
8. Have Group 1 leave the room with the same directions you gave to Group 2 earlier (see step 1).
9. Explain to Group 2 that they have become trainers and will teach Group 1 a social skill (giving recognition to an employee for good performance).
10. Have Group 2 read the instructions (for Group 2).

**Figure E.4   Job Breakdown Sheet for Training Purposes**

DEPARTMENT _____ JOB _____
BREAKDOWN MADE BY _____
DATE _____

| IMPORTANT STEPS | KEY POINTS |
|---|---|
| (What To Do)<br>　A logical segment of the operation,<br>　when something happens to advance<br>　the work | (How To Do It)<br>Anything that may:<br>　Make or break the job<br>　Injure the worker<br>　Make the work easier to do |
|  |  |
|  |  |
|  |  |
|  |  |
|  |  |

11. Have Group 2 memorize the On-The-Job Key Behaviors in Figure E.2.
12. You now have two alternative methods to follow (see student instructions for Group 2 and Optional Method). Please choose one.
13. Have the trainers (Group 2) read and memorize the steps of giving recognition (Figure E.3). Then have the trainers practice the three steps on each other so that they are able to do the task.
14. Call Group 1 back into the classroom. Depending upon which method you have chosen, have the trainers (Group 2) choose one or two trainees.
15. Have the trainers teach the three steps of giving recognition to the trainees. *NOTE*: Read the student instructions carefully so you know what is to happen.
16. When all the trainees have learned the three steps of giving recognition explain the importance of generalization in teaching social skills; i.e., social skills are generalized by practicing the skills across people and contexts (practice giving recognition for a different performance to a different person).
    TIME: 15 minutes.

## Suggestions To Instructor

You may want to follow up the exercise with a discussion about development of the steps to be taught with O.J.T. These steps were provided for this exercise (i.e., the cup folding steps and the giving recognition steps). However, a supervisor would have to develop the steps to be taught before O.J.T. was attempted. Figure E.4 is a form which can be used in developing the steps in the task. For more information see: Graig, R. L., ed. *Training and Development Handbook*. New York: McGraw-Hill, 1976 (Second Edition), Chapter 32.

*NOTE*: This follow-up discussion is highly recommended.

# BIBLIOGRAPHY

Adkins, D. C. (1974) *Test Construction: Development and Interpretation of Achievement Tests* (2nd ed). Columbus, OH: Merrill.

Allen, C. R. (1919) *The Instructor, the Man and the Job.* Philadelphia: J. B. Lippincott Co..

Alssaid, L. L., and Hutchinson, W. R. (1977) Comparison of modeling techniques in counselor training. *Counselor Education and Supervision, 17,* 36–41.

Altmann, H. A., and Firnesz, K. M. (1973) A role playing approach to influencing behavioral change and self-esteem. *Elementary School Guidance and Counseling, 7,* 276–81.

Ammons, R. B. (1954) Knowledge of performance, survey of literature, some possible explanations and suggested experimentation. WADC Technical Report 54–14, Wright Air Development Center.

Anderson, J. R. (1978) Arguments concerning representations for mental imagery. *Psychological Review, 85,* 249–77.

Annett, J. (1961) The role of knowledge of results in learning: A survey. U.S. NAVTRADEVCEN Technical Document Report 342–3, May.

Atkinson, R. C. (1972) Ingredients for a theory of instruction. *American Psychologist, 27,* 921–31.

Atwater, S. K. (1953) Proactive inhibition and associative facilitation as affected by degree of prior learning. *Journal of Experimental Psychology, 46,* 400–404.

Bandura, A. (1969) *Principles of Behavior Modification.* New York: Rinehart & Winston.

Bandura, A. (1971) *Psychological Modeling: Conflicting Theories.* Chicago: Aldine-Atherton.

Bandura, A. (1977) *Social Learning Theory.* Englewood Cliffs, NJ: Prentice-Hall.

Bandura, A. (1977a) Toward a unifying theory of behavioral change. *Psychological Review, 54,* 191–215.

Bandura, A.; Adams, N. E.; and Beyer, J. (1977) Cognitive processes mediating behavioral change. *Journal of Personality and Social Psychology, 35,* 125–39.

Bandura, A., and Jeffery, R. W. (1973) Role of symbolic coding and rehearsal process in observational learning. *Journal of Personality and Social Psychology, 26,* 122–30.

Bandura, A.; Jeffery R.; and Bachicha, D. L. (1974) Analysis of memory codes and cumulative rehearsal in observational learning. *Journal of Research in Personality, 7,* 295–305.

Bandura, A. and Menlove, F. L. (1968) Factors determining vicarious extinction of avoidance behavior through symbolic modeling. *Journal of Personality and Social Psychology, 8,* 99–108.

Bandura, A., and Mischel, W. (1965) Modification of self-imposed delay of reward through exposure to live and symbolic models. *Journal of Personality and Social Psychology, 2,* 698–705.

Bandura, A.; Ross, D.; and Ross, S. A. (1963) A comparative test of the status, envy, social power, and secondary reinforcement theories of identification learning. *Journal of Abnormal and Social Psychology, 67,* 527–34.

Baron, R. A. (1970) Attraction toward the model and model's competence as determinants of adult imitative behavior. *Journal of Personality and Social Psychology, 14,* 345–51.

Berenson, J. K. (1975) Behavior and attitude change in emotionally disturbed children through the combined use of modeling, role playing, and reinforcement. Unpublished doctoral dissertation, University of Massachusetts.

Bernardin, H. J. and Beatty, R. W. (1983) *Performance Appraisal: Assessing Human Behavior at Work.* Boston, MA.: Kent.

Breham, J. W., and Cohen, A. R. (1962) *Explorations in Cognitive Dissonance.* New York: Wiley.

Brock, T. C., and Blackwood, J. E. (1962) Dissonance reduction, social comparison, and modification of other's opinions. *Journal of Abnormal and Social Psychology, 65,* 319–24.

Bryon, J. H. and Test, M. A. (1967) Models and helping: Naturalistic studies in aiding behavior. *Journal of Personality and Social Psychology, 6,* 400–407.

Burnaska, R. F. (1976) The effects of behavior modeling training upon managers' behaviors and employee perceptions. *Personnel Psychology, 29,* 329–36.

Byham, W. C., Adams, D., and Kiggins, A. (1976) Transfer of modeling training to the job. *Personnel Psychology, 29,* 345–50.

Campbell, J. P. (1971) Personnel training and development. *Annual Review of Psychology*, Palo Alto, CA: Annual Reviews.

Candler, A., and Goodman, G. (1977) The relationship of authoritarianism and behavior modeling in prospective teachers. *Social Behavior and Personality, 5*, 125-29.

Carlsmith, J. M.; Collins, B. E.; and Helmreich, R. L. (1966) Studies in forced compliance: I. The effect of pressure for compliance on attitude change produced by face-to-face role playing and anonymous essay writing. *Journal of Personality and Social Psychology, 4*, 1-13.

Cascio, W. F. (1982) *Costing Human Resources: The Financial Impact of Behavior in Organizations*. Boston, MA: Kent.

Chasnoff, S. (1976) The effects of modeling and ambiguity tolerance on interview behavior. *Counselor Education and Supervision, 16*, 46-51.

Cheek, L. M. (1973) Cost effectiveness comes to the personnel function. *Harvard Business Review*, May–June, 79.

Clore, G. L., and Jeffery, K. M. (1971) *Emotional role playing, attitude change and attraction toward a disabled person*. Paper presented at the Midwestern Psychological Association Convention, Detroit, Michigan.

Cobb, R. M. (1974) Acquisition and retention of cooperative behavior in young boys through instruction, modeling and structured learning. Unpublished doctoral dissertation, Syracuse University.

Cohen, A. R., and Latane, B. (1962) An experiment on choice in commitment to counterattitudinal behavior. In J. W. Bruhm and A. R. Cohen (eds.), *Explorations in Cognitive Dissonance*. New York: Wiley.

Cominsky, I. J. (1982) Transfer of training in counselor education programs: A study of the use of stimulus variability and the provision of general principles to enhance the transfer of the skill of reflection of feeling. *Dissertation Abstracts International*, July 43 (1-A), 76.

Cook, T. D. and Campbell, D. T. (1979) *Quasi Experimentation: Design and Analysis Issues for Field Settings*. Chicago, IL: Rand and McNally.

Cook, D. W., and Kunce, J. T. (1977) Reducing counselor anxiety by using modeling strategies. *Journal of Employment Counseling, 14*, 110–15.

Cook, D. W., and Kunce, J. T. (1978) Paramodeling effects in counselor training. *Journal of Employment Counseling, 15*, 62–66.

Corsini, R. J. (1966) *Roleplaying in psychotherapy: A manual*. Chicago, IL: Aldine.

Culbertson, F. M. (1957) Modification of an emotionally held attitude through role playing. *Journal of Abnormal and Social Psychology, 54*, 230–33.

Dalton, R. F. (1973) An application of principles of social learning to training in communication of empathy. (Doctoral dissertation, The Pennsylvania State University, 1972). *Dissertation Abstracts International, 33*, 5597-A. (University microfilm no. 73-7422).

Dalton, R. F., Jr., and Sundblad, L. M. (1976) Using principles of social learning for communication of empathy. *Journal of Counseling Psychology, 23*, 454-57.

Davis, K., and Jones, E. E. (1960) Changes in interpersonal perception as a means of reducing cognitive dissonance. *Journal of Abnormal and Social Psychology, 61*, 402-10.

Dean, M. L. (1975) The effects of class, sex, and ethnic group variables upon the ability to delay gratification in children and the acquisition of delay behavior through modeling and role playing (Doctoral dissertation, The University of New Mexico, 1974). *Dissertation Abstracts International, 35*, 4645-B.

Decker, P. J. (1980) Effects of symbolic coding and rehearsal in behavior-modeling training. *Journal of Applied Psychology, 65*, 627-34.

Decker, P. J. (1982) The enhancement of behavior modeling training of supervisory skills by the inclusion of retention processes. *Personnel Psychology, 32(2)*, 323-32.

Decker, P. J. (1983) The efforts of rehearsal group size and video feedback in behavior modeling training. *Personnel Psychology, 36*, 763-73.

Decker, P. J. (1984) Effects of different symbolic coding stimuli in behavior modeling training. *Personnel Psychology, 37*(4), 711-720.

Dempster, F. N. (1981) Memory span: Sources of individual and developmental differences. *Psychological Bulletin, 89*, 63-100.

Dietz, D. W. (1982) On the job training and the training within industry program. In Carl Heyel (ed.), *The Encyclopedia of Management*, 3rd. Ed. New York: Van Nostrand Reinhold Co., pp. 770-72, 1247-49.

Dolly, J. P.; Meredith, V. A.; and Saunders, J. C. (1977) The effect of negative feedback on modeling behavior. *The Journal of Educational Research, 8*, 324-27.

Dorster, J. (1972) Effects of instruction, modeling and role rehearsal on interview verbal behavior. *Journal of Consulting and Clinical Psychology, 39*, 202-9.

Dowling, T. H., and Frantz, T. T. (1975) The influence of facilitative learning. *Journal of Counseling Psychology, 22*, 259-63.

Duncan, C. P. (1953) Transfer in motor learning as a function of degree of first-task learning and inter-task similarity, *Journal of Experimental Psychology, 45*, 1-11.

Ebel, R. L. (1972) *Essentials of Educational Measurement*. Englewood Cliffs, NJ: Prentice-Hall.

Ekman, P. A. (1958) A comparison of verbal and non-verbal behavior as reinforcing stimuli of opinion responses. Unpublished dissertation, Adelphi College.

Epstein, M. L. (1980) The relationship of mental imagery and mental rehearsal to performance of a motor task. *Journal of Sport Psychology, 2*, 211–20.

Fahmy, S. A. (1953) Conditioning and extinction of a referential verbal response class in a situation resembling a clinical diagnostic interview. *Dissertation Abstracts, 13*, 873–74.

Fast, D. (1974) A new approach to quantifying training program effectiveness. *Training and Development Journal, 26(6)*, 8–14.

Festinger, L. (1957) *A Theory of Cognitive Dissonance*. New York: Harper and Row.

Festinger, L. and Carlsmith, J. M. (1959) Cognitive consequences of forced compliance. *Journal of Abnormal Social Psychology, 58*, 203–10.

Fitts, P. M. (1965) Factors in complex skill training. In R. Glaser (ed.), *Training Research and Education*. New York: Wiley, 177–97.

Fleishman, E. A. (1975) Toward a taxonomy of human performance. *American Psychologist, 30*, 1127–49.

Fox, W. M. (1983) Behavior Modeling: An overview. An unpublished manuscript, University of Florida.

French, J. R. P. (1945) Role playing as a method of training foremen. *Sociometry, 8*, 410–22.

Friedenberg, W. P. (1971) Verbal and non-verbal attraction modeling in an initial therapy interview analogue. Unpublished masters thesis, Syracuse University.

Friedman, P. H. (1971) The effects of modeling and role-playing on assertive behavior. In R. D. Rubin, et al. (eds.) *Advances in behavior therapy*. New York: Academic Press, 149–69.

Fyffe, A. E. and Oei, T. P. (1979) Influence of modeling and feedback provided by the supervisors in a microskills training program for beginning counselors. *Journal of Clinical Psychology, 35*, 651–56.

Gagne, R. M.; Baker, K. E.; and Foster, H. (1950) On the relation between similarity and transfer of training in the learning of discrimination motor tasks. *Psychological Review, 57*, 67–79.

Gagne, R. M. and Foster, H. (1949) Transfer to a motor skill from practice on a pictured representation. *Journal of Experimental Psychology, 39*, 342–54.

Gelfand, D. M., and Singer, R. D. (1968) Generalization of reinforced personality evaluations: A further investigation. *Journal of Clinical Psychology, 24*, 24–26.

Gerst, M. S. (1971) Symbolic coding processes in observational learning. *Journal of Personality and Social Psychology, 19*, 7–17.

Gilbert, T. F. (1967) Praxeonomy: A Systematic Approach to Identifying Training Needs. *Management of Personnel Quarterly*, 20–23.

Goldsmith, J. B., and McFall, R. M. (1975) Development and evaluation of an interpersonal skill-training program for psychiatric inpatients. *Journal of Abnormal Psychology, 84*, 51–58.

Goldstein, A. P.; Martens, J.; Hubben, H.; vanBelle, H.; Schaaf, W.; Wiersma, H.; and Goedhart, A. (1973) The use of modeling to increase independent behavior. *Behavior Research and Therapy, 11*, 31–42.

Goldstein, A. P., and Sorcher, M. (1974) *Changing Supervisory Behavior.* New York: Pergamon Press.

Goldstein, A. P.; Sprafkin, R. P.; Gershaw, N. J.; and Klein, P. (1980) *Skill-Streaming the Adolescent: A Structured Learning Approach to Teaching Prosocial Skills.* Champaign, IL: Research Press.

Goldstein, I. L. (1974) *Training Program Development and Evaluation.* Monterey, CA: Brooks Cole.

Goldstein, I. L. (1980) Training in Work Organizations. *Annual Review of Psychology, 31*, 229–72.

Gormally, J.; Hill, C.; Otis, M.; and Rainey, L. (1975) A microtraining approach to assertion training. *Journal of Counseling Psychology, 22*, 299–303.

Gronlund, N. E. (1976) *Measurement and Evaluation in Teaching* (3rd ed.). New York: Macmillan.

Hamilton, D. L.; Thompson, J. L.; and White, A. M. (1970) Role of awareness and intentions in observational learning. *Journal of Personality and Social Psychology, 16*, 689–94.

Harvey, O. J., and Beverly, G. D. (1961) Some personality correlates of concept change through role playing. *Journal of Abnormal and Social Psychology, 63*, 125–30.

Hayes, S. C.; Rincover, A.; and Volosin, D. (1980) Variables influencing the acquisition and maintenance of aggressive behavior: Modeling versus sensory reinforcement. *Journal of Abnormal Psychology, 89*, 254–62.

Heitbrink, P. G. (1971) The effectiveness of behavior modeling and instruction in vocational counseling with schizophrenic and normal subjects. *Dissertation Abstracts*, 32(6-B), 3636 (No. 72–1322).

Hendrickson, G., and Schroeder, W. (1941) Transfer of training in learning to hit a submerged target. *Journal of Educational Psychology, 32*, 206–13.

Hicks, D. J. (1965) Imitation and retention of film-mediated aggressive peer and adult models. *Journal of Personality and Social Psychology, 2*, 97–100.

Hildum, D. C., and Brown, R. W. (1956) Verbal reinforcement and interviewer bias. *Journal of Abnormal and Social Psychology, 53*, 108–11.

Hogan, P.; Hakel, M. D.; and Decker, P. J. (1984) The relative efficacy of trainee-generated versus trainer-provided rule coding for observational learning generalization. Submitted to *Journal of Applied Psychology.*

Hrapsky, J. S. (1981) Effects of training in visual observation upon subsequent visual-motor performance. *Dissertation Abstracts International*, vol. 42 (3-13), 1212.

Hundleby, G., and Zingle, H. (1975) Communication of empathy. *Canadian Counselor, 9*, 148–52.

Huyck, E. T. (1975) Teaching for behavioral change. *Humanist Educator, 14*, 12–20.

Ilgen, D. R.; Fisher, C. D.; and Taylor, M. S. (1979) Consequences of individual feedback on behavior in organizations. *Journal of Applied Psychology, 64(4)*, 349–71.

Ivey, A. (1971) *Microcounseling: Innovations in Interviewing Training.* Springfield, IL: Thomas.

Jaffee, P. G. (1974) Modeling and instructional treatments with asocial psychiatric patients. Unpublished doctoral dissertation, University of Western Ontario.

Janis, I. L., and King, B. T. (1954) The influence of role playing on opinion change. *Journal of Applied Social Psychology, 48*, 211–18.

Janis, I. L. and Mann, L. (1965) Effectiveness of emotional role playing in modifying smoking habits and attitudes. *Journal of Experimental Research in Personality, 1*, 84–90.

Jeffery, R. W. (1976) The influence of symbolic and motor rehearsal on observational learning. *Journal of Research in Personality, 10*, 116–27.

Kanfer, F. H.; Duerfeldt, P. H.; Martin, B.; and Dorsey, T. E. (1971) Effects of model reinforcement expectation to perform and task performance on model observation. *Journal of Personality and Social Psychology, 20*, 214–17.

Kanfer, F. H., and Goldstein, A. P. (1980) *Helping People Change.* New York: Pergamon Press.

Kazdin, A. (1973) Covert modeling and the reduction of avoidance behavior. *Journal of Abnormal Psychology, 81*, 87–95.

Kazdin, A. (1974) Effects of covert modeling and model reinforcement on assertive behavior. *Journal of Abnormal Psychology, 83*, 240–52.

Kazdin, A. (1975) Covert modeling, imagery assessment, and assertive behavior. *Journal of Consulting and Clinical Psychology, 43*, 716–24.

Kazdin, A. E. (1980) *Behavior Modification in Applied Settings.* Homewood, IL: Irwin Dorsey Press.

Kazdin, A. E. (1982) The separate and combined effects of covert and overt rehearsal in developing assertive behavior. *Behavior Research and Therapy, 20*, 17–25.

Kazdin, A. E. and Mascitelli, S. (1982) Behavioral rehearsal, self-instructions, and homework practice in developing assertiveness. *Behavior Therapy, 13*, 346–60.

Kirkpatrick, D. L. (1967) Evaluation of Training. In Craig, R. L., and Bittel, L. R. (eds.), *Training and Development Handbook*. New York: McGraw-Hill.

Kleinasser, L. D. (1968) The reduction of performance anxiety as a function of desensitization, pretherapy vicarious learning, and vicarious learning alone. Unpublished doctoral dissertation, Pennsylvania State University.

Kloba, J. A., Jr. (1975) The effects of model status and trainee dependency-independency on adolescent learning of a helping skill using the microcounseling training paradigm (Doctoral dissertation, The University of Rochester, 1975). *Disseration Abstracts International, 36*, 2027-A. (University Microfilms No. 75-22, 797).

Kloba, J., Jr., and Zimpfer, D. (1976) Status and independence as variables in microcounseling training of adolescents. *Journal of Counseling Psychology, 23*, 458-63.

Knowles, M. S. (1970) *The Modern Practice of Adult Education*. New York: Association Press.

Kohlenberg, R.; Phillips, T.; and Proctor, W. (1976) A behavioral analysis of peaking in residential electrical-energy consumers. *Journal of Applied Behavior Analysis, 9*, 13-18.

Komaki, J. (1977) Alternative evaluation strategies in work settings: reversal and multiple baseline designs. *Journal of Organizational Behavior Management, 1(1)*, 53-77.

Kraut, A. I. (1976) Developing managerial skills via modeling techniques: Some positive research findings—a symposium. *Personnel Psychology, 29*, 325-28.

Krumboltz, J. D.; Varenhorst, B. B.; and Thoresen, C. E. (1975) Nonverbal factors in the effectiveness of models in counseling. *Journal of Counseling Psychology, 22*, 542-46.

Lamel, P. A. (1971) Imitation learning of information processing. *Journal of Experimental Child Psychology, 12*, 223-27.

Latham, G. P. and Saari, L. M. (1979) The application of social learning theory to training supervisors through behavior modeling. *Journal of Applied Psychology, 64*, 239-46.

Latham, G. P. and Wexley, K. N. (1977) Behavioral observation scales for performance appraisal purposes. *Personnel Psychology, 30*, 255-68.

Latham, G. P. and Wexley, K. N. (1981) *Increasing Productivity Through Performance Appraisal*. Reading, MA: Addison-Wesley.

Latham, G. P. and Yukl, G. A. (1975) A review of research on the application of goal setting in organizations. *Academy of Management Journal, 18*, 824-45.

Lazarus, A. A. (1966) Behavior rehearsal vs. non-directive therapy vs. advice in effecting behavior change. *Behavior Research and Therapy, 4*, 209-12.

Lefkowitz, M. M.; Blake, R. R.; and Mouton, J. C. (1955) Status factors in pedestrian violation of traffic signals. *Journal of Abnormal and Social Psychology, 51*, 704-6.

Liebert, R. M., and Swenson, S. A. (1971) Abstraction, inference, and the process of imitative learning. *Developmental Psychology, 5*, 500-504.

Lippitt, R. (1943) The psychodrama in leadership training. *Sociometry, 6*, 289-92.

Lira, F. T.; Nay, R.; McCullough, J. P.; and Etkin, M. (1975) Relative effect of modeling and roleplaying in the treatment of avoidance behaviors. *Journal of Consulting and Clinical Psychology, 43*, 608-18.

Locke, E. A. (1968) Toward a theory of task motivation and incentives. *Organizational Behavior and Human Performance, 3*, 157-89.

Locke, E. A.; Shaw, K. N.; Saari, L. M.; and Latham, G. P. (1981) Goal-setting and task performance: 1969-1980. *Psychological Bulletin, 90*, 125-52.

Loughlin, P. R., Moss, I. L., and Miller, S. M. (1969) Information-processing in children as a function of adult model, stimulus display, school grade, and sex. *Journal of Educational Psychology, 60*, 188-93.

Lovaas, O. I.; Koegel, R.; Simmons, J. Q.; and Stevens, J. (1973) Some generalization and follow-up measures on autistic children in behavior therapy. *Journal of Applied Behavior Analysis, 6*, 131-66.

Lumsdaine, A. A. (1961) The analysis of student response as a factor in instruction. In A. A. Lumsdaine (ed.), *Student Response in Programmed Instruction*. Washington, D.C.: National Academy of Sciences–National Research Council, Chapter 1.

Lumsdaine, A.; Sulzer, R.; and Kopstein, F. (1961) The effect of animation cues and repetition of examples on learning from an instructional film. In A. A. Lumsdaine (ed.), *Student Response in Programmed Instruction*. Washington, D.C.: National Academy of Sciences, National Research Council, Chapter 17.

Luthans, F., and Kreitner, R. (1975) *Organizational Behavior Modification*. Glenville, IL: Scott, Foresman.

MacKay, D. G. (1981) The problem of rehearsal or mental practice. *Journal of Motor Behavior, 13(4)*, 274-85.

Mager, R. F. and Pipe, P. (1970) *Analyzing Performance Problems*. Belmont, CA: Fearon.

Mandler, G. (1954) Transfer of training as a function of response over learning. *Journal of Experimental Psychology, 47*, 411-417.

Mandler, G. and Heinemann, S. H. (1956) Effects of overlearning of a verbal response on transfer of training. *Journal of Experimental Psychology, 52*, 39-46.

Mann, B. and Decker, P. J. (1984) The effect of key behavior distinctiveness on generalization and recall in behavior modeling training. In press, *Academy of Management Journal*.

Mann, J. H. (1956) Experimental evaluations of role playing. *Psychological Bulletin, 53,* 227–34.

Marholin, D., and Gray, D. (1976) Effects of group response-cost procedure on cash shortages in a small business. *Journal of Applied Behavior Analysis, 9,* 25–30.

Marlatt, G. A. and Gordon, J. R. (1980) Determinants of relapse: Implications for the maintenance of behavior change. In P. O. Davidson and S. M. Davidson (eds.), *Behavioral Medicine: Changing Health Life Styles.* New York: Brunner/Mazel, 410–52.

Marx, R. D. (1982) Relapse prevention for managerial training: A model for maintenance of behavior change. *Academy of Management Review, 7(3),* 433–41.

McClure, L. F.; Chinsky, J. M.; and Larcen, S. W. (1978) Enhancing social problem-solving performance in an elementary school setting. *Journal of Educational Psychology, 70,* 504–13.

McCormick, E. J. (1970) *Job Analysis: Methods and Applications.* New York, AMACON-American Management Assoc.

McFall, R. M. and Galbraith, J. R. (1977) *Two studies examining feedback in assertion training.* Unpublished manuscript, University of Wisconsin.

McFall, R. M., and Marston, A. R. (1979) An experimental investigation of behavior rehearsal in assertive training. *Journal of Abnormal Psychology, 76,* 295–303.

McFall, R. M. and Twentyman, C. T. (1973) Four experiments on the relative contributions of rehearsal, modeling, and coaching to assertion training. *Journal of Abnormal Psychology, 81,* 199–218.

McGehee, W. and Thayer, P. W. (1961) *Training in Business and Industry.* New York: Wiley.

McGehee, W. and Tullar, W. L. (1978) A note on evaluating behavior modification and behavior modeling as industrial training techniques. *Personnel Psychology, 31,* 477–84.

McKeon, W. J. (1981) How to determine offsite meeting costs. *Training and Development Journal, 35,* 116–22.

Meichenbaum, D. H. (1971) Examination of model characteristics in reducing avoidance behavior. *Journal of Personality and Social Psychology, 17,* 298–307.

Meisel, J. (1972) The effect of model-observer similarity on imitation of negative attributes (Doctoral dissertation, Stanford University, 1971). *Dissertation Abstracts International, 32,* 6080-B. (University microfilm no. 72-71, 617).

Melnick, J. (1973) A comparison of replication techniques in the modification of minimal dating behavior. *Journal of Abnormal Psychology, 81,* 51–59.

Melnick, J. and Stocker, R. (1977) An experimental analysis of the behavioral rehearsal with feedback technique in assertiveness training. *Behavior Therapy, 8,* 222–28.

Meyer, H. H. and Raich, M. S. (1983) An objective evaluation of a behavior modeling training program. *Personnel Psychology, 36(4)*, 755–61.

Michael, D. and Maccoby N. (1961) Factors influencing the effects of student participation on verbal learning from films: Motivating versus practice effects,
"feedback," and overt versus covert responding. In A. A. Lumsdaine (ed.),
*Student Response in Programmed Instruction*. Washington, D.C.: National
Academy of Sciences–National Research Council, chapter 18.

Milby, J. B. (1970) Modification of extreme social isolation by contingent social reinforcement. *Journal of Applied Behavior Analysis, 3*, 149–52.

Miller, N. E. and Dollard, J. (1941) *Social Learning and Imitation*. New Haven: Yale
University Press.

Miller, R. B. (1966) *Task Taxonomy: Science of Technology?* Poughkeepsie, New
York: IBM.

Moore, M. L. and Dutton, P. (1978) Training Needs Analysis: Review and Critique.
*Academy of Management Review, 3*, 532–45.

Moreno, J. L. (1923) *Das Stegreif theater*. Potsdam: Kiepenherer.

Moses, J. L. and Ritchie, R. J. (1976) Supervisory relationships training: A behavioral evaluation of a behavior modeling program. *Personnel Psychology, 29*,
337–44.

Nelson, J. E. (1982) Assertiveness training using rehearsal and modeling with male
alcoholics. *Dissertation Abstracts International*, December Vol. 43 6-B), 1983.

Noble, G.; Egan, P.; and McDowell, S. (1977) Changing the self-concepts of seven-
year-old deprived urban children by creative drama or video feedback. *Social
Behavior and Personality, 5*, 55–64.

Noel, W. (1976) *Experiencing as systematic training: Its effects on communication
between black and white high school students*. (Unpublished dissertation)
Amherst: University of Massachusetts.

Nugent, G. C.; Tipton, T. J.; and Brooks, D. W. (1980) Use of introductory organizers in television instructions. *Journal of Educational Psychology, 72*, 445–51.

Odiorne, G. S. (1970) *Training by Objectives: An Economic Approach to Management*. New York: Macmillan.

O'Reilly, C. A., III; Parlette, G. N.; and Bloom, J. R. (1980) Perceptual Measures of
Task Characteristics: The Biasing Effects of Differing Frames of Reference
and Job Attitudes. *Academy of Management Journal, 23*, 118–31.

O'Toole, W. M. (1979) Effects of practice and some methodological considerations in
training counseling interviewing skills. *Journal of Counseling Psychology, 26*,
419–26.

Paivio, A. (1971) *Imagery and verbal processes*. New York: Holt, Rinehart and
Winston.

Parr, G. D. (1974). The effects of modeling, behavior rehearsal and counselor sex in assertive counseling with adolescents. Unpublished doctoral dissertation, University of Colorado.

Paulos, R. W., and Liebert, R. M. (1972) Influence of modeling, exhortative verbalization and surveillance on children's sharing. *Developmental Psychology, 6,* 402-8.

Perkins, S. and Atkinson, D. (1973) Effect of selected techniques for training resident assistants in human relations skills. *Journal of Counseling Psychology, 20,* 89-94.

Perry, M. A. (1975) Modeling and instructions in training for counselor empathy. *Journal of Counseling Psychology, 22,* 173-79.

Petroski, R. A.; Craighead, L. W.; and Horan, J. J. (1983) Separate and combined effects of behavior rehearsal and self-other modeling variations on the grooming skill acquisition of mentally retarded women. *Journal of Counseling Psychology, 30,* 279-82.

Porras, J. I. and Anderson, B. (1981) Improving managerial effectiveness through modeling-based training. *Organizational Dynamics,* 60-77.

Porras, J. I.; Hargis, K.; Patterson, K. J.; Maxfield, D. G.; Roberts, N.; and Bies, R. J. (1982) Modeling-Based Organizational Development: A Longitudinal Assessment. *The Journal of Applied Behavioral Science,* Vol. 18, Page 433-446.

Porter, L. W. and Lawler, E. E. (1968) *Managerial Attitudes and Performance.* Homewood, IL: Irwin.

Primo, S. L. (1974) Locus of control of reinforcement as a cognitive characteristic of observers in a vicarious learning situation (Doctoral dissertation, University of Pittsburgh, 1973). *Dissertation Abstracts International, 34,* 5205-B. (University microfilm no. 74-8683).

Protas, E. J. (1981) A comparison of a model demonstration and a roleplaying simulation on the transfer of learning to a clinical evaluation and history in physical therapy students. *Dissertation Abstracts International,* September 42(3-A), 1113-1114.

Prout, M. F. (1974) An analogue study assessing the effects of three training procedures on non-verbal assertive behavior. An unpublished doctoral dissertation, The American University.

Pylyshyn, Z. (1973) What the mind's eye tells the mind's brain: A critique of mental imagery. *Psychological Bulletin, 80,* 1-24.

Quay, H. (1959) The effect of verbal reinforcement on the recall of early memories. *Journal of Abnormal and Social Psychology, 59,* 254-57.

Rachman, S. (1972) Clinical applications of observational learning, imitation and modeling. *Behavior Therapy, 3,* 379-97.

Rennie, D., and Toukmanian, S. (1974) Acquisition of counseling skills by introverted and extroverted counselor trainees under conditions of experiential and didactic training. Paper presented to the symposium on Personality and Applied Psychology, Canadian Psychological Association Annual Meeting, Windsor, June.

Rickard, H. C., and Joubert, C. E. (1968) Subject-model sexual status and observer performance. *Psychonomic Science, 10,* 407–8.

Ritter, B. (1969) The use of contact desensitization, demonstration-plus-participation and demonstration alone in the treatment of acrophobia. *Behavior Research and Therapy, 7,* 157–61.

Robinson, S. E.; Froehle, T. C.; and Kupius, D. J. (1979) Effects of sex of model and media of model presentation on skill development of counselor trainees. *Journal of Counseling Psychology, 26,* 74–80.

Ronnestad, M. H. (1977) The effects of modeling, feedback, and experimental methods on counselor empathy. *Counselor Education and Supervision, 16,* 194–201.

Rosen, J. (1978) The efficacy of modeling and instructional techniques for counselor acquisition of nonverbal empathy skills (Doctoral dissertation, Indiana University, 1978). *Dissertation Abstracts International, 39,* 5334-A. (University microfilm no. 7906027)

Rosengren, T. M. (1972) A leaderless group model designed to increase self-reliant verbal behavior. *Dissertation Abstracts International, 1972, 32(3-A),* 976–977.

Rosenthal, T. L.; Zimmerman, B. J.; and Durning, K. (1970) Observationally induced changes in children's interrogative classes. *Journal of Personality and Social Psychology, 16,* 681–88.

Rossenblith, J. F. (1959) Learning by imitation in kindergarten children. *Child Development, 30,* 69–80.

Ryan, E. D. and Simons, J. (1981) Cognitive demand, imagery, and frequency of mental rehearsal as factors influencing acquisition of motor skills. *Journal of Sport Psychology, 3,* 35–45.

Ryan, E. D. and Simons, J. (1982) Efficacy of mental imagery in enhancing mental rehearsal of motor skills. *Journal of Sports Psychology, 4,* 41–51.

Sagotsky, J. (1977) The effects of consistent and inconsistent verbalizations and behavior modeling on the cooperative and competitive behavior of second and fifth grade children (Doctoral dissertation, The Ohio State University, 1977). *Dissertation Abstracts International, 38,* 969-B. (University microfilm no. 77-17, 132)

Salzinger, K., and Pisoni, S. (1957) Reinforcement of verbal affect responses of schizophrenics during the clinical interview. Presented at American Psychological Association, New York.

Sarason, I. G., and Ganzer, V. J. (1973) Modeling and group discussion in the rehabilitation of juvenile delinquents. *Journal of Counseling Psychology, 20,* 442–49.

Satterwhite, F. H. (1971) Interaction of model and observer's cognitive styles in an observational learning paradigm (Doctoral dissertation, University of Washington, 1970). *Dissertation Abstracts International, 3,* 5214-A. (University microfilm no. 71-8541).

Schinke, S. P., and Rose, S. D. (1976) Interpersonal skill training in groups. *Journal of Counseling Psychology, 23,* 442–48.

Schuh, A. J., and Young, Y. P. (1978) Indicators of attitude shift from role playing. *Bulletin of the Psychonomic Society, 11,* 283–84.

Scott, W. A. (1957) Attitude change through reward of verbal behavior. *Journal of Abnormal and Social Psychology, 55,* 72–75.

Shaw, M. E., Corsini, R. J., Blake, R. R., and Mouton, J. S. (1980) *Role playing: A practical manual for group facilitators.* San Diego: University Associates, Inc.

Sheffield, F. and Maccoby, N. (1961) Summary and interpretation of research on organizational principles in constructing filmed demonstrations. In A. A. Lumsdaine (ed.), *Student response in programmed instruction.* Washington D.C.: National Academy of Sciences–National Research Council, Chapter 9.

Silverman, M. S., and Quinn, P. F. (1974) Co-counseling supervision in practicum. *Counselor Education and Supervision, 13,* 256–60.

Smith, P. E. (1976) Management modeling training to improve morale and customer satisfaction. *Personnel Psychology, 29,* 351–59.

Smith, R. L. (1982) An evaluation of the effectiveness of graduated phase modeling in improving communication skills and self-perceived relationship quality among dating couples. *Dissertation Abstracts International,* Feb. 42(8-B), 3404.

Sodetz, A. R. (1972) The effect of videotape microtraining on counselor behavior. Unpublished doctoral dissertation, University of Missouri.

Solomon, R. L. (1949) An extension of controlled group design. *Psychological Bulletin, 46,* 137–50.

Sorcher, M. and Spence, R. (1982) The Interface Project: Behavior modeling as social technology in South Africa. *Personnel Psychology, 35,* 557–81.

Spiegler, M. D.; Liebert, R. M.; McMains, M.; and Fernandez, L. E. (1969) Experimental development of a modeling treatment to extinguish persistent avoidance behavior. In R. Rubin and C. Franks (eds.), *Advances in Behavior Therapy, 1968.* New York: Academic Press.

Spool, M. D. (1978) Training programs for observers of behavior: A review. *Personnel Psychology, 31,* 853–88.

Sterosahl, K. O., and Ascough, J. C. (1981) Clinical uses of mental imagery: Experimental foundations, theoretical misconceptions, and research issues. *Psychological Bulletin, 89*, 422–38.

Stone, G. L., and Jackson, T. (1975) Internal-external control as a determinant of the effectiveness of modeling and instructions. *Journal of Counseling Psychology, 22*, 294–98.

Stone, G. L. and Kelley, K. (1980) Effects of helping skills on attitudes toward psychological counseling. Paper presented at the Iowa Educational Research and Evaluation Meeting. Iowa City, IA.

Stone, G. L. and Vance, A. (1976) Instructions, modeling and rehearsal: Implications for training. *Journal of Counseling Psychology, 23*, 272–79.

Stroll, H. (1982) The effects of modeling, rehearsal, and verbal coding strategies on facilitation and transfer of children's cooperative and game behavior. *Dissertation Abstracts International*, 43(1-B), 298.

Sutton, K. (1970) Effects of modeled empathy and structured social class upon level of therapist displayed empathy. Unpublished master's thesis, Syracuse University.

Thompson, A. J. M., and Blocher, D. H. (1979) Co-counseling supervision in microcounseling. *Journal of Counseling Psychology, 26*, 413–18.

Thorndike, E. L. and Woodworth, R. S. (1901) (I) The influence of improvement in one mental function upon the efficiency of other functions. (II) The estimation of magnitudes. (III) Functions involving attention, observation, and discrimination. *Psychological Review, 8*, 247–61.

Tibbitts, S. T. (1974) The effects of expectancy and inconsistent vicarious consequences on the acquisition and performance of imitative responses (Doctoral dissertation, University of Montana, 1974). *Dissertation Abstracts International, 35*, 2472-B. (University microfilm no. 74-24,019).

Toffler, A. (1970) *Future Shock*. New York: Random House.

Training Within Industry Report, 1940–1945, War Manpower Commission, Bureau of Training, Washington, D.C., Sept. 1945.

Tureen, R. G. (1972) Comparison of left and right-hand performances in tactuo-spatial perception (Doctoral dissertation, Wayne State University, 1969). *Dissertation Abstracts International, 32*, 7327-B. (University microfilms no. 72-16, 236).

Twentyman, G. T. and Zimering, R. T. (1979) Behavioral training of social skills: a critical review. *Progressive Behavior Modification, 7*, 319–400.

Uhlemann, L.; Lee, G; and Stone, G. (1976) Effects of modeling and instructions on low-functioning trainees. *Journal of Counseling Psychology, 23*, 509–13.

Underwood, B. J. (1951) Associative transfer in verbal learning as a function of response similarity and degree of first-line learning. *Journal of Experimental Psychology, 42*, 44–53.

Van Sickle, D. J. (1975) Anxiety and assertive training: A program evaluation and therapy outcome study. Unpublished doctoral dissertation, University of Utah.

Vroom, V. H. (1964) *Work and Motivation*. New York: Wiley.

Walsh, W. G. (1971) The effects of conformity pressure and modeling on the attraction of hospitalized patients toward an interviewer. Unpublished doctoral dissertation, Syracuse University.

Walter, G. A. (1973) Promoting performance-oriented behavior change: The effects of video tape feedback and modeling. *Academy of Management Proceedings*, 457–62.

Walter, G. A. (1976) Changing behavior in task groups through social learning: Modeling alternatives. *Human Relations, 29*, 167–78.

Warren, M. W. (1969) *Training for Results*. Menlo Park: Addison-Wesley.

Watts, M. W. (1973) Behavior modeling and self-devaluation with video self-confrontation. *Journal of Educational Psychology, 64*, 212–15.

Weiss, H. M. (1977) Subordinate imitation of supervisor behavior: The role of modeling in organizational socialization. *Organizational Behavior and Human Performance, 19*, 89–105.

Weiss, H. M. and Nowicki, C. E. (1981) Social Influences on Task Satisfaction: Model Competence and Observer Field Dependence. *Organizational Behavior and Human Performance, 27*.

Wexley, K. N. and Latham G. P. (1981) *Developing and Training Human Resources in Organizations*. Glenview, IL: Scott, Foresman.

Wexley, K. N. and Thornton, C. L. (1972) Effect of verbal feedback of test results upon learning. *Journal of Educational Research, 66(3)*, 119–21.

White, D. K. (1977) The effects of videotaped feedback on the assertive behavior of selected counselor education students in an assertive training program (Doctoral dissertation, University of Missouri, Kansas City, 1976). *Dissertation Abstracts International, 38*, 6440A.

Willis, J. and Gueldenpfenning, J. (1981) The relative effectiveness of lecturing, modeling, and role playing in training para-professional reading tutors. *Psychology in the Schools, 18*, 323–29.

Wilson, S. H. (1976) Determining the effects of two differential self-modeling techniques on the acquisition of appropriate counseling behaviors of counselor trainees (Doctoral dissertation, University of Tennessee, 1975). *Dissertation Abstracts International, 36,* 5066-A.

Wittrock, M. G. and Lumsdaine, A. A. (1977) Instructional psychology. *Annual Review of Psychology, 28,* 417–59.

Yamamoto, K. and Inomata, K. (1982) Effect of mental rehearsal with part or whole demonstration models on acquisition of backstroke swimming skills. *Perceptual and Motor Skills, 54,* 1067–70.

Young, R. K. and Underwood, B. J. (1954) Transfer in verbal materials with dissimilar stimuli and response similarity varied. *Journal of Experimental Psychology, 47,* 153–59.

Zemke, R. (1982) Building behavior models that work—the way you want them to. *Training,* January, *19,* 22–25.

Zimbardo, P. G. (1965) The effect of effort and improvisation on self-persuasion produced by role playing. *Journal of Experimental Social Psychology, 1,* 103–20.

Zimmerman, B. J. and Rosenthal, T. (1974) Observational learning of rule-governed behavior by children. *Psychological Bulletin, 81,* 29–42.

## Appendix A References

Angelone, M. W. (1983) The application of behavior modeling to empathy training and its influence on managerial flexibility and level of empathy. *Dissertation Abstracts International,* June 43(12-A) 3788-3789.

Argyle, M.; Trower, P. E.; and Bryant, B. M. (1974). Explorations in the treatment of neurosis and personality disorders by social skills training. *British Journal of Medical Psychology, 47,* 63–72.

Boland, J. M. (1974) *An experimental investigation into the outcomes of assertion training with non-assertive clients.* Unpublished doctoral dissertation, University of Nebraska-Lincoln.*

Bouffard, D. L. (1973) *A comparison of response acquisition and desensitization approaches to assertion training.* Unpublished doctoral dissertation, Indiana University.*

Braukmann, G. J.; Fixen, D. L.; Phillips, E. L.; Wolf, M. M.; and Maloney, D. M. (1974) An analysis of a selection interview training package for predelinquents at Achievement Place. *Criminal Justice and Behavior, 1,* 30–42.

Buttrum, S. M. (1974) *The use of behavioral rehearsal, modeling, projected consequences and cognitive modification in assertive training.* Unpublished doctoral dissertation, University of Western Ontario.*

Charonko, J. J. (1979) The effects of microcounseling and monitor modeling upon the acquisition of group leadership skills (Doctoral dissertation, West Virginia

University). *Dissertation Abstracts International, 40,* 1274-A. (University Microfilms No. 7920691).

Cobb, R. M. (1974) *Acquisition and retention of cooperative behavior in young boys through instructions, modeling and structured learning.* Unpublished doctoral dissertation, Syracuse University.*

Donk, L. (1972) Attending behavior in mental patients. *Dissertation Abstracts International, 33,* 72–22.569.

Doty, D. W. (1975) Roleplaying and incentives in the modification of the social interaction of chronic psychiatric patients. *Journal of Consulting and Clinical Psychology,* 1975, *43,* 676–82.

Dunn, R. (1975) *Comparative effects of three counselor training techniques on reflecting of feeling.* Paper presented to the Canadian Psychological Association Annual Meeting, Quebec City, June, 1975.

Eoyang, J. (1979) Effects of modeling, rehearsal, and feedback on helper goal-setting behavior (Doctoral dissertation, The University of Oklahoma, 1978). *Dissertation Abstracts International, 39,* 3486-B. (University Microfilms No. 7824589).

Erdman, C. D. (1974) The effects of didactic, modeling, and laboratory training on the display of counselor expertness (Doctoral dissertation, The Ohio State University). *Dissertation Abstracts International, 34,* 4038-B. (University Microfilm No. 74-3159).

Evans, D.; Uhlemann, M.; and Hearn, M. (1975) *Microcounseling and sensitivity training with hotline workers.* Unpublished paper, London, Ontario, University of Western Ontario.

Fox, W. M. (1983) Behavior Modeling: An overview. An unpublished manuscript, University of Florida.

Fyffe, A. E. and Oei, T. P. S. (1979) Influence of modeling and feedback provided by the supervisors in a microskills training program for beginning counsellors. *Journal of Clinical Psychology, 35,* 651–56.

Gluckstern, N. B. (1972) Parents as lay counselors: The development of a systematic community program for drug counseling. (ERIC Document Reproduction Service No. ED 065 812)

Goldsmith, J. B., and McFall, R. M. (1975) Development and evaluation of an interpersonal skill-training program for psychiatric inpatients. *Journal of Abnormal Psychology, 84,* 51–58.

Goldstein, A. (1973) *Structured Learning Therapy: Toward a Psychotherapy for the Poor.* New York: Academic Press.

Gustafson, K. (1975) *An evaluation of enriching intimacy—a behavioral approach to the training of empathy, respect-warmth, and genuineness.* Unpublished dissertation, Amherst University of Massachusetts.

Gutride, M.; Goldstein, A.; and Hunter, G. (1972) *The use of modeling and role playing to increase social interaction among schizophrenic patients*. Unpublished manuscript, Syracuse University.

Gutride, M. E.; Goldstein, A. P.; and Hunter, G. F. (1973) The use of modeling and role playing to increase social interaction among asocial psychiatric patients. *Journal of Consulting and Clinical Psychology, 40*, 408–15.

Haase, R. and DiMattia, D. (1970) The application of the microcounseling paradigm to the training of support personnel in counseling. *Counselor Education and Supervision, 10*, 16–22.

Haase, R.; DiMattia, D.; and Guttman, M. (1972) Training of support personnel in three human relations skills: A systematic one-year follow-up. *Counselor Education and Supervision, 11*, 194–99.

Haase, R.; Forsyth, D.; Julius, M.; and Lee, R. (1971) Client training prior to counseling: An extension of the microcounseling paradigm. *Canadian Counselor, 5*, 9–15.

Hearn, M. (1976) *Three modes of training counsellors: A comparative study*. Unpublished dissertation, London, Ontario, University of Western Ontario.

Heimberg, R. G.; Cunningham, J.; Heimberg, J. S.; and Blankenberg R. (1982) Social skills training to prepare disadvantaged youth for the job interview: A controlled evaluation. *Behavior Modification, 6*, 299–322.

Hersen, M.; Eisler, R. M.; and Miller, P. M. (1974) An experimental analysis of generalization in assertive training. *Behavior Research and Therapy, 12*, 295–310.

Hersen, M.; Eisler, R. M.; Miller, P. M.; Johnson, M. B.; and Pinkston, S. G. (1974) Effects of practice, instructions, and modeling on components of assertive behavior. *Behavior Research and Therapy, 11*, 443–51.

Hollandsworth, J. G.; Glazeski, R. C.; and Dressel, M. E. (1978) Use of social skills training in the treatment of extreme anxiety and deficient verbal skills in the job interview setting. *Journal of Applied Behavior Analysis, 11*, 259–69.

Holstein, S. J. (1974) *The modification of maladaptive mother-child interaction through modeling and behavior rehearsal*. Unpublished doctoral dissertation, University of North Carolina at Chapel Hill.*

Ivey, A. (1971) *Microcounseling: Innovations in Interviewing Training*. Springfield, IL: Thomas.

Ivey, A. E., and Authier, J. (1978) *Microcounseling: Innovations in interviewing, counseling, psychotherapy, and psychoeducation*. Springfield, IL: Thomas.

Kelly, J. A.; Laughlin, C.; Claiborne, M.; and Patterson, J. A. (1979) A group procedure for teaching job interviewing skills to formerly hospitalized psychiatric patients. *Behavior Therapy, 10*, 299–310.

Kerrebrock, R. (1971) Application of the microcounseling method using videotape recordings to the training of teachers in basic counseling techniques. Unpublished dissertation, Los Angeles, University of California, *Dissertation Abstracts International, 32,* 740A.

LaGreca, A., and Santogrossi (1980) Social skills training with elementary school students: A behavioral group approach. *Journal of Consulting and Clinical Psychology, 48,* 220-28.

Leonard, P. (1977) Comparative effectiveness of four instructional fidelity levels in learning skills associated with termination of counseling contact. *Dissertation Abstracts, 37(9-A),* 5569-5570.

Lomont, J. F.; Gilner, F. H.; Spector, N. J.; and Skinner, K. K. (1962) Group assertion training and group insight therapies. *Psychological Reports, 25,* 463-70.

Loogin, H. F., and Rooney, W. M. (1973) Assertive training as a programmatic intervention for hospitalized mental patients. *Proceedings of the 81st Annual Convention of the American Psychological Association, 8,* 461-62.

Manderino, M. A. (1974) *Effects of a group assertive training procedure on undergraduate women.* Unpublished doctoral dissertation, Arizona State University.*

McFall, R. M., and Galbraith, J. R. *Two studies examining feedback in assertion training.* Unpublished manuscript, University of Wisconsin.*

McFall, R. M. and Twentyman, C. T. (1973) Four experiments on the relative contributions of rehearsal, modeling, and coaching to assertion training. *Journal of Abnormal Psychology, 81,* 199-218.

Mehnert, I. B. (1974) *The effects of an abbreviated training paradigm on females learning assertive behavior.* Unpublished doctoral dissertation, University of South Dakota.*

Melnick, J. (1973) A comparison of replication techniques in the modification of minimal dating behavior. *Journal of Abnormal Psychology, 81,* 51-59.

Moreland, J. R.; Ivey, A. E.; and Phillips, J. S. (1973) An evaluation of microcounseling as an interviewer training tool. *Journal of Consulting and Clinical Psychology, 41,* 292-300.

Morrill, C. M. (1973) *A behavioral group method for teaching interpersonal skills to children.* Unpublished doctoral dissertation, University of Missouri-Columbia.*

Murphy, P. J. (1979) Model-reinforcement counseling versus rational behavior therapy for reducing anxiety of in-training (Doctoral dissertation, Indiana State University). *Dissertation Abstracts International, 39,* 7164-A. (University Microfilm No. 7912925)

Orlando, N. (1974) The mental patient as a therapeutic agent: Self-change, power and coring. *Psychotherapy: Theory, Research, and Practice, 11,* 58-62.

O'Toole, W. M. (1979) Effects of practice and some methodological considerations in training counseling interviewing skills. *Journal of Counseling Psychology, 26,* 419-26.

Parr, G. D. (1974) *The effects of modeling, behavior rehearsal and counselor sex in assertive counseling with adolescents*. Unpublished doctoral dissertation, University of Colorado.*

Paulson, T. L. (1974) *The differential use of self-administered and group-administered token reinforcement in group assertion training for college students*. Unpublished doctoral dissertation, Fuller Theological Seminary Graduate School of Psychology.*

Petrick, S. (1976) *An evaluation of a combined group therapy and communication skills training program for psychiatric inpatients*. Unpublished dissertation, Lincoln University of Nebraska.

Phelps, A. T. (1979) Development and evaluation of an instructional counseling procedure for the treatment of reticence (Doctoral dissertation, University of California, Los Angeles). *Dissertation Abstracts International, 39*, 4064-A. (University Microfilms No. 7901389)

Ronnestadt, M. H. (1977) Effect of modeling, feedback, and experimental methods on counselor empathy. *Counselor Education and Supervision, 16*, 194–201.

Sarason, I. G., and Ganzer, V. J. (1973) Modeling and group discussion in the rehabilitation of juvenile delinquents. *Journal of Counseling Psychology, 20*, 442–49.

Schinke, S. P.; Gilchrist, L. D.; Smith, T. E.; and Wong, S. E. (1978) Improving teenage mothers' ability to compete for jobs. *Social Work Research and Abstracts, 14*, 25–29.

Schinke, S. P., and Rose, S. D. (1976) Interpersonal skill training in groups. *Journal of Counseling Psychology, 23*, 442–48.

Stone, G. L. and Vance, A. (1976) Instructions, modeling, and rehearsal: Implication for training. *Journal of Counseling Psychology, 23*, 272–79.

Teevan, K. G. and Gabel, H. (1978) Evaluation of modeling-roleplaying and lecture-discussion training techniques for college student mental health paraprofessionals. *Journal of Counseling Psychology, 25*, 169–71.

Tofte-Tipps, S.; Mendonca, P.; and Peach, R. V. (1982) Training and generalization of social skills: A study with two developmentally handicapped, socially isolated children. *Behavior Modification, 6*, 45–71.

Thorpe, G. L. (1973) *Short-term effectiveness of systematic desensitization, modeling, and behavior rehearsal, and self-instructional training in facilitating assertive-refusal behavior*. Unpublished doctoral dissertation, Rutgers University.

Toukmanian, S. G. and Rennie, D. L. (1975) Microcounseling versus human-relations training. *Journal of Counseling Psychology, 22*, 345–52.

Twentyman, C. T., Jensen, M., and Kloss, J. (1978) Social skills training with the complex offender. *Journal of Clinical Psychology, 34*, 320–26.

Twentyman, C. T., and Martin, B. (1978) Modification of problem interaction in mother-child dyads by modeling and behavior rehearsal. *Journal of Clinical Psychology, 34*, 138–43.

Wallace, W. G.; Horan, J. J.; Baker, S. B.; and Hudson, G. R. (1975) Incremental effects of modeling and performance feedback in teaching decision-making counseling. *Journal of Counseling Psychology, 22*, 570–72.

Werner, J. S.; Minkin, N.; Minkin, B. L.; Fixen, D. L.; Phillips, E. L.; and Wolf, M. M. (1975) "Intervention package": An analysis of prepared juvenile delinquents for encounters with police officers. *Criminal Justice and Behavior, 2*, 55–84.

Wolfe, J. L., and Fodor, I. G. (1977) Modifying assertive behavior in women: A comparison of three approaches. *Behavior Therapy, 8*, 567–74.

Zashin, M. M. (1981) A prosocial behavior training program: Modeling, role playing, and training in verbal self-instruction as techniques for teaching prosocial behaviors to groups of behaviorally disturbed. *Dissertation Abstracts International*, September, 42(3-B) 1199.

* A review of this work is readily available:

Twentyman, C. T. and Zimering, R. T. (1979) Behavioral training of social skills: A critical review. In Hersen, M.; Eisler, R. M.; and Miller P. M. (eds.), *Progress in Behavior Modification* (Vol. 7). New York: Academic Press, 319–400.

## Appendix B References

Kazdin, A. E. (1980) *Research Design in Clinical Psychology.* New York: Harper and Row.

Kimble, G. A. (1961) *Hilgard and Marquis' conditioning and learning.* New York: Appleton-Century-Crofts.

Mahoney, M. J. (1971) The self-management of covert behavior: A case study. *Behavior Therapy, 2*, 575–78.

Premack, D. (1965) Reinforcement theory. In D. Levine (ed.) *Nebraska Symposium on Motivation.* Lincoln: University of Nebraska Press.

Skinner, B. F. (1953) *Science and human behavior.* New York: Macmillan.

# Index

## Subject Index

# Name Index

# About the Authors

PHILLIP J. DECKER, Ph.D., is an Assistant Professor of Management at the School of Business of the University of Missouri-St. Louis. He also holds an appointment in the Psychology Department of UMSL. Dr. Decker received his Ph.D. in Industrial/Organizational Psychology from the Ohio State University. He teaches primarily personnel/human resource and training courses; his research has been primarily in behavior modeling and employee selection. Dr. Decker has published the results of his research in the *Journal of Applied Psychology, Personnel Psychology*, and *The Academy of Management Journal*. He has worked in a consulting capacity with companies such as Hughes Aircraft, General Electric, Ford Motor Co., and Emerson Electric.

BARRY R. NATHAN is an Assistant Professor of Psychology at the University of Missouri-St. Louis and also holds an appointment in the Business School. He received his Ph.D. and M.A. degrees from the University of Akron and his B.S. in zoology from the University of Maryland. In addition to Behavior Modeling, his research interests include issues in performance appraisal, employee motivation, and personnel selection. As a consultant and trainer he has assisted organizations in performance appraisal, interviewing, and employee communication. Dr. Nathan is a member of the American Psychological Association and the Academy of Management.